CW01085115

OUTSIDE THE MAINSTREAM

OUTSIDE
—— THE ——
MAINSTREAM

A HISTORY OF
SPECIAL EDUCATION

J. S. Hurt

B. T. Batsford Ltd · *London*

Photoset by Deltatype Ltd, Ellesmere Port, Cheshire
and printed in Great Britain by
Biddles Ltd
Guildford & Kings Lynn

Published by B. T. Batsford Ltd
4 Fitzhardinge Street, London W1H 0AH

British Library Cataloguing in Publication Data

Hurt, J. S.
  Outside the mainstream : a history of
  special education.
  1. Exceptional children——Education——
  Great Britain——History
  I. Title
  371.9.'0941   LC3986.G7

ISBN 0–7134–5291–9

TO DAVID

born with Down's Syndrome

'Experience has . . . led many of those who are concerned to the conclusion that every child, no matter how severely handicapped, should have the opportunity to develop to the fullest extent of which he is capable, and that it cannot be right to exclude any child from the scope of the educational services.'

William van Straubenzee, House of Commons, 13 July 1970.

CONTENTS

INTRODUCTION

As the title implies, this book is concerned with those children whose schooling and education took place outside the ordinary school system, thus its cover is greater than that normally included under the title 'special education'. The first two groups of children for whom special arrangements were made were those seen as posing a threat to social order: the pauper child and the socially deviant child. The first three chapters of this study deal with their education and socialisation, while they remained outside the mainstream of education.

The original intention was to avoid such an arbitrary terminal point, as a study of the orphaned or abandoned child, as well as of all those who are taken into care, should go further. Similarly any historical study of the delinquent child should carry beyond 1933, the year in which the Home Office took direct control of the approved schools, down to the present day. Tempting though it was to involve oneself in the literature of criminology and penology, the economic constraints in which publishers operate prevailed. The remaining chapters deal with what is more traditionally seen as within the sphere of special education, the education of the physically or mentally handicapped child. Specialists in the various fields that I have attempted to cover will no doubt be aware of many lacunae and of aspects left untreated in my attempt to keep this book to a reasonable length. These shortcomings are particularly apparent in the last chapter dealing with the post-war years, an era whose specialist literature deserves a book in itself for an adequate survey.

I wish to acknowledge my indebtedness to Taylor and Francis Ltd for permission to include material first published under the title 'Reformatory and Industrial Schools before 1933' in *History of Education*, XIII (1984) and to Carfax Publishing Co. for their agreement to my reproducing the substance of my 'The Epileptic Child and Special Education before 1939' which appeared in *Educational Review*, XXXIV (1982).

It is also a pleasant task to thank the University of Birmingham for their assistance in granting me study leave to work on this book and for their financial help enabling me to visit various archives. My final thanks are to my wife, Grenda, for encouraging me to write this book in the first place, to our elder son whose condition inspired the study, and to Cathy Baker who masterminded the production of the final typescript.

INSTITUTIONAL LIFE FOR THE CHILDREN OF THE POOR: WORKHOUSE SCHOOLS BEFORE 1870

Children in workhouse, reformatory, and industrial schools formed part of a small group for whose welfare the state, prompted by a realization of the social danger they posed, assumed responsibility. 'Their fathers are dead, or are unknown, or are in prison, or have deserted them, or are not even able to feed them, much less to educate them. To them the State is *loco parentis*',[1] declared the Newcastle Commissioners two decades before compulsory education became the general rule. The schools such children attended performed a dual function. Their purpose was to protect their charges by segregating them from adult contamination, be it that of the prison inmate, the prostitute or unmarried mother in the female ward of the workhouse, or the habitual pauper in the male ward. At the same time the schools protected society from the young delinquent, beggar, or vagrant child. Lunatic asylums performed a similar dual role. By the end of the century the segregation of feeble-minded children and adults, as earlier the provision of separate workhouse wards for able-bodied male and female adults, seemed a necessary means of checking the propagation of social undesirables.

The schools' aim was the elimination of the children's hereditary criminal or pauper taint. Similarly the later development of schooling for the mentally and physically handicapped held out the hope of training such children to lead financially independent lives without recourse to poor relief. Expenditure on the schools described in this and succeeding chapters seldom found many advocates. Posts in workhouse, reformatory, and industrial schools offered the prospect of low salaries, long hours spent in uncongenial surroundings, and a lack of professional status and social esteem. This deterred all but the poorly qualified from applying for posts as teachers or industrial trainers. The offer of free board, lodging, and shelter from the vicissitudes of the outside world, while dealing with children to whom one could feel morally superior, may have attracted those seeking a haven from the pressures of everyday life. Some took posts in workhouses because they had failed elsewhere, as did the two of the Education Department reported to the Poor Law Board in 1867 as having been dismissed from elementary schools in consequence of immorality and 'very immoral and disgraceful conduct'.[2]

The prospect for pupils on discharge was equally discouraging. As few employers wanted to take them, their future lay in those areas where recruitment remained difficult however depressed the economy. Another consideration was to place children as far away as possible from their old haunts, friends, and relations. The colonies were a useful outlet for both sexes, while the army or a seafaring life held out the lure of a disciplined and hierarchical environment as an added bonus for the disposal of boys.

When dealing with juvenile deviants, be they delinquent or pauper, the state showed greater readiness to curb parental rights than in other instances. The first legislation to protect children from parental cruelty did not reach the statute book until 1889, yet an act passed in 1822 had given animals some protection. Similarly, early legislation to protect children did not affect respectable parents in their homes. It dealt with orphans, as did Hanway's Acts of 1762 and 1767, and the Factory Act of 1802, or with children outside the home, as did the flood of Factory Acts after 1833. The practice of separating children from their parents, whose unworthiness was thought to stand self-revealed when they applied for relief in the workhouse, provides the first substantial denial of a parent's rights to his child. The workhouse pauper ceased to be a free man and became subject to a special code of laws that applied to his status. Separated from his wife, *a mensa et thoro* ('from bed and board'), he could only see his children at stipulated times, and had to have his children educated without reference to his opinions or wishes. 'The law therefore overrides the authority of an ignorant and probably degraded parent, where it clashes with the welfare of society.' Pauper parents enjoyed one legal right. They had to give their consent before a child was sent to a district school, that is, a school serving a number of unions, and, after 1851, to another workhouse school within twenty miles of the home union.[3]

The earliest legislation to deal with vagabonds, dating from the fourteenth century, was essentially punitive in nature. Tudor acts, however, aimed not only at punishment but also at supporting those unable to work or who could not find any. Overseers of the poor, and the magistracy, were to establish Industrial schools for children and were to set them to work. However, both John Locke in 1696 and the Select Committee on Poor Laws in 1817 found that the authorities preferred the simpler and less expensive solution of giving parents money for the upkeep of their children rather than undertaking the long-term expense of providing vocational training. Within the context of the post-war depression the 1817 Select Committee argued that if a mother and father could afford to maintain two of their children, others over the age of three could be set to work, given a bellyful of bread daily together with warm-water gruel in winter, and sent to church every Sunday. Notwithstanding the earlier failure of charity schools to be self-supporting the Committee pursued the chimera of economic self-sufficiency and even looked to a surplus from the sale of goods produced by the children. If necessary, the new voluntary parochial schools could be mobilized: 'such schools now generally established and supported by voluntary contributions . . . appear to afford the means by which education and industry may be most advantageously united.' The Report concluded its educational recommendations by looking to the faithful execution of the existing law and the lodging of the children of 'extensive parishes' where the daily attendance of the younger ones would be impracticable. The Committee's recommendations were followed in at least one recorded instance. At Southwell in 1822 a building adjoining the workhouse was set aside for children of labourers with large families; here they were fed, taught, returned to their homes at night, and given Sunday dinner if they attended church.

Apart from a few isolated examples little attention was given to the question of educating pauper children, as distinct from providing industrial or vocational training, before 1834. Hanway's Act of 1767, dealing only with pauper children in the Metropolitan Bills of Mortality parishes and excluding the City of London, speaks of their education and maintenance in its preamble. A local act passed the same year allowed Plymouth to appoint a pious, sober and discreet person to teach the three Rs. In this maritime town the syllabus was to include the art of navigation, and such parts of mathematics as were relevant and within the children's capacity.[4] Given that the Royal Commission on the Poor Laws was appointed in early 1832, a year before the Treasury made its first grant for the building of schoolhouses, it is not surprising that the enquiry, the report, and subsequent legislation gave no more than scant attention to the education of pauper children. The lengthy instructions to the assistant commissioners, apart from a few scattered references to the maintenance and the welfare of children, devoted only two lines to their education. Commissioners had to enquire whether existing workhouses and similar institutions had scholars attached to them, whether the children were kept apart from other inmates, and whether their religious and moral education received attention.[5] In practice the Commissioners' concern with the concept of 'less eligibility', whereby as a preventative device discipline inside the workhouse was to render the pauper's condition irksome, virtually excluded any consideration of remedies such as the development of education that might have helped to eradicate pauperism and destitution. Only two of the 26 assistant commissioners seem to have thought about education in this light. So great was the concern of the period to remove the social threat of pauperism at the least possible expense to the propertied classes that the Commissioners saw its elimination as the first task facing the legislature. Once this issue had been successfully tackled, only then would attention be given to national education, by using income from existing endowments (much of which was currently 'applied in a manner unsuited to the present wants of society'[6]), a suggestion that had the merit of apparently involving no Treasury expenditure.

Discussion on the nature of the education the workhouse should offer came only later. Although James Kay has received much of the credit for developing pauper education, his interest in the subject did not grow until the late 1830s, after he had written a report on the existing apprenticeship system, a matter that inevitably involved some consideration of industrial training. His friendship with E. Carleton Tufnell, with whom he visited David Stow's Scottish model school, helped further in nurturing his interest in the matter. Although the application of the workhouse test was to be the means of restricting the number of adult applicants, he argued that children needed a more positive approach if hereditary pauperism was to be eradicated. 'We must rely on an improved industrial training as the chief available means for reducing the burthen, by changing the condition of the great numbers of pauper children, the descendants of former generations of paupers.' The test of the effectiveness of any educational system would be the extent to which ex-workhouse children remained in post as 'good servants or good workmen', or took refuge, once again, in the workhouse. Although the physical condition of the children was not to be above that of the household of an independent labourer, different considerations applied to their training. Education was 'to be regarded as one of the most important means of eradicating the germs of pauperism from the rising generation, and of securing in the minds and in the morals of the people the best protection for the institutions of society.' Accordingly it was impossible to avoid a commitment to giving them an adequate education 'on the grounds of the deficiency of provision for the self-supporting classes.' On the contrary, 'the nature of the duty of society towards the dependent class may serve to illustrate its responsibilities towards every other class.' The abolition of the earlier system of compulsory apprenticeship in 1844 strengthened his case: 'the pauper child . . . now depends on the physical, moral, and mental vigour he may acquire in the school for the means of pushing his way in life so as to secure independence.'[7]

In seeking an antidote for 'hereditary pauperism' through education, contemporaries showed little awareness of its social and economic causes. Without a rapid expansion of the economy, children of paupers were likely to stay at the bottom of the pile through no fault of their own. On the other hand, despite their moralizing on the subject, commentators were right in being aware of the way in which such a situation bred low expectations and a readiness to accept economic dependence as a way of life. Yet although some saw that a man might become unemployed through no fault of his own, the way in which he dealt with the problem was still seen as a test of his moral fibre. Writing in the aftermath of the 'railway mania' one inspector conceded that a man might become unemployed through fluctuations in trade, in employment, especially on the railways, or Irish immigration. The way in which these factors produced pauperism, though, 'mainly depends on the provident habits and fortitude with which our poorer classes generally, are enabled to struggle with adversities and maintain their independence. These are qualities which are alone the result of a moral and industrial discipline.'[8]

Not only was there no serious discussion in the early 1830s of the kind of education the proposed workhouses should offer, but the newly appointed commissioners, in dealing with pauper children, soon departed from one of the *Report's* main recommendations about workhouse organization. Whereas earlier legislation had distinguished two broad categories of pauper – the vagrant and the 'deserving' poor – the *Report* of 1834 identified four – able-bodied males, able-bodied females, the aged and impotent, and children, each of which was to be housed separately. 'We supposed the use of four buildings in every union', Nassau Senior recollected in 1862.

With one exception, the district school, the plan of establishing separate workhouses for the four main groups of paupers was quietly dropped. The expense was too great, the number of potential inmates, especially in rural unions, too small. The common workhouse, containing society's economic and social casualties, became the norm. Despite this the Poor Law Commissioners made strenuous efforts to salvage one specialist workhouse, the district school taking children from a number of unions, from the wreckage. Local initiative took the lead. The Select Committee on the Poor Law Amendment Act of 1834, sitting in 1838, heard that the West London Union was already negotiating with the East London and Kensington Unions to establish a joint school that W. E. Hickson, an early propagandist for national education and member of the handloom commission, hoped might 'become a model school for the rest of the country . . . .' It also took evidence from Dr Kay, who pointed to the main problems of providing education in a small workhouse school, problems that were never satisfactorily solved even by the end of the century. The most important was that of obtaining suitable teachers at salaries guardians were likely to offer, at a time when the supply of reasonably competent candidates was extremely limited. Other difficulties included the generally unsatisfactory nature of the education then being offered and the lack of means of isolating children from adult paupers. In addition to Kay's evidence the Select Committee must also have had in mind the case of the Bedford guardians, who had requested permission to limit workhouse education to reading only, an action that resulted from their concern not to put pauper children at an advantage over poor children not in the workhouse.[9]

Kay argued that, in contrast to small workhouse schools, large district ones offered advantages stemming mainly from the economies of scale. To obtain satisfactory teachers the 39 unions in Norfolk and Suffolk would have had to pay men £35 to £40 a year and women £20, together with board and lodging. With the cost of paying industrial teachers, the salary bill would have been £3,361 – 16s a year. In addition, the initial equipping of the schols would have cost an estimated £4,700. If there were four schools for the two counties, each housing 400 to 500 children, the poor law authorities could save at least £2,000 a year while still offering attractive salaries. The four principal teachers and their wives could be paid £120 a year plus keep, while assistant teachers and industrial instructors could be induced to serve in workhouse schools at lower but still reasonable rates of pay. In addition chaplains could be appointed at £60 a year to oversee the children's religious education. With an efficient religious and moral training, the acquisition of various trade skills and their habituation to hard work, children would be able to find employment without the guardians having to pay apprenticeship premiums. The Committee's recommendation, 'That the Commissioners be empowered, with the consent of the guardians, to combine parishes or unions for the support and management of district schools, and to regulate the distribution of the expenses of such establishments',[10] laid down the guidelines for future legislation.

By this time the Poor Law Commissioners, having dealt with the immediately pressing problem of forming unions, possessed the means by which they could make provision for the education of pauper children. They accordingly asked their assistant commissioners to report on the state of workhouse education. The first three reports published, Kay's on the training of pauper children, Richard Hall's on the education of pauper children in the unions of Berkshire and Oxfordshire, and William Day's on certain Shropshire unions, with suspiciously fortuitous unanimity recommended the formation of district schools. In concurring with this the Commissioners used the opportunity to point to the need for further legislation, their existing means of taking such action being 'circuitous and inefficient'. In response to their prompting Lord John Russell unsuccessfully introduced bills in 1840 and again in 1841, the year in which Lord Melbourne's administration finally lost its precarious hold over the House of Commons. The Act passed three years later contained weaknesses. In deference to ratepayer fears of incurring excessive demands school districts were not allowed to borrow more than one-fifth of average expenditure, an inadequate amount to secure the erection of a suitable building. Further restrictions showed due respect to the strength of early nineteenth-century English landed society's resistance to outside interference in the affairs of its immediate neighbourhood. No part of any combination of parishes was to be more than 15 miles away from any other part. In addition, a majority of the guardians of every parish or union had to give their consent in writing to the formation of a school district. Any school formed under the Act was to be managed by a board consisting of guardians elected from the participating unions, an arrangement Dr Kay had suggested in 1838 as a means of obtaining guardians who would take an interest in the school. As the financial and geographical restrictions proved too onerous, a further act of 1848 removed them. The need for guardians to give written consent for the incorporation of their unions into school districts remained on the statute book until 1882.[11]

The 1844 Act also repealed Hanway's Acts of 1762 and 1767 which had required the metropolitan parishes to send their infant poor away from London in an attempt to reduce the high rate of infant mortality then prevalent in the London workhouses. Such children were farmed out to contractors who formed what might be seen as prototype district schools. In such establishments children were the victims of two financial pressures, one exercised by the guardians wanting to pay the lowest possible tariff for their children's accommodation, the other from the contractor wanting to maximize his profit. Of these schools Drouet's at Tooting was the least satisfactory. Here the proprietor supplemented his contractual earnings with a second business deal under which pauper girls made shirts for London shops. As Drouet's extra profit was made at the expense of the time the girls should have spent on their schooling, his financial acumen earned inspectoral censure. Another contractor's school, Aubin's at Norwood, also created problems for the Poor Law Commissioners, whose authority over such places remained obscure in law until 1849: in that year an act brought those still in existence, two at Margate for scrofulous adults and for children respectively, and a third for the poor of Newington at Brixton, clearly within their jurisdiction. On first inspection Kay had found the means adopted for religious instruction at Norwood inadequate and not meeting the legal requirements of the 1834 Act, the moral training 'in every respect extremely defective', while the children's industrial training was confined to 'occupations of the most cheerless description, useless in preparing them for any future duties, and pernicious because they disgusted them with labour.' Their recreation was 'not encouraged by any systematic arrangements'. Finally, the school was insufficiently furnished with the implements of instruction used currently in National and British and Foreign Society schools. In accordance with Kay's recommendation the Poor Law Commissioners appointed a chaplain, the best they could do to improve matters, given their limited powers. Despite this initiative Kay later argued that the defects inseparable from contractors' establishments were such as to make any extension of the system undesirable. Although standards at Norwood improved, an outbreak of cholera, killing 150 children at Tooting in 1849, brought the practice of mass child-farming to an end. At Drouet's subsequent trial for manslaughter, a charge on which he was acquitted, sufficient evidence was produced of poor feeding, bad housing, and insufficient care of the children for *The Times* to declare: 'There is but one favourable point in this terrible tragedy, which is, that the deaths of these 150 Tooting children will effectually break up the child-farming system – and for ever.'[12] In one respect the paper's leader writer proved a false prophet. Baby farming still caused scandals a generation later. On the other hand Drouet's school ceased operation on the death of its proprietor, in the same year as his trial. The Central London School District purchased Aubin's premises while two more districts, the South Metropolitan and the North Surrey, were formed in the aftermath of the trial. From the late 1840s the newly appointed inspectors of poor law schools had the duty of suggesting possible combinations of unions from which guardians might form school districts. Despite official support there were only six district schools in 1861, three attached to Metropolitan unions and three based on provincial ones. In that year the Newcastle Commissioners recommended the building of more district and separate schools, the latter being ones physically separated from the workhouse. The Poor Law Board continued to support a policy of erecting such schools until the late 1870s when the last school district, Brentford, was formed, by which time the policy of herding pauper children together in large numbers was coming under attack.[13] When a series of scandals earned district schools the pejorative title 'barrack schools' in the 1890s there were still ten, six attached to Metropolitan unions and four to provincial ones. From then onwards their numbers gradually shrank.

However, until at least the middle of the nineteenth century residence in a district school seemed to many the route to pauper child's salvation, especially if that child were orphaned or deserted. Such children, it was argued, were victims of circumstances beyond their control. As such they should be removed from the children of vagabonds so that they would not earn the stigma of the workhouse or be corrupted by association with adult paupers and their children. Hence the deserted or orphaned child should grow up well away from the workhouse, for he 'cannot be a pauper in the sense in which the term is commonly understood, that is, he cannot be indigent as the consequence of his own want of industry, skill, frugality, or forethought, and he ought not, therefore, be taught to despise himself'. Away from the workhouse he would enjoy better opportunities than before; 'the pauper apprentice and the juvenile vagrant were, under the old system, brethren of the same class – outcasts.' With the children separated from adult paupers it would be possible to produce God-fearing independent labourers who would not become a public burden later in life by graduating to an adult ward of the workhouse or a prison cell. In a properly equipped and supervised school Kay's desiderata of a good workhouse education would be met.

> The teachers will rear them in habits of industry, cleanliness, punctuality, and order. They will be taught to speak the truth, and trained to be kind to their fellows, to be respectful to their superiors . . . they will be informed how they may best secure themselves against the vicissitudes of life, and what are the consequences of vice.
> Sanctions of religion should be the foundation of this instruction . . . the claims which religion has upon their thoughts, and the influence which it ought to exert on them . . . should be carefully depicted.

Training of this nature required unremitting daily effort to secure its objectives.

> To produce a punctual discipline of the hours allotted to rising and going to bed; to prayers, meals, exercises, and school; to ensure exact discipline in the movements of the children at these several periods; to preserve uninterrupted decorum in attitude, expression, and manner during meals and religious services . . . must be the subject of a continued effort.[14]

Under a properly organized system of industrial training designed to equip boys for the lowly positions they could expect to occupy on discharge, they would learn to make and mend shoes and tailor their clothing, a training in self-sufficiency that was thought to be particularly valuable for those going into the army or emigrating to the colonies. For those going to sea there could be extra training in seamanship and naval drill. The larger numbers of children in a district school, as well as making possible their classification by age and ability, also justified the purchase of special equipment for their training. The latter consideration became more important in the 1860s when the staples of small schools, tailoring and shoemaking, crafts which required little capital outlay for teaching, took on more and more the character of sweated trades. Training boys for the sea or as band boys for the army required classes of at least a hundred pupils to make the project pedagogically and financially worthwhile. A set of masts and rigging cost £100. Brass instruments for band boys cost £60, together with the recurring cost of the bandmaster's and drill master's wages. Again, in a large school girls would be habituated to hard work, an essential preliminary to the drudgery of domestic service, by spending long hours washing and ironing clothes. Destined to become the wives of labourers, they would supplement their general training by learning the more specialist skills of preparing 'a frugal meal, consisting of cheaper but wholesome materials, such as could be afforded by a workman.'[15]

Furthermore, district schools gave poor children one of the few opportunities they had of receiving any education, before the introduction of universal elementary education. Although the schools were primarily for deserted and orphaned children, guardians could send any child provided the parents consented. This arrangement allowed a struggling family to put some of its children into a workhouse, thereby reverting to a practice John Locke had recommended in 1697. However, the unpopularity of the workhouse and the new poor laws, parental reluctance to allow a family to be split except in dire emergency, and the guardians' reluctance to spend money on education, made such a practice rare. In a few instances, though, guardians allowed poor children, not necessarily with parents on relief, to attend a nearby workhouse school. Such arrangements, though of doubtful legality, were in the spirit of W. E. Hickson's proposals that the poor law system should provide the basis of a national system of education. Dr Kay had also advocated a measure of integration by recommending that unions with only a few children needing education should establish schools outside the workhouse to be attended by children from the parish. If there were good parochial schools already in existence workhouse children should attend them, provided the guardians had sufficient control over the schools. Eventually the little-used Denison's Act of 1855 allowed guardians to pay the school fees of children whose parents were on outdoor relief, to attend any school.[16]

Whatever the kind of school guardians provided, or failed to provide, the central government found its powers severely limited. The terms of the 1834 Act gave local boards ample justification for dragging their heels, if they so wished. Initially the Poor Law Commission's life was five years, a period marked by opposition from a small group that denounced, *inter alia*, the Act's infringement of local gentry autonomy. It is easy, however, to exaggerate the strength of this early opposition: historians have, until recently, been considerably influenced by the violent resistance of a few northern towns and *The Times* campaign against the new poor law. The issue did not feature prominently in the general election campaign of 1837, Benjamin Disraeli's denunciation of the new Act in his address to Maidstone's electorate being one of the few made in southern England.[17] The early years were ones of strained counsels within the Commission itself and doubts about its powers over unions created under local acts. Uncertainty remained until 1844, when the case of *Queen v. the Guardians of the Poor of the City of Oxford* (Queen's Bench Division, 1844) put the power of the Poor Law Commissioners to regulate the proceedings of guardians appointed under a local act beyond all doubt. However, *Regina v. the Parish of St Pancras* protected the constitution of such a board of guardians and the manner of its appointment from the Commission's interference. Only in 1867, after the passage of twelve continuation acts, did the central government agency, a board from 1847 onwards with a president answerable to the House of Commons, finally become established. Despite this the central authority's powers remained seriously limited. Even their right to supervise workhouse education appeared in general terms as one of a series of powers contained in an omnibus clause. The 1834 Act did not allow the Commissioners to order the erection of a workhouse or school without the consent of a majority of the guardians or ratepayers. Even where buildings already existed they could not order the execution of minor works costing more than £50. Once there was a workhouse, they could require the appointment of a teacher, and regulate his duties, but could not 'any further enforce any system of education'. Again, although the 1844 Act gave the central government certain limited powers in forming school districts, it could not require the newly-created school district to build a school nor any of the constituent unions to send their children to it. In practice, once a union had started a school its guardians were reluctant to lose control over 'their' children, if only because they feared greater expense. Paradoxically, the offer of grants towards the salaries of teachers and industrial teachers, made in particular to improve the quality of schooling in small schools, lessened any financial advantage to be derived from parting with a school, thereby making some distant district school even less attractive in an age of strong local loyalties.

When one turns to small workhouse schools one can see why many contemporaries at first thought that the district school offered children far better prospects than did small schools, for not until the 1850s and 1860s did concern begin to be voiced about the psychological effects of keeping large numbers of children in impersonal institutions. Thus J. C. Symons, an assistant poor law inspector for the counties of Gloucester and Worcester, reported that in none of his 19 unions was 'the provision of buildings or grounds sufficient for the proper efficient education and training of the children'. Eight unions had no facilities for the employment of children out of doors, 'in only thirteen were any trades taught, and then in very small rooms, so that only forty-five boys were taught' in the two counties. Children usually slept three abed, except in Worcester where there could be as many as five in the same bed. At Cheltenham 134 children had a total area of 168' × 63' for their buildings and playground. Such was their frustration at these cramped quarters that they had eventually rioted and attacked the schoolmaster.

In Symons's area and elsewhere workhouse masters and mistresses frequently secured teaching posts for their own children or other young relatives. Whether related or not, teachers were subordinate to the workhouse superintendent on whose good will they depended for their daily creature comforts. The protection teachers needed from their less well-educated superiors, intent on using them as additional servants or demanding the services of the children when they were supposed to be in the classroom, was something the Education Department could not provide. At the heart of any such struggle were the different concepts of the purpose of the workhouse and the contrasting value systems of two government departments. The Poor Law Board was 'stereotyped by law, destitute of internal degeneration into mere formality'. Boards of Guardians, imbued with this spirit, had good reason to believe their worst prejudices confirmed. Education required an expenditure that was at variance with the concept of less eligibility and one that seemed to give pauper children an unfair advantage over those of the independent labourer struggling to find the weekly school pence. As Symons wrote, 'The whole spirit and economy of the workhouse are alien to the requirements of a school of religion and industry.'[18]

Even the offer of a grant towards the cost of teachers' salaries, first fixed at £30,000 for a full financial year in 1846, was of only limited assistance. In improving the standards of workhouse teachers the government departments concerned, the Education Department and the Poor Law Board, faced two major problems. First, the shortage of suitably qualified teachers was a general one. Hence the offer of slightly improved salaries alone was not enough. Second, the attitude of poor law guardians, which was frequently one of indifference to pauper education, constituted a further obstacle. To improve the quality of teacher supply in the elementary schools, the Education Department introduced a wide-ranging series of regulations in 1846, which are best known for the inauguration of the pupil–teacher system, the Queen's scholarship, the teacher's certificate, and the steps taken to improve and expand the training colleges. The attention given to these initiatives has obscured the measures introduced at the same time to provide trained teachers for pauper and penal schools, and improve the salaries of workhouse teachers.

Kay-Shuttleworth (Dr Kay had assumed the additional name on his marriage in 1842) realized the need for a 'cautious and patient administration' in dealing with the guardians, as the majority of existing workhouse teachers would be found to be inefficient. He accordingly proposed a four-fold scale certificate to make the objectives of the examination seem reasonable to both guardians and teachers, while giving the latter the prospect of higher remuneration if they took steps to improve their general competence. Until the proposed normal school, or training college, started operating, he saw dismissal as being confined to *extreme cases*, involving the removal of immoral and extremely ignorant men and those who had been habitual paupers. With the start of the normal school he looked to an annual flow of fifty trained masters into the workhouse schools.[19]

Unfortunately the new college, despite the abolition of fees in November 1854 in order to attract more students, produced not a stream but a trickle. Of 120 students admitted between the beginning of 1850 and March 1855, 19 fell by the wayside, through a variety of causes ranging from death and breaking their contracts to expulsion. With 37 still in residence, the remaining 64 included 46 teaching in workhouse schools, three in penal or prison schools, eight in schools in the colonies, two in other schools 'connected with the government' and five, by special leave, in other schools. A further analysis shows that 33 of the 46 were in union workhouse schools and twelve in district or industrial schools, with one unclassified.

This was a poor return for the government's investment of £41,007 14s 2d in the purchase and adaptation of Kneller Hall, Twickenham, followed by a further £21,131 19s 1d spent between 1850 and 1855. Its headmaster was the Rev William Temple who, when the school closed in December 1855, spent a short time as an HMI before becoming headmaster of Rugby School, and subsequently Archbishop of Canterbury via the sees of Exeter and London. The assistant head was Francis Palgrave who worked later in the Education Department, where he produced his *Golden Treasury* (1861). Unfortunately guardians had failed to match the enterprise of the central government in providing Kneller Hall as a training college, by building the necessary district schools in which to employ the teachers. Finding jobs for them in small workhouse schools was a temporary expedient, making the best of a bad situation.

Students, who had come to Kneller Hall in the expectation of earning comparatively high salaries in district schools, felt an understandable sense of injustice. The workhouses in which they found themselves having to teach were condemned by the Rev H. Moseley in his report on Kneller Hall as 'alike unfit for the residence of children and teachers'. The future teacher's rooms were poorly furnished, and unheated. Petty tyrannies of the guardians included instances of the denial to a teacher of leave to attend church on Sunday and a refusal to supply a shaving mirror. Other problems confronted the new teacher. As a result of local opposition the proposed practising schools for students to learn how to deal with pauper and criminal children were never built. Although the Kneller Hall student, despite this handicap, was alleged to emerge well trained to give lessons, he was quite unprepared for that side of his duties to which the workhouse superintendent attached most import- ance, the supervision of children on their domestic duties in their quarters. 'Unless district schools are built', Moseley concluded, 'Kneller Hall ought not to exist.' His advice was taken, and Kneller Hall became the home of the Royal Army School of Music, where today bandsmen practise under Heathrow's flight path.[20]

Despite the problems facing him, Kay-Shuttleworth pitched his expectations high. As a condition of receiving a grant towards teachers' salaries, guardians were required to supply 'convenient and respectably furnished apartments' and rations 'the same in kind and quantity as the master of the workhouse'. In addition teachers were to be subject to no menial duties, have proper assistance for the management of the children when not in school, and have time for leisure and for training their pupil-teachers. Schools were to have a well-ordered arrangement of desks and benches, as well as a sufficient supply of books. Kay-Shuttleworth, looking to training in coopering, basket making, tinman's and blacksmith's work, carpentry and printing, in preference to tailoring and shoemaking, condemned such 'mean mechanical drudgery' as sorting hair and bristles, picking oakum, heading pins, making hooks and eyes, and chopping billets. Domestic work for girls was to include training in all the services of a housemaid, which was possibly to be combined with lessons in cottage economy. Such hopes were not always realized even by the end of the century, let alone in the 1850s.[21]

The Poor Law Board agreed with Kay-Shuttleworth on the need to handle guardians carefully, as any attempt by the inspectorate to wield its new powers energetically would have had a boomerang effect. In December 1848 an official warned him, 'I am convinced that if we use it at all freely or effectively, if we exercise an authority over schoolmasters or schoolmistresses without due consideration for the wishes of the guardians, if we at all hold the disposal of the grant over their heads by way of menace, we shall end in a great many cases by having the grant flung back in our faces, or no education given at all. The truth is that we can do no good at all except by carrying the Boards of Guardians with us in all our movements.' In similar vein the Poor Law Board agreed that although school inspectors could point out a teacher's deficiencies to him they hoped that inspectors would not intimate that his salary would depend on obtaining a certificate. The demarcation line drawn between the Poor Law Board and the Education Department severely curtailed the authority of the latter's inspectorate. Although responsible for the organization, discipline, and instruction in the schools, they were to send any suggestions concerning the classification of inmates, comments on the buildings, or anything that would modify the rules and regulations of the Poor Law Board, through the Education Department to the Board and not communicate directly with the guardians. Subsequent ambiguities were usually resolved in the P.L.B.'s favour; thus, even a suggestion that boys and girls should be separated in a certain school was deemed to come within the Board's jurisdiction. Again, the P.L.B. refused to allow the Education Department to deal directly with guardians in implementing its scheme by which schools could buy books cheaply. Last, the action of a good-natured poor law school inspector who told a teacher of a better post paying £3 10s a year more brought a complaint from the employing union. In commenting on the guardians' attitude one inspector minuted that they preferred pedagogic mediocrity to efficiency. Many guardians found the appointment of a poorly qualified candidate administratively convenient, whatever the educational consequences might have been, 'as it will probably be of a more permanent nature than that of a highly qualified teacher'. The latter with his inspector's backing was likely to be a bird of passage winging his way to a better paid post, leaving them with the time-consuming task of finding a replacement.[22]

A return made of teachers serving in workhouse schools in 1847 shows the extent of the problem facing the Education Department. In 30 of the 103 unions in the counties, running alphabetically from Bedford to Dorset, there were no teachers. By a generous interpretation 37 of the 62 schoolmasters employed can be considered to have had some relevant experience as former students or teachers in some kind of school. The schoolmasters' previous callings also included tailoring, cabinet making, shoemaking and baking, experience that could be used in industrial training and, a point of importance to the guardians, gave them a dual role in the workhouse. Forty-two of the 83 schoolmistresses claimed some previous teaching experience. Their former trades included making dresses, mantuas, and straw bonnets, working as sewing women and in domestic service. Amongst the best paid were a married couple at Stockport whose combined salary was £84 a year without board. The lowest paid were a couple at Penrith on £2 12s 0d a year each without board. Between these two extremes two men received less than £10 a year, 27 earned £10 to £20 a year, a further 24 were on £21 to £30, five on £31 to £40 and two on £41 to £50 a year. Apart from the woman at Penrith, two other women earned less than £10 a year, 72 were on £10 to £20 a year, and a further seven on £21 to £30. Thus few enjoyed the salaries of £35 for a man and £20 for a woman plus board, that Kay-Shuttleworth saw as the going rate to secure satisfactory teachers. In contrast the headmaster of the Central London

District School was earning £140 a year in 1861, with board and lodging, a salary that reflected the shortage of trained teachers at the time of his appointment. On the top of a financial Everest, he overshadowed his counterparts at other district schemes on £90 to £100 a year. Even thirty years later there were apparently no more than twelve teachers earning more than £60 a year in district and other large schools, of whom only three had £100 or more a year.[23]

Thus, inspection and certification made possible the introduction of uniform salary scales set at a higher level than those previously paid. The three main categories of the certificate – efficiency, competency, and probation – were each further subdivided into three levels, with a tenth and lowest level, permission. For a certificate of probation a candidate had to read fluently, write correctly a few simple sentences dictated from the New Testament, write and work sums correctly using the first four simple rules of arithmetic, simple and compound, and answer correctly a few simple questions concerning the life of Jesus Christ and his Disciples. When inspection began 'the performance of those receiving certificates of probation was generally not superior in penmanship, style, or accuracy to what could be found on the slate of a ten-year-old in an ordinary school'. At the top grade of efficiency a candidate had to show evidence of sound attainments in Biblical knowledge, English grammar, composition, etymology, decimal arithmetic, geography, especially of the British Empire and Palestine, the outlines of English history, and a knowledge of school management and organization. A teacher of three years' experience in a workhouse school, holding a certificate of efficiency, became eligible in the mid-1850s for a first class Queen's scholarship entitling him to free residence and tuition in a training college plus an annual allowance of £3 to £6 for incidental expenses. A teacher with a competency certificate, an achievement within the range of a pupil-teacher who had failed his Queen's scholarship examination, could redeem himself after three years in a workhouse school, by winning his scholarship without a grant.[24]

At first the pay structure took no cognizance of the size of a school, so a man in the top grade could earn £60 a year by teaching a handful of children, the good fortune of a man of Biggleswade with only six pupils. To remedy anomalies such as these the pay structure included a capitation element from 1850 onwards, an alteration that penalized the more efficient schoolmaster, as his competence lost him both pupils and income as soon as his scholars were ready for the labour market. In contrast, the elementary schoolteacher found that a reputation for competence brought him more pupils and a higher salary if he was paid a proportion of the school fees. Moreover, the workhouse teacher could lose or gain pupils through circumstances beyond his control. In times of economic prosperity guardians found little difficulty in placing children in jobs outside, while at the same time the total number of workhouse inmates declined. Conversely a trade depression was the teacher's economic salvation. When the new salary scales were first introduced, few earned the possible maximum of £60 a year, plus board and lodging assessed as worth a further £15 a year. In 1852, while five per cent and two per cent of the masters and mistresses respectively held certificates of efficiency, only seven per cent of the schools had the hundred pupils necessary to give teachers the maximum capitation grant and a total salary of £60.[25] The average pay of 35 men and eight women holding efficiency certificates was £66 and £54, including their board. By contrast 36 men and 18 women with first-class certificates in elementary schools averaged £113 and £65 respectively. To make service in workhouse schools more attractive R.R.W. Lingen, secretary to the Education Committee, proposed a new scale offering £90 a year plus board, a suggestion that would have upset the internal hierarchy of the workhouse. It would, the P.L.B. objected, have put the teacher on a 'higher salary scale than a very large proportion of workhouse masters and mistresses'. Holding no kind of formal qualification, they found their better educated subordinates a threat to their authority and personal esteem. Even a holder of a certificate of competency, eligible for a proposed salary of £35 to £45 or £25 to £35, depending on sex, would have been on a par with many workhouse masters and mistresses. However, the capitation fee was increased in two stages, eventually allowing a teacher to earn the maximum salary with only 50 pupils; women teachers found their original salaries, two-thirds of a man's, raised to four-fifths. These salary scales remained in existence until workhouse teachers were put on the Burnham scale after the First World War, by which time only a handful of teachers in small workhouses remained, some of whom were receiving salaries comparable to those paid to elementary school teachers.[26]

Although the pay of workhouse teachers clearly lagged behind that of certificated teachers in elementary schools, the comparison is in one respect misleading. The latter formed an elite. In 1859 elementary schools contained 6,878 certificated teachers of whom 40 per cent had been trained. The average annual pay of uncertificated masters in schools, subject to occasional inspection, was £45 12s 0d, of mistresses £28 7s 9d, with half of the two groups enjoying rent-free accommodation. Pay in private schools, catering for those middle-class parents who might have kept their sons at school until the age of fourteen at the most, could be as low as in a workhouse school. In Lancashire the headmaster in a country school might earn £75 a year but the usher, or second master, was on £30. In North Wales and parts of the marches, in the few private schools for which information is available, the average salary was £38 2s 6d. In Northumberland the top rate for an assistant master was £60 a year with residence. Although salaries in Norfolk's private schools ranged between £50 and £100 a year, one master was on £30. Private schools in extra-Metropolitan Surrey and Sussex, charging day boys' fees of £6 6s to £12 12s a year, offered an average of £41 and residence. Schools paying such low salaries could not pick and choose. E. C. Tufnell, who had been instrumental in securing the dismissal of masters from workhouse schools for gross ignorance or immorality, maintained that 'In almost every case they have become ushers in gentlemen's schools'.[27]

Although the pay of an uncertificated teacher could be broadly comparable to that offered in the workhouse, conditions of service were not. The teacher in a voluntary school, working nominally a five-hour stint a day, five days a week, forty-four weeks a year, under the 'occasional supervision of his social superiors', led in comparison a seemingly idyllic life, whatever the social slights he might have suffered and the extraneous duties he was expected to perform. The workhouse teacher, with little or no free time, usually had an uneasy relationship with the workhouse master and matron, 'bitter enemies to all whom they cannot trample on'. Although such teachers were not supposed to carry out duties unconnected with their defined role, in practice they must have found it hard to resist such pressures. To some it was a matter of self-interest to help with keeping the accounts and other records if they hoped to become workhouse masters themselves, one of the few avenues of promotion open to them.

Just how far state inspection and certification of teachers helped to improve standards is difficult to assess. Certainly inspection seems to have removed the obviously incompetent, if only because guardians became chary of employing teachers who might be refused the grant, a misfortune that would have put the salaries on the rates. An advertisement for a job involving long hours of work in an institution generally held in low esteem, teaching children reputed to be completely ignorant, a proportion scrofulous or suffering from some other bodily or mental infirmity, for £30 or £40 a year, did not attract the well qualified. Instead guardians were beset, one inspector wrote, by a busy and roving race, composed of damaged schoolmasters and mistresses, 'unfortunate' tradesmen and farmers, 'learned' labourers and journeymen, 'distressed' widows and daughters, armed with a goodly pile of 'the best possible testimonials' from 'persons of the highest respectability', some of which were forged. Since the turnover of such teachers, 'the most restless of that unquiet profession', could involve as many as 185 changes in 64 schools over a four-year period, guardians faced with dismay the often recurring prospect of filling such posts, a task that one inspector saw as causing more trouble than any other workhouse appointment.[28]

Table 1

The Certification of Workhouse Teachers

		1851			1862		
		Men	Women	Totals	Men	Women	Totals
Efficiency	I	10	1		25	9	
	II	6	4		18	8	
	III	17	3	41	40	16	116
Competency	I	27	12		54	32	
	II	47	37		22	32	
	III	71	61	255	31	45	216
Probation	I	78	109		64	127	
	II	58	100		30	76	
	III	36	72	453	14	48	359
Permission		16	51	67	2	11	13
Special		4	4	8	1	1	2
Total		**370**	**454**	**824**	**301**	**405**	**706**
Refused Certificate		14	38		8	22	

Source: P.P. 1852, XXXIX, p. 54; P.P. 1863, XLVII, p. 335

Table 1, showing the grading of teachers in 1851, soon after inspection began, and in 1862, the last year for which these data are available before the transfer of the inspectorate to the P.L.B., suggests an improvement that to some extent may be deceptive. When teachers stayed in a particular post for a few years, inspectors upgraded them not for showing greater competence but to give them a salary increment in recognition of their fidelity and as an encouragement to stay put.

Comparing the quality of education offered in over 700 workhouse schools with that available to a child of an independent labourer poses a number of problems. What may have been true of a small school in a rural union was not necessarily so in a large workhouse school in an industrial area. Given the limited job opportunities available to women in rural areas at this time, women teachers in rural union schools might have been of a higher calibre than those in urban areas. In addition, with small classes, children could have had much more individual attention than in a larger class in an urban union. Similarly, the quality of education available outside the workhouse varied considerably from, on the one hand, a school with a trained and certificated master, to a small dame's school where the education was of a quality still disputed amongst historians. Furthermore, workhouse children divided into two broad categories: the permanent inmates consisting of orphaned or deserted children, and those of parents who sought short-term relief, the ins-and-outs, who could account for anything between one-third and one-half of the total juvenile inmates. The latter were a particularly nomadic tribe. For example, Wolverhampton workhouse held 179 children on 1 December 1860, of whom 101 were still there a year later. In the interim, however, there had been 945 admissions and 859 discharges.[29] The presence of an unknown proportion of children suffering from some form of mental or physical handicap must have added to the teacher's problems of dealing with an ever-changing group of scholars of differing attainments, ages, and abilities.

However, before the implementation of universal compulsory education legislation, the permanent workhouse child had in theory a better opportunity than many others of obtaining some basic education, provided the guardians honoured the P.L.B. regulations in the spirit as well as the letter. He should have received instruction in arithmetic, included in the syllabus from 1842 onwards, reading, writing, and the principles of the Christian religion, for at least three working hours of every day, and such other instruction 'as may fit them for service, habits of usefulness, industry, and virtue'.[30] If indeed this rule was observed, the regular tuition received daily even under a poorly qualified teacher could have been of greater benefit to workhouse children than they would have derived from irregular attendance at a poorly run school outside.

Narrow though this syllabus may seem, many other schools offered little more. The Newcastle Report provides returns made by managers and proprietors of schools in the ten areas covered by the assistant commissioners. As their compilers doubtless wanted to give as good an impression as possible their claims have to be treated cautiously – a claim to teach geography, for example, might have been based on little more than teaching the names of some of the capital cities of Europe. Public day schools, that is non-profit making ones, usually of a religious foundation, showed the following percentages of children learning reading, writing and arithmetic: 95.1, 78.1, and 69.3 respectively. In private schools, run for profit, the corresponding figures were 93.5, 43.2, and 33.8. Thus, if the returns are at all reliable, a child in a workhouse school was three times as likely to learn some arithmetic as one in a private school taking children of the labouring classes. The opportunity which children, outside the workhouse, had of extending their education beyond the three Rs was greater in the publicly supported schools than in private ones. In public schools the percentages learning geography, English grammar, and English history were 39.4, 28.0, and 19.5 respectively. The corresponding figures for private schools were 20.1, 21.2, and 17.9.[31] The children's chances of studying these more esoteric subjects were further reduced by the intermittent nature of their attendance.

There were two small groups of workhouse children to whom the above discussion does not apply. In the early 1860s there were still three West Riding, Yorkshire, unions and eight in Wales without a workhouse and accordingly without a school. A certain number of unions preferred to send their children to a local school, a move that avoided the expenditure of running one themselves and providing a teacher with board and lodging. As early as 1852 17 unions relied on local schools of varying quality. Before 1870 some National Society schools were reluctant to accept workhouse children for fear that 'respectable' parents would threaten to withdraw their own, thereby endangering the school's income from fees and voluntary contributions. After 1870 such schools had no option if they wanted to receive the Education Department's annual grant, a condition of which required them to be open to all comers.

At first sight the appointment of the Newcastle Commission gave an opportunity of making a thorough comparison between conditions in workhouse schools and in those others available for working-class use. Unfortunately the Poor Law Act, 1850, confined the statutory right of entry to workhouse to the poor-law inspectorate. J. F. Stephen, secretary to the Commission, created baronet in 1891 on his retirement from the high court, saw Lord Courteney, President of the Poor Law Board, informally about this matter in early October 1859 before writing formally enclosing a list of the unions whose public elementary schools the Assistant Commissioners would visit. 'It is not at all improbable', Lord Courteney minuted, 'that guardians will be jealous of a visit from a third inspector'. W. G. Lumley, his assistant, revealingly observed, 'Many of these zealous men will find ample scope for their pens in the workhouse management.' On 20 October the P.L.B. guardedly offered such assistance 'as they properly can, consistently with the nature of their own offices, and the powers of the guardians of each union'. The letter continued:

I am desired, however, to point to the Education Commissioners that neither the Board nor their inspectors have any legal power to ensure admission into a workhouse for any person but those whose right to enter is provided by statute, or, consequently to give any person the right to examine such school; and also that the government of each workhouse, and the power to grant and refuse admission (with the above exception) rests with the guardians.

The following month, John Jenkins, one of the Assistant Commissioners, asked for a letter of introduction to the officials of the Merioneth Union as 'we have miles of mountain ground cutting off one portion of a parish from another, and the population of one know as little of the educational provision made for the other portion of their parish as they know of the state of education in Australia or New Zealand. The relieving officers can best supply this information.' The best the P.L.B. could do was to give Jenkins a letter of introduction requesting the reader to give such information and assistance as it might be in the reader's power to afford.[32]

Despite these legal barriers, some Assistant Commissioners managed to visit workhouse schools. Generally, they were impressed by what they saw. Two Assistant Commissioners, the Rev J. Fraser and the Rev T. Hedley, visited schools in rural unions. Hedley wrote approvingly of the beneficial effects of the recent introduction of industrial training. Fraser reported favourably on the classroom instruction, in a passage as interesting for what it says about the schools as for what it reveals of his own social assumptions: 'The instruction given is not ambitious in its range, but thoroughly sound of its kind.' The reading of the girls in Hereford workhouse he thought the best he had heard in the county for articulation and freedom from provincialism. 'It struck me that the condition of the workhouse schools very nearly approached the ideal of what elementary education in this country under our confessedly difficult circumstances ought to be, perfectly unassuming, and perfectly in keeping with what the children's future career is likely to be.' As none of the schools he visited held more than twenty pupils at the time of his visit, conditions, for reasons discussed above, may well have been unusually favourable. Although it is not clear whether Dr W. B. Hodgson visited the one workhouse school in that part of the Metropolis assigned him, he dissented from Fraser's rustic paternalism: 'It is not sought to do for them what is sought for ordinary pupils in schools. They are only paupers, and a very plain education – very plain indeed – is thought sufficient for them.'[33]

Although Patrick Cumin, another Assistant Commissioner and later Secretary to the Education Department (1884–90), was satisfied with the classroom instruction he saw, he criticized the workhouses for their failure to segregate children from adults and exercise control over their young inmates. In one instance, he stated, the wall was low enough to enable boys to escape, be absent for days, and commit all manner of crimes in the meantime. Cumin, as did the poor law inspectors, spoke disapprovingly of the practice of allowing pauper women, alleged in many cases to be prostitutes or mothers of illegitimate children, to use the lying-in wards, to look after young children, or to work alongside older girls. Even after allowing for contemporary moral obloquy, consequential exaggeration, and the new middle-class morality of the age, the Commission's disquiet on this point seems well-founded. The Report also dwelt on what today would be described as the psychological effects of long-term institutionalization, especially when it was unaccompanied by any form of physical activity or industrial training: 'The bad influences of workhouses are not confined to the formation of vicious habits'; they have 'an even stronger and better marked tendency to produce helplessness, and to prevent the growth of independence of character, than to encourage vice.' On leaving the workhouse, Cumin continued, with a compassion tinged with conventional moralism, 'Boys who have never been accustomed to handle a spade, and girls who have never been accustomed to scrub floors, naturally rebel when they can spend their lives in eating, sleeping, reading, and play.'[34]

Despite Kay-Shuttleworth's early commitment to industrial training, the offer of a grant to assist in paying the relevant instructors had not been made until 1855, shortly before the Newcastle Commissioners reported. Thus it was easy to find much that was wrong with workhouse training; less defensible is the extent to which similar shortcomings were still coming to light fifty years later. In theory the schoolmaster was responsible for industrial training, a task for which he was usually ill-equipped. As he lacked the necessary expertise and equipment, he seldom discharged this part of his duties. For the pauper child this was doubly disadvantageous, as he accordingly lacked both the training and physical stamina with which to hold down the type of job he was likely to obtain on discharge in an economy still heavily dependent on muscle power. Behind Cumin's censorious comments, however distasteful they may sound today, lies a grain of truth. Unless a boy or girl possessed the necessary physique, developed through hard manual work, that child was unprepared for the unskilled labouring work he or she was likely to find in mid-nineteenth century England. Such children had to overcome another hurdle, the harshness with which employers treated those bearing the workhouse stigma. Given their background, it was easy for such children to appear stupid on discharge. They had led extremely restricted lives during which they had been allowed no personal possessions, had never been able to handle money or carry out the simple transactions of everyday life, and they lacked social skills and the basic knowledge of everyday matters that people outside took for granted. Hence employers readily complained or refused to take them. Farmers found that the workhouse boy 'has learnt to handle a spade, but he knows nothing of the farmyard, and he is not inured to the weather'. With many workhouses lacking adequate ground on which to train agricultural labourers it is not surprising that boys sent to farmers were unaccustomed to doing a full day's work, and had no experience of ploughing, or handling horses. Such lack of training merely reinforced their awkwardness and timidity, causing them to flee to the workhouse as a refuge from employers who treated them more harshly than they treated the children of their labourers.[35]

It is not easy to determine how quickly guardians took advantage of the new grant offered. Some workhouses, already employing tradesmen and artisans for general maintenance purposes, must have seized on the newly available official bounty by dubbing their employees 'industrial instructors'. Certainly a return made in 1860 shows how easily the instructors could perform a dual role. As the 11 bandmasters, 6 drill masters, and one instructor in seamanship could only be employed in instructing the children, the Poor Law Board met the whole of their salaries. The balance – 39 tailors, 46 shoemakers, 34 gardeners, 32 houseworkers, 22 sewing women, 24 laundryworkers, 4 cooks, 12 agricultural workers, 3 painters, 5 bakers, 6 carpenters, one clog maker, 4 engineers (usually boilermen), and one in a smithy – drew two-thirds of their pay from the state if living in, or one-half if living out. To qualify for the grant a school had to have about thirty children, six of whom had to be under instruction. As the latter condition was one the inspectorate found it hard to dispute, one wonders why guardians were so slow to take advantage of the offer. Part of the explanation lies in the small size of many workhouse schools: 568 had less than 50 pupils in 1852. A more sinister explanation, advanced by one inspector, is that guardians were reluctant to provide industrial training as they would have had to feed the children better and their clothes and shoes would have worn out more quickly. Many workhouses, he complained, were not *work-houses*.[36]

In contrast the Newcastle Commissioners, swayed by E. C. Tufnell's evidence on the superiority of the education offered in district schools, as employing better paid teachers and providing a superior system of industrial training to children who were necessarily segregated from adult paupers, condemned the small workhouse school despite the evidence they had heard in its support. While the overwhelming majority of pauper children – 37,545 in March 1859 – attended these schools, separate schools held 4,381, and district ones, 2,682. Convinced that the latter two types of schools tended to emancipate children from pauperism, they recommended an extensive building programme, placing their emphasis in particular on the provision of district schools.[37] The call for more district schools came at the very time that philanthropically-minded pioneers were beginning to seek an alternative to institutional care for the pauper child.

THE WORKHOUSE
AND BEYOND

From the 1850s concern grew about the wisdom of keeping children in workhouses and other institutions in large numbers, while at the same time unofficial visitors started to penetrate beyond the porter's lodge. A small group of philanthropic women, taking up the plight of female and juvenile inmates and the state of workhouse medical services, began to develop aftercare services for children, at first mainly for girls, on their discharge. In so doing they were entering one of the few spheres thought appropriate to middle-class women of the time, while restricting their concern to matters generally conceded to come within a woman's traditional role. Their implicit criticism of the workhouse regime inevitably brought them into the male-dominated political world, for it challanged the accepted canons of contemporary social policy.

At about the same time some of the first recorded visitors were seeing workhouse inmates, the Rev H. Moseley suggested a plan by which children could be taken out of the workhouse and placed in parish schools. Under his plan the houses of teachers in voluntary schools would be enlarged to board the children, the cost of whose food and clothing would fall on the parish. Over the country as a whole each school would have had to take three or four children. Such a radical change in accepted poor law policy found ready criticism. As approximately 90 per cent of voluntary schools were in association with the Anglican Church, nonconformists had a ready-made grievance. A further objection was that the plan was a recipe for administrative chaos, involving both the Poor Law Board and the Education Department. Difficulties in providing industrial training gave a third pretext for defending the *status quo*. Writing more than a century before E. Goffman published his *Asylums: essays on the social situation of mental patients and other inmates* (1961), Moseley pointed out some of the detrimental consequences of congregating the social casualties of the day in large numbers in institutions.

There is . . . this defect, common to all pauper schools, and to ragged and reformatory schools also, that they aggregate the evil which it is their object to remedy, and deal with it not in fragments with other elements tending to neutralize it, but alone in the lump.

The public opinion of a large school is more powerful than the authority of its teachers . . . in the pauper school it has a tendency to be on the side of pauperism; in the reformatory school, of larceny; and in the ragged school, of rags.[1]

Shortly before Moseley raised these issues HMI Joseph Fletcher, honorary secretary to the Statistical Society, had expressed doubts about the wisdom of embarking on a policy of building district schools. After making a lengthy survey of the farm school system used on the continent for pauper and criminal children, he argued that the district schools, then in the course of erection near London, had yet to prove their worth, 'while we have ample testimony in favour of the farm school system'. He was even able to cite E. C. Tufnell as being on the side of the angels. In default of district schools, Tufnell wanted schools separated from the workhouse presenting 'the aspect of a well-ordered family', in which 'habits of industrious application are acquired, and the right principles of action inculcated, so that education in its highest sense is imparted to the pupils. . . .' Farm schools on the Continent, Fletcher concluded, held a social position precisely analogous to that of our workhouse ones. In such schools a training in vigorous rural industry, conducted on the principles of a Christian family, would yield 'the greatest attainable moral vigour'. Although he was making a plea for what later became known as scattered or cottage homes, he did so in the context of a predominantly rural and agricultural economy that was already rapidly yielding to an urbanized, industrial one that would offer a diminishing number of job opportunities to the young agricultural worker.

In possible reaction to the sustained campaign in *The Times* and the revelation of scandals at Andover, Blean, and Hoo workhouses a number of articles and pamphlets began to take up the cause of the workhouse child. Amongst the first was the *Church of England Magazine*'s 'The Union Workhouse' which pointed out the value of visiting children in workhouses, as well as visiting them later when they were in service or apprenticeship. The article also urged visitors to take toys, but not food, and to arrange half-day treats outside. Other publications include May and Archer, *A Plan for Rendering the Union Workhouses National Houses of Mercy* (1850), G. W. Shepherd's *Sunshine in the Workhouse* (1858), her *Christmas Eve in the Workhouse* (1859) and *Experiences of a Workhouse Visitor* (1857), Hannah Archer's *Scheme for Befriending Orphan Pauper Girls* (1861), and 'Workhouses and Women's Work' in the *Church of England Monthly Review*.

At the first annual conference of the National Association for the Promotion of Social Science, held at Birmingham in 1857, Louisa Twining read a paper on workhouses. Although the subsequently published transactions of the Association only reproduced an abridged version of her lecture its references to recent revelations of conditions in certain London workhouses aroused sufficient unease for the Association to sanction the formation of the Workhouse Visiting Society the following summer. Its first stated aim was to befriend 'destitute and orphan children in the schools, and after they have been placed in situations'. Louisa Twining, its secretary, had begun to visit an old woman in the Strand workhouse, London, in 1853, more than twenty years before the first generally accredited election of a woman guardian. Although the Poor Law Board shortly afterwards decided not to allow visits by groups of women, Miss Twining was able to continue her solitary visits to individuals. Four years later the P.L.B. relented sufficiently to permit group visits provided the guardians gave their permission, a concession the Strand guardians then refused to make. Fears lest officious lady visitors would interfere with the running of a workhouse or suggest changes involving expense made guardians wary of the new Society. The guardians of St Pancras workhouses, for example, agreed a *modus vivendi* by which members of the Society undertook not to interfere, an arrangement that led to harmonious relations on visits which afforded the pauper women 'a great deal of consolation'. Non-interference became the Society's rule. One of the few politically safe areas in which members could take action was through the provision of books, and of religious texts for the walls of wards, a form of expenditure that the Poor Law Board's auditors would have disallowed. Texts came from the Book Society, the Society for Promoting Christian Knowledge, and the National Society, books from the Religious Tract Society, the Pure Literature Society, the journal *Scripture Truths*, and from the Society for the Gratuitous Supply of Admonitions and Prayers to Workhouses, Hospitals etc.[2]

Worthy though such literature may have been, it did little to inspire young children or relieve the tedium of their surroundings. A survey made thirty years later of libraries and newspapers in workhouses shows little improvement. Southampton workhouse, with a library of about 500 books and a printed catalogue, was one of the most lavishly provided. The list shows a heavy preponderance of such didactic and improving literature as *An Alarm to Unconverted Sinners* and *Admonitions against infidelity*. Many of the books were very old, the oldest being *Youth's Magazine* (1805). There was little that was suitable for those of limited reading ability, whether child or adult. Some workhouses became the recipients of books discarded by the local free library, others depended on local charity and special efforts at

Christmas. Yet another source was the use of collecting boxes at railway stations, the only way in which Ashbourne's paupers received any newspapers or magazines. This general lack of suitable reading material for children must have seriously impeded their general personal and mental development.[3]

Thus, for fear of giving offence and risking subsequent refusal of admission, visitors could do little except provide literature, hold short religious services, and talk to the children and elderly women. William Crooks's experience later in the century shows just how rigidly the workhouse superintendent could control admission to his house. Even after Crooks was elected to the Poplar Union he found that the superintendent could refuse him admission except on regular house committee days. It required an order from Sir Henry Fowler, president of the Local Government Board, in 1893 to give guardians right of access to all parts of the workhouse containing women and children, provided their proceedings were in accordance with such rules as the guardians determined. In other words, the right of access to all except guardians remained tightly controlled.[4]

Although workhouse visitors found their scope for initiative circumscribed, they and other philanthropically-minded women could assist pauper children in other ways. Growing dissatisfaction with the workhouse regime and the training provided prompted them to seek alternatives to the workhouse altogether and to establish after-care associations. However, one of the first attempts at boarding out was made by the guardians of the Norwich Union. At first the Norwich guardians, a prime example of an 'entrenched preindustrial oligarchy fearful of losing their power' formed under a local act, had strenuously resisted the encroachment of the 1834 Act on their autonomy. By 1845, however, the board had become alarmed at the lack of segregation of their children in the local workhouse, 'a medieval ecclesiastical building'. They accordingly put the older boys in a separate house with the schoolmaster, from which they went out to daily employment in the city. With the establishment of a separate building for girls in 1850 and the acquisition of further premises in 1853 only infants and the younger girls remained in the original workhouse.[5]

Humanitarian motives were more apparent in a scheme the Rev J. Armistead, vicar of Sandbach, described to the Select Committee on Poor Relief in 1861, in which he sent girls to widows of the parish and to his National Society school. He argued for an extension of his methods so that workhouse children could be brought up in foster homes, dressed in the same way as other children and sent to the village school. Girls would then be able to find jobs in gentlemen's households, situations that were beyond the reach of girls brought up in the workhouse. They would also see their foster homes as their natural ones, returning to them if necessary between jobs . Another early pioneer was the Hon Mrs Emmeline Way, who started a home at Brockham, near Reigate, Surrey, in which she trained ex-workhouse girls for domestic service. Others followed her example at Bristol in 1860, and Southall in 1863, the year in which Mrs Way opened her second home. At first guardians used their powers under the Industrial Schools Act, 1857, to pay for the maintenance of children they sent her. As this home was a voluntary one the legality of the guardians' action was open to question. The passage of the Education of Pauper Children Act, 1862, resolved the issue by permitting the Poor Law Boards to certify various institutions, including those for idiotic, blind, deaf, and dumb children so that guardians could contribute towards their maintenance. Other early promoters of the boarding-out movement included Miss Boucheret who described her experiences in the *English-woman's Review* (January 1867), the guardians of Eton Union and of King's Norton Union, near Birmingham, and Colonel W. E. Grant, whose pamphlet *Advantages of the Boarding Out System* (1869) received considerable publicity.[6]

By the end of the decade the Poor Law Board had cautiously agreed that Mrs Archer, the wife of the chairman of Highworth and Swinton Union, should put into effect the plan she had outlined in her pamphlet for boarding out pauper girls within the confines of the union. Prompted by this increasing voluntary effort and unofficial criticism the Poor Law Board, the Local Government Board from 1871 onwards, commissioned a report on the boarding-out system in Scotland, where because of a shortage of workhouses the practice had a long history, and a second on boarding out within the union in England. The survey showed 28 unions boarding out 415 children, in some cases apparently without the formal approval of the central authority. Warminster, Ringwood, Devizes, Highworth and Swinton Unions, with over fifty children boarded out, had been doing so for 20, 12, 9, and 6 years respectively. Other unions with over ninety children boarded out had started within the last year or so. The report, which also shows three poor law districts with no children boarded out, illustrates the diversity of poor law practice in regard to children. In a more specialized study it would be possible to pursue such themes as regional differences, change over time, the personal influence of inspectors of workhouses and inspectors of schools, and the interplay between the guardians, people un-accustomed to interference in running their local affairs, and the central government. Here one can only state one's awareness of issues that render generalizations suspect. Soon after J. J. Henley had reported favourably on the practice in Scotland, G. J. Goschen, president of the P.L.B., received a delegation of women, said to be the first ever to wait on a government department. Headed by Miss Preusser, who had seen boarding out practised in her native Germany and wanted to board out Bethnal Green children outside the union, the members presented a petition signed by over 3,000 women.[7]

The circular letter accompanying Goschen's boarding out Order of November 1870, allowing children to board out beyond the union's limits, admitted the disadvantages of the small workhouse school: the imperfect classification of children, their incomplete segregation from adults, their tendency to look on the workhouse as their natural home, and the difficulty of obtaining competent teachers. These drawbacks constituted

> difficulties of too formidable a character, both in social and educational respects, to justify any preference for the system if any other practice should appear to offer reasonable chances of success.

Although Goschen argued that children would receive a better education in district and separate schools than if they were boarded out, he admitted their deleterious effects on children, and on girls in particular:

> The monotony and confinement of pauper schools must necessarily be unbroken, and prevent to a great extent the development of many of the faculties of mind and body which, in the case of children who must look forward to a hard industrial life, it is most important to expand.

The accompanying Order steered a careful course between the Scylla of the baby-farming scandals of a decade or so earlier and the even earlier abuses of the contractors' establishments, and the Charybdis of subverting the principles of the New Poor Law. The maximum payment of 4s a week for a child's maintenance, exclusive of clothing, medical and school fees, was set at a level to avoid making boarding out a covert form of outdoor relief for the foster parents, while not allowing the fostered child to become materially better off than an independent labourer's one. In addition children were not to be boarded out with persons in receipt of poor relief, nor with relations, except in special circumstances. There was an absolute ban on homes in which the father was a night worker or ones with adult lodgers. As one of the objectives of the new scheme was to allow unions in large urban areas to make use of facilities offered them for training children in homes in agricultural areas, foster homes in towns with a population of under 15,000 were especially favoured by officialdom. Larger towns, where abuses were less likely to be detected, were to be avoided. So as to set an example of the dignity of honest labour, foster parents engaged in manual labour received preference over those in sedentary occupations. To oversee the scheme the Poor Law Board broke new ground by going outside the guardians in enlisting the assistance of voluntary agencies, the proposed boarding-out committees, to supervise the childrens' welfare by making regular visits and reporting to the relevant guardians. As a further safeguard against ill-treatment the Board looked to schoolmasters' reports. Although the Board had possessed powers since 1847 allowing inspectors to visit any place where a person in receipt of relief was lodged, it was not until November 1885 that it appointed Miss M. H. Mason, at first on a temporary basis, to visit boarded-out children.[8]

Thus the publication by Mrs Nassau Senior, the political scientist's daughter-in-law, of her report in 1874 helped to reinforce both official and unofficial doubts about the wisdom of keeping children in work-house schools. She condemned the regime as morally and physically harmful, especially in the case of girls. While the scholastic training of children in the Metropolitan pauper schools was satisfactory, it did not meet the girls' requirements. She recommended an extension of boarding out and the development of small units of twenty to thirty children, so as to break up the existing schools. The proposed smaller units would allow children something approaching normal family life. Failing the implementation of these changes she advocated using some of the larger establishments as infants' schools in which older girls could look after the inmates, an arrangement that would give them a more comprehensive training as domestic servants than they then received. Other suggested forms of reorganization included using some schools as hospitals, while yet others were set aside for dividing the remaining children between the long-stay inmates and ins-and-outs. Despite the Board's failure to implement these proposals, she took action to see that one of her ideas bore fruit. The following year she founded the Metropolitan Association for Befriending Young Servants, the plan of which she had sketched out in a letter to Goschen the previous November.[9]

Over the next thirty years the boarding-out movement made some headway. On 1 January 1907, 8,659 children classified as outdoor paupers were boarded out, 6,806 within the union and 1,853 without. Better progress was made using cottage and scattered homes which housed roughly one-quarter of children on indoor relief, 15,889 out of 60,421. A third of all indoor pauper children were still in workhouses, of whom 14,676 were in ordinary wards while the remainder were in infirmaries and asylums. 11,809 were in poor law schools, of whom half were still in district ones. The balance, 11,225, were in various certified schools and homes. It is to these various categories that we must now turn our attention to see how they had fared over the three decades. One small group, those still taught in a school within a workhouse, can be dismissed quickly. By 1907, as a result of the spread of universal education, most guardians had closed their small schools. Only 565 now attended schools of which 'little can be said except in condemnation.'[10]

The large Metropolitan district schools, albeit housing only a small minority of all workhouse children, aroused disquiet for much of the period. Various forms of ophthalmia had been present from the earliest days. Children at the Central London District School, for example, had brought it with them when they moved from their old premises at Norwood to Hanwell in 1856. It remained a scourge, though less virulent in form, until at least the end of the century. Only one school, the North Surrey District School at Anerley, had managed to eradicate the infection for most of the period. The circumstances of the management committee's success were mainly fortuitous. Described in 1872 by Edward Nettleship as 'a great ophthalmic infirmary', it had acted on his advice to set up an isolation unit for infected children 'and then only through the adventitious availability of a suitable building during reconstruction work that resulted from the outbreak of ophthalmia in the first place'. Rather than maintain the isolation unit after the completion of the rebuilding work, Anerley resorted to the simple expedient of excluding all affected children. This enabled the school to maintain a clean bill of health for most of the remainder of the century, apart from a minor outbreak in the 1880s when some infected children inadvertently slipped through the screening process. The management committee of the Central London District School at Hanwell, whose members came from some of London's wealthiest parishes, showed a particularly cavalier attitude towards the health of their charges. Only after outbreaks of eye infection in 1874 and 1888, severe enough to warrant official reports and a question in the House of Commons from A. J. Mundella, did they call in Sydney Stephenson, a distinguished ophthalmologist, and agree to building an ophthalmic school costing £30,000, in 1889. Four years later the school became available for the general use of the Metropolis. Despite these ameliorative steps, the Departmental Committee which reported on the Metropolitan poor law schools in 1896 concluded that the incidence of ophthalmia was little less than twenty years earlier, when Nettleship had made his report. The Committee found that the Hackney guardians had done little to adopt remedial measures, children had less than the recommended minimum cubic air space, there was no attempt at isolating sufferers, and children had not been outside the schools for two years. At Brentwood the guardians 'put every pressure upon the medical officer to ignore the ophthalmia, and let other children come and mix with them'. Following the Departmental Committee's recommendation Stephenson inspected 17,002 children in over a hundred institutions. Between the two surveys the virulence of ophthalmic complaints and their incidence had diminished. Whereas Nettleship had found 42 per cent of the children suffering from 'bad granular lids', defined by Stephenson as trachoma, the latter found 4.91 per cent. Similarly the incidence of 'discharge' fell from 11.90 to 4.06 per cent, while ophthalmic corneal discharge similarly fell from 9.10 to 1.28 per cent. Overall, Nettleship had found more than two-thirds of the children with some kind of eye defect. Whereas thirty years earlier purulent ophthalmia, a complaint that caused at least one half its victims either to lose their sight or have it severely damaged, had been a matter of serious concern, Stephenson did not find a single case in the schools. Trachoma remained the most prevalent form of ophthalmic complaint; 'If we could get rid of it', Stephenson wrote, 'the burning question of ophthalmia would cease to exist in the Metropolitan pauper schools'. The main causes of improvement were thought to be an increased attention now paid to ophthalmia both inside and outside the schools, together with the bettering of the school environment. Buildings that had been thought healthy in the 1850s were no longer considered adequate by the late 1890s. In 1862 Hanwell, where the corridors were 'the lungs of the establishment' and were held responsible 'in no small degree [for] the high standard of health the school maintains', was later described as being 'built as if for the express purpose of limiting the entry of light and air'. In 1890 the building's main frontage running for six hundred feet was broken up, the drainage improved, and a gymnasium built. The boys' school at Sutton had been constructed in 1854 'upon a plan that nobody would nowadays dream of adopting'. By the late nineteenth century its means of ventilation were considered inadequate. Despite the greater availability of information on sanitary and health matters those schools that were in a bad condition in 1874 remained at the top of the ophthalmic league in 1896.

As in other instances, guardians feared the reaction of their ratepayers to having to find more money, more than the power of the L.G.B. to withhold the next precept from the Metropolitan Common Fund for failing to execute an order relating to structural alterations to a workhouse or the appointment of officials. Unfortunately for poor parishes expenditure relating to the erection or repair of buildings fell on local rates, while the cost of the maintenance of a London school fell on the Metropolitan Common Fund. Moreover, the guardians' scant regard for the inspectorate meant that they did not attach any greater importance to an inspector's recommendation than to an ordinary individual's though 'perhaps it might be more authoritative'. Seeing themselves as officialdom's equals in discussing any suggestions, they were accused by a frustrated bureaucracy of picking and choosing as they pleased, especially when public expenditure was involved. Thus even when the Sutton Board had itself commissioned a report, its chairman could blithely state that they 'had not felt themselves called upon to take any notice' of it.[11]

Concern over the incidence of ophthalmia was part of a wider uneasiness about the wisdom of keeping children in workhouses, and in district schools in particular. Improvements that took place in other Metropolitan schools failed to assuage this concern, particularly when abuses or scandals came to light. Because of structural inadequacies, 26 boys died in a fire at the Forest Gate Schools in 1889; two more died there from ptomaine poisoning and 148 were ill after eating soup made from fly-blown meat four years later. At Brentwood a nurse received five years' penal servitude for ill-treating the infants in her charge over a long period; so thirsty were these children at times that they drank water from puddles and water closets. The Departmental Committee subsequently appointed found that girls were generally known by their numbers, that opportunities for organized games and outside visits were the exception rather than the rule, overcrowding and the resulting pervasive institutional smell a cause for complaint, and a rigid discipline the norm. On the other hand the girls at St George's in the East school, Brentwood, Essex, now had one consolation: they no longer had to have their hair cropped. The children at Anerley enjoyed a heated swimming bath and a gymnasium, while the babies had a nursery. Sick children could go to a convalescent home at Broadstairs, Kent. Other recent changes included the appointment of a visiting dentist and an improved course of technical instruction.

Although it was possible to argue that, despite the various imperfections that came to light, the children's creature comforts compared favourably with those available to their social peers outside, their moral or psychological condition was worse. Dr Barnardo, for example, thought that the 'dull monotony of institutional life, and its yearly routine which reduces everything to the dead level of a colourless experience . . . has much to answer for in the evil habits contracted by these girls'. The aggregation of children who 'had nothing in common but their poverty and their unfortunate and often degrading antecedents' led the Committee to recommend the closing of the District Schools. Turning Kay-Shuttleworth's earlier argument on its head, they decided that the schools reinforced rather than removed the taint of pauperism. They failed to encourage childrens' mental development and aspiration for higher things. In saying this they were at one with Miss W. L. Hall, secretary of the Association for the Advancement of Boarding Out, who had informed the House of Lords' Select Committee of 1889 that the only way of counteracting the hereditary taint of pauperism was to remove children from the workhouse. The Committee decided that the boarding-out system was the best as it gave pauper children the healthiest and most natural life they could have, as well as offering them the best chance of escaping their former pauper associations and becoming absorbed into the respectable working population. Following the publication of the Report the number of children in large district schools fell from 7,395 in 1895 to 3,591 by 1907.[12]

Alternatives to workhouses and their schools remained unpopular with guardians for a number of reasons. In 1903, one of the few years for which there are details of pauper children of school age in school, 15,167 of the 31,778 attended public elementary schools. The remainder were at poor law schools – 4,130 were in district ones, 9,962 in separate schools, 1,672 in traditional workhouse schools, and a further 847 in institutions belonging to the Metropolitan Asylums Board, with 516 in the training ship *Exmouth* and 331 elsewhere.[13] As when guardians were first urged to form district schools, local boards were reluctant to see buildings they had either erected or had available, lying underused or empty merely because of a change in attitude towards child care. Guardians still had to provide indoor relief for tramps' children and those of the able-bodied poor, both of which groups had to take their children with them should they decide to discharge themselves, an action they sometimes took at a moment's notice. A nucleus of permanent children was useful to the smooth running of the workhouse in many ways. They could for instance assist with the daily discipline and internal economy of the childrens' ward, thereby making the handling of temporary sojourners easier for authority. To have had only short-stay children in the workhouse and to have sent 'permanent' children elsewhere, while still providing schooling, would have added to both unit and total costs. Moreover, some of the new forms of child care deprived guardians of direct control over 'their' children, as had the earlier district schools. Although all unions could board out their children, in 1907 only 93, of which 26 were Metropolitan, were doing so.[14] Guardians worked through an intermediary, the Association for the Advancement of Boarding Out, which put them in touch with the locally convened voluntary committees that shared responsibility for the children's welfare with the Poor Law Board. As guardians could not claim travelling expenses for visiting children outside the boundaries of their unions, unless they possessed an unusual sense of altruism they were dependent on Miss Mason's and the local committee's vigilance in seeing that their children were properly treated.

Despite the precautions the Local Government Board had built into the scheme some homes were unsatisfactory. Aspirant foster parents applied for children for motives that ranged from altruism at one extreme to a desire for cheap servants at the other, an ambition the Board attempted to thwart by imposing an upper age limit of ten except for those boarded out with their younger siblings. Miss Mason found on her early inspections that the least satisfactory homes were in areas whose local committees were the slackest. One committee, nominally with ten members, had only two active ones responsible for 56 children. On a number of occasions evidence of ill-treatment came to light only by chance or when children left their foster homes. Miss Mason found that the children's fear of returning to the workhouse was so great that unless they were actually starved or badly beaten they preferred to be fostered out. At times it proved impossible to extract information from obviously ill-treated children when they had been removed from their homes. As a result of the abuses she found in her early years of duty, both Barnardo's and the Council of the Children's Holiday Fund appointed lady inspectors.

The difficulty of finding suitable foster parents, combined with her reluctance to remove children from their new homes, made Miss Mason ready to accept standards of hygiene lower than those countenanced by the Board's regulations for workhouses. She found many instances of girls who were outwardly clean, thus satisfying the superficial inspection made by members of many of the voluntary committees, who on closer examination revealed filthy underclothing and bodies black with dirt of long standing, covered with purpura and fleabites. She did not reject a house, unless 'Its condition and smell are likely to be actually dangerous to health', with up to four children of the same sex in a bed, or bedding 'unless almost black, and not always even then'. She passed nits in the hair unless the hair was nearly matted with them, as well as body dirt of four or more weeks' standing. Yet at the other extreme, as the Poor Law Report of 1909 makes clear, some children were treated with loving care in their homes. All enjoyed the advantage, denied most other pauper children, that with the stigma of the workhouse less apparent they had a better chance of fitting in with the local community and its schools.[15]

Children boarded out within the union were not so lucky. Bereft of the supervision of a locally based committee that Miss Mason's visits reinforced, and denied membership of a medical panel, they had to rely on the spasmodic and uncertain support of the relieving officer. Not only was the latter wont to take the standard of the home of an applicant for outdoor relief as his norm, but he used boarding out, despite regulations to the contrary, as a covert form of outdoor relief. The appointment of a boarding out committee was optional. If there were no committee, guardians had to ensure that the relieving officer and a medical officer visited the children. As there was no effective mechanism to ensure that such visits were made, children could go for long periods without ever seeing an official. When the guardians did appoint a committee, they could dispense with both officials and rely on the diligence of one of their own members to report on the foster homes once every six weeks. In neither case did Miss Mason hold any responsibility for children boarded out within the union.[16] In response to criticisms made by the Royal Commission in 1909 the Local Government Board issued an order in December of that year requiring guardians to appoint a boarding out committee which could consist either entirely of non-guardians, or a mixture of guardians and non-guardians. The Order provided for the appointment of a woman visitor, required the medical officer to report on all children quarterly, and transferred the duties of the relieving officer to the woman visitor or a member of the committee. The following year the Board increased its staff of women inspectors to six to supervise the fostering of the 9,000 children boarded out both within and without the union. Finally, the Boarding Out Order, 1911, abolishing any remaining administrative distinctions between the supervision of the two classes of children, required all committees to appoint women to at least one-third of their places, and placed the duty of medical inspection on the elementary school.[17]

Another group, almost as neglected by officialdom before the late 1900s as children boarded out within the union, were those in certified institutions, holding 8,000 in 1908, and uncertified ones, holding 3,000. By 1908 there were 269 schools certified under the Education of Pauper Children Act, 1862. Over the intervening forty years two modifications were made to the original act. From 1868 onwards guardians were permitted to send blind, deaf and dumb children to uncertified schools. In 1882 they were allowed to pay the voluntary agencies more than the original limit of the notional cost of a child's maintenance in a workhouse, as this figure did not allow anything for a child's education. As the 1862 Act predated universal compulsory education, Poor Law Inspectors, certifying a school, had looked solely at its sanitary condition. Such schools also lay outside the orbit of the Elementary Education Act, 1876, which required children to satisfy certain standards of attainment and attendance before being granted permission to work. Following a complaint from the Metropolitan Board of Guardians in 1883 about the lack of information they had on Roman Catholic schools that they were in effect subsidizing, the Poor Law Inspectorate began to visit 23 of the larger ones, a duty handed over to the Board of Education in 1904.

The Local Government Board's only responsibility for the remaining certified schools was to visit them annually, a task not always carried out, to ensure that the children were properly fed and clothed, and not overcrowded. On such visits inspectors did not always know how many children a particular school held, a circumstance that enabled managers to hide children they did not wish to be seen. Hence evidence of ill-treatment, illegal employment, overcrowding, and illicit farming out of children at a profit to the school came to light only by chance. Apart from those children in approximately twenty schools inspected by the Board of Education for grants as public elementary schools before 1904, the educational standard of the others remains unknown. The Local Government Board did not know if a particular school was designated a public elementary school for grant-receiving purposes: the Local

Education Authority had no right of admission to schools not so designated to check on school attendance and other matters. As a result of these revelations the Board of Education assumed responsibility for the remaining schools certified under the 1862 Act.[18]

Children in cottage and scattered homes constitute the last category of indoor pauper children that needs consideration. By 1907 fifty unions had placed 8,420 in grouped cottage homes, while 47 used scattered homes for 4,963. In both instances the basic unit contained approximately ten to fifteen children supervised by a matron if the children were young, or a married couple if the children were older. Children from the homes attended the local elementary school. Cottage homes owe their origins to the initiative of those voluntary societies in the 1860s that had set up institutions comparable to industrial and reformatory schools. By the late 1870s the Local Government Board had approved plans for the building of five cottage homes for 934 children to operate on a group or family system. A Report suggested that the capital cost of such schools need not be higher than that of a large district school, while running costs might be lower. Not only could a married couple provide a wide range of services more cheaply than two single persons, but the cottage homes would benefit from the labour supplied by the boys and girls. In addition the wider syllabus of industrial training would 'produce healthy heads of families, and the progenitors of children free from the hereditary taints now common to that class'. Scattered homes developed more slowly, the first nine being opened in Sheffield in 1896.[19] By the end of the Second World War the disadvantages for a child of life in a large institution were widely accepted. The Curtis Committee, realizing that 'something must be provided which gives the child the feeling that there is a secure and affectionate personal relation in his life', argued the need to place all children in care in small groups in small nurseries, grouped or scattered homes if they could not be boarded out or provided for in voluntary homes.[20]

Despite the various methods available by 1914 for the care of pauper children, the typical child had spent his formative years in a workhouse children's ward and school, or a district or separate school. Although there was an increase in the number of children sent to local public elementary schools this resulted more from considerations of expediency than of humanity. Guardians closed small schools because of the increasing difficulty they experienced in obtaining suitable staff. It seems that board schools accepted the pupils more readily than did ones connected with the Church of England, as 'people of the parish . . . have a sort of feeling that there is something unsavoury about the very person of a pauper child'. Where such schools refused to accept pauper pupils the Education Department forced the managers' hands by pointing out that they received their grants for public elementary schools. Before 1891 and the general abolition of school fees managers had had the last word, for they could charge the maximum fee of ninepence a week, thereby effectively debarring pauper children whose fees the guardians paid. The passage of the Elementary Education Act, 1876, helped to accelerate the decline of the small workhouse school. Even before that date one Poor Law Inspector had introduced an examination of the children in the three Rs, under the standards of the Revised Code. Many teachers unable to meet his requirements had resigned. With the increased demand for teachers in new schools in the 1870s and 1880s guardians were unable to staff small schools at the small salaries they could offer, with teachers of a sufficient calibre to meet the requirements of the new Act. From 1895 onwards the Board actively encouraged guardians to send children to local day and Sunday schools to enable them to mix with other children as much as possible. At the same time the President reminded guardians that the 1842 regulations concerning workhouse uniform were not mandatory. Paupers on leave from the workhouse, a group that could include children going to school, did not have to wear clothing 'in any way distinctive or conspicuous in character'. Despite these good intentions children from the workhouse did not always mix with other children at playtime and, even when they were not wearing uniform, their clothes marked them out from others.[21]

The requirement that children over the age of 10 had to possess a certificate of proficiency or of previous attendance from a certified efficient school, a term that included workhouse schools, necessitated changes in the Local Government Board's 1847 regulations as well as a fresh appraisal of the schools. Their inspectorate was told to refuse certificates only 'where the workhouse is thoroughly bad . . . and where also there are means of remedy at hand that the guardians refuse to adopt. The Board hope that the inspector will be especially cautious in the selection of schools that are to be so marked.' At least one inspector heeded the advice. On forwarding his list of schools to be certified as efficient he had borne in mind, he wrote,

> the injunction not to be very strict in judging of the efficiency of a school, but to take into account all the circumstances which may have unfavourably affected the result of the exertions of the teacher.

Inspectors knew that they could do little about the teacher. Two years earlier Tufnell, in response to a suggestion that the test for higher grades of the certificate should be made more rigorous, had written:

> In these small schools, where the teacher has to put up with many inconveniences and often snubs from the master of the workhouse and ignorant guardians, we must take what we can get, and to exact [higher] requirements . . . would result in our getting no teachers at all.

Once certified, a school had to offer instruction for four hours a day to children over the age of seven, the time being divided between the morning and afternoon sessions. Previous to this, although the Board's regulations had required three hours' instruction a day, it had been powerless to stipulate when such instruction was given. In addition schools had to keep attendance registers in a prescribed form, possess a timetable, and prepare lists of pupils to be examined in the standards of the Revised Code.[22]

It was one matter to make new regulations, it was another to enforce them through the agency of an inspector making an annual visit of which prior notice had been given. Moreover, the annual grant paid to the workhouse was in respect of the teacher, not of the children's performance and attendance. Thus poor law inspectors, unlike those of the Education Department, could not reduce the grant if they found that the children did not make the prescribed number of attendances. 'The school inspector is of no account, and the guardians know it.'[23]

Except for the introduction of drawing into a few of the larger schools and the need to meet the requirements of the 1876 Act, the regulations issued by the Poor Law Board in 1847 set the pattern of workhouse education until after the turn of the century. Thus the pauper child did not generally benefit from the extension to the school curriculum made by the Education Department when it offered financial inducement for teaching such subjects as English, history, geography, elementary science, object lessons, and manual training. Such history, geography, and natural science as a child learnt came incidentally, if at all, from reading lessons, a process that the restricted life of a workhouse made all the more difficult for a teacher whose general knowledge may have been meagre in the first place. 'The confinement between four walls takes all the intelligence out of them.'[24] The transfer of inspection from the Education Department to the Poor Law Board for the period from 1864 to 1904, when it was returned to the Board of Education in belated response to the recommendations of the Cross Commission in 1888 and the Departmental Committee on Metropolitan Schools in 1896, re-inforced the intellectual purdah separating the workhouse child from his peers outside.[24]

For much of the period after 1870 workhouse teachers suffered almost equal isolation. Slowly, however, there was an improvement in their prospects and conditions of service. In 1873 the Education Department allowed those holding Local Government Board certificates of competency or efficiency to be examined for the Education Department's teacher's certificate. The five out of the first six who passed the examination then found a further hurdle to surmount. To obtain their full certificate or parchment they had to teach for two years in a school recognized as efficient by the Education Department, and be passed by one of the Department's inspectors, but service in a poor law school and inspection by one of the Board's inspectors did not count towards qualifying for the coveted parchment. The one concession the Education Department was prepared to make was to allow the newly-trained teacher, straight from college, to count his time in a workhouse school as his probationary period. He then had to move to a public elementary school for examination by an inspector of the Education Department. Not until 1890, after considerable pressure from work-house teachers who wanted to qualify for the better-paid posts in district schools, did the Education Department agree to examine them in their place of employment for their parchment. Even then they remained less well paid than their colleagues in board schools. By the late 1900s the London Poor Law schools offered headmasters and headmistresses average salaries of £190 and £120 respectively, while the London School Board paid headmasters £200 to £500 a year and headmistresses £150 to £300 a year. Assistant masters and mistresses in the capital's poor law schools averaged £120 and £100 a year respectivly. No head of a London Poor Law school received as much as he would under the London School Board, while only two assistants were paid on the L.S.B.'s scale. Men in London's Board schools earned £90 to £200 a year and women received £80 to £150 a year on incremental scales, while the highest paid male assistant in a London poor law scheme received £175 a year and the lowest paid had to be content with £60 a year.[25]

In contrast to the slight improvements gained by workhouse teachers, the lot of pupil teachers worsened. When Kay-Shuttleworth moved to the Education Department as its first Secretary he, and later his successor R. R. W. Lingen, found that the poor law regulations stood in the way of apprenticing pauper children as pupil-teachers. As paupers they could not earn any money or even possess their own clothes or books. The Education Department accordingly arranged for the pauper apprentice to receive his accumulated pay, on the expiry of his article, as an exhibition to a training college. The number of such children was always small, 81 in 1862 and 56 the following year, of whom 40 were in district or large separate schools. To be apprenticed, a pupil-teacher had to work in a school containing a minimum of forty scholars, a requirement that made approximately half all workhouse schools ineligible. Transfer to larger schools would not have solved the difficulty as both apprentice and teacher had to come from the same school. The onus on the guardians to feed, clothe, and buy books for the apprentice between the ages of 13 and 18 acted as a further deterrent. Pupil teachers disappeared altogether from workhouse schools by the 1880s. New regulations required the Education Department's inspectorate to examine certain aspects of the candidate's work, testing by Poor Law inspectors not being accepted. Moreover, the fees charged by training colleges rose to a level that made the pupil-teacher's accumulated earnings insufficient to take him through the two-year course. Bereft of the consolation of teaching pupil teachers at a slightly higher level than normally required in the classroom, poorly paid workhouse teachers remained an underprivileged group until after the First World War. Teachers in workhouse schools could only have moved at considerable risk to their pension prospects. The Poor Law Officers' Superannuation Act, 1898, put the cost of paying a pension on the last employing union. Hence, unions were reluctant to take on an employee with only a few years to serve before retirement. If a teacher moved from a workhouse to an elementary school he found that his service in his previous post carried no recognition for pension purposes under the Elementary School Teachers' Act, 1898 which, moreover, applied solely to certificated teachers. Given all these disadvantages trained teachers shunned workhouse schools. For example, of the 2,192 former students of St John's College, Battersea, who could be traced in 1906, only seven were teaching in workhouse schools (although this may be somewhat atypical, for St John's could attract some of the ablest students of each year's cohort).[26]

When Tillard and Synge inspected 28 of the larger district and separate schools on behalf of the Board of Education they found both teachers and pupils still living in an educational ghetto. They issued their report only three years after the ending of the practice of examining individual children in the three Rs, a practice that the Board of Education's inspectorate had abandoned more than a decade earlier. Thus, teaching and curriculum had remained based on the Revised Code of 1862 for more than forty years. Although they professed to have seen a great improvement in the schools already they had to admit that some of the older teachers would never be anything but wooden and mechanical, and that it was still possible to find one headmaster who 'believes in the three Rs and no nonsense'. Whatever might have been the comparative merits of small workhouse schools earlier in the century, the introduction of universal elementary education and the improvement of its quality in the latter decades had bypassed the pauper child. Narrowly educated, he was now about a year behind his contemporaries in an ordinary school. The general standards of the schools varied considerably. At one extreme were those controlled by guardians who still regarded a school as little more than a sideshow and took little interest in it. In such cases guardians had done little to implement recommendations concerning repairs or additions to staff. At the other extreme, amongst the 28, were rare instances of schools as efficient as the best local authority ones. Outside these extremes the authors maintained that the average poor law school compared fairly well with the average public elementary one. These larger schools now offered better conditions of service to their teachers, most of whom lived outside and enjoyed the same holidays as other teachers. In contrast to evidence presented to the Royal Commission on the Poor Laws, they reported:

> Into scales of payment we did not make any inquiry, but it came to our knowledge that in many poor law schools the guardians now adopt the scale of salaries for teachers in public elementary schools used by the local education authority.

Despite the brave gloss Tillard and Synge put on matters, they thought that the schools would be run more effectively by the local education authority, that the isolation of their teachers should be ended, and that there should be free interchange between them and elementary school teachers. In making these recommendations they were endorsing the sentiments expressed by Moseley half a century earlier and reiterated by Poor Law Inspector Holgate when he appeared before the Cross Commissioners.[27] Assimilation took place after the First World War when the newly appointed Burnham Committee recognized the service of teachers in poor law schools, along with that in reformatory and industrial ones, as qualifying for increments on the Burnham Scale. Similarly the Teachers' Superannuation Acts of 1918 and 1922 allowed service in these schools to count for pension purposes.

Yet the poor law school and even the idea of the district school lingered on. The Poor Law Institutions Order of 1913 requiring all healthy children over the age of three to be removed from workhouses at the end of six weeks, suspended during hostilities, was reintroduced in an advisory form in 1920. The unions in Cornwall proposed to comply with the letter of the Order, but not its spirit, by turning Truro workhouse into a district school taking two hundred children from neighbouring unions, a plan dropped twelve months later. Although the 1913 Order became mandatory in 1930, workhouses continued to contain a nucleus of 2–3,000 healthy children throughout the interwar years. In 1930, a year after the abolition of the boards of guardians, there still remained 40 poor law schools, five district schools and 11 schools administered by the Metropolitan Asylums Board, containing a total of 9,652 children. The Local Government Act, 1929, together with the Poor Law Act of the following year, allowed local education authorities to provide education in the remaining poor law schools and, if they acted as agents of the new Public Assistance Committees, to become responsible for the children's care. Hospital schools, accounting for 28 of the 56 schools just mentioned, began to pass from the control of the P.A.Cs. to that of the Public Health Committees. By 1938 there remained 20 poor law schools, 13 of which were educating 2,566 healthy children, and seven hospital schools with 210 pupils. The schools had 103 full-time members of staff of whom 80 and 12 were recognized as certificated and uncertificated teachers respectively. Despite this improvement in staffing, only the exceptional child stood any chance of climbing the educational ladder. Of 1,122 children leaving school in 1937–8, nine went to secondary school and a further 90 to other institutions offering some form of post-elementary education or training. Few were able to take advantage of any local authority scholarships to secondary schools that were available (such as those of the London County Council, for example, which had opened their scholarships to poor law children in 1908.[28])

For much of the period under discussion the demands made on children's labour under the guise of industrial training had hampered their scholastic development. Before 1897, when the Local Government Board issued its first set of regulations to limit the time thus spent by children, some guardians expected children to work under conditions that would have been in breach of the Elementary Education Acts outside the workhouse. Under an order introduced that year part-time exemption from schooling was permitted at 11 and full-time at 14. No child under the age of 11 could do more than one hour's work a day, a limit that rose in stages to eight hours for those totally withdrawn from schooling at 14. Schools, previously required to give instruction every working day, now closed one day a week and six weeks a year. Unions had to prepare and exhibit timetables of industrial work. How far this order was obeyed must remain a matter largely for conjecture, as it must with almost every other order. Suffice it to say that although the Elementary Education Act, 1893, had raised the minimum age for part- or full-time exemption from schooling to 11, members of the 1896 Departmental Committee found six schools employing boys of 10, a seventh girls of the same age, and an eighth girls of 8 on a part-time basis. When a school alternated classroom tuition with industrial training on a diurnal basis, children could be working a ten-hour day. Twelve years later Tillard and Synge found instances of the total withdrawal of children from the classroom at the age of 13 or on reaching a certain standard. Most schools adopted a policy of partly withdrawing children at the age of 12 or on reaching Standard IV or V. In some cases strong girls were withdrawn without fulfilling these conditions.[29]

In many instances the guardians' concern was not to give children a training that might be useful in later life but to keep down running expenses:

> Many guardians look upon the children as machines, for the purpose of reducing the expense to the union to the lowest possible amount. The so-called industry . . . is literally making use of the children's labour as cheap labour in the workhouse.[30]

Once children in small workhouses started going to outside schools, industrial training went by default in the absence of a schoolmaster. Such supervision as they received out of school hours usually came, if at all, from the porter, another minor official, or a pauper. Consequently they did not gain the kind of preparation for the world beyond school their peers outside received, such as running errands, helping their parents domestically or in their paid work, or having a part-time job. Patching, repairing, and cobbling, marked the usual limits of boys' experience in the overmanned trades of tailoring and shoemaking. Other work for them included assisting workmen, cleaning, sweeping, and polishing. Much of the time was probably spent in idleness, especially at week-ends, an idleness that combined with a routine of daily monotony to give William Crooks, MP, an abiding memory of his workhouse childhood.[31]

Girls undoubtedly suffered more than boys, as the daily running of a workhouse encompassed jobs that fell within women's traditional role. Domestic tasks in district schools were essentially large-scale ones, of little value in training a girl for domestic service in a small household. With poor-quality supervisory staff directing them, girls had to scrub 'vast corridors and endless dormitories', wash large quantities of crockery and cutlery, or prepare food for its subsequent rough-and-ready cooking. The bigger the workhouse or school, the greater the sub-division of labour. Thus a girl might learn to starch a collar but never to iron, to peel potatoes by the bushel but never to cook them. At one London school where 1,684,000 towels and 35,000 other articles were washed yearly, girls were mere drudges, loading and unloading boilers or turning mangles.[32] Consequently, unless a girl became a member of a small privileged elite preparing food for the senior workhouse staff, she never learnt the use of ordinary domestic utensils, how to lay a fire, or set a table. The ignorance of many ordinary domestic utensils and processes shown by girls on first going out to service was often mistaken for stupidity by unsympathetic employers.

The crude cooking methods described by Dr Edward Smith in his report to the Poor Law Board in 1866 demonstrate the inadequacy of the workhouse kitchen as a training ground for future domestic servants. In nearly all the workhouses he visited there was a proportion, he thought too large a proportion, of children whose health and strength were not equal to that found among their contemporaries in the community at large. Although he held it to be important not to allow the children to acquire tastes that they might not be able to satisfy in later life, they should be enabled as a matter of public policy to grow up strong and healthy. In the long run an abundant supply of food, he argued, was cost-effective. A sound diet would avoid the procreation of future inmates of workhouses and of physically and mentally inferior citizens. A study made ten years later of children's diet in the Metropolitan schools reveals a number of similarities with prison dietaries. Meals were monotonous, bland, cheap and easy to prepare and serve, but thought to be nutritious. Thus breakfast at Bethnal Green School consisted of a daily serving of 5 oz bread and one-and-half pints of oatmeal gruel, at St George's in the East children had 6 oz bread and a half-pint of milk a day. Supper at both schools had bread as its main constituent with the addition of cheese, milk, or broth. The mid-day meal offered the greatest variety over the course of the week. At Bethnal Green children had 5 oz meat and 8 oz potatoes or vegetables three days a week, 4 oz bread and one-and-half pints of pea soup twice a week, 12 oz suet pudding twice a week, and mid-day meals at St George's in the East were basically similar. Matters were no better at the Swinton Schools, near Manchester, at the end of the century where gruel or porridge had been served for breakfast for at least sixty years. Supper consisted of bread and milk. The mid-day meals did not contain any fresh vegetables, fish, or butter. An ounce of meat was given twice a week as a constituent of potato hash or pea soup. Apart from requiring separate dietary tables in 1856 for children under the age of five and for those between five and nine, the consolidated order of 1847 remained in force until 1900, when the Board gave guardians wider latitude than before. Christmas Day in the Workhouse, a day immortalized by George Sims, must have seemed a gastronomic oasis in a desert of gruel. If the infrequency with which Christmas treats are mentioned in the *Journal of the Workhouse Visiting Society* (1859–6) is a reliable guide it was an oasis few children reached. The ones reported, at Kirkdale Industrial School and St Giles's Workhouse School, were at well-known institutions and so could have been deemed news-worthy. On the other hand celebrations, treats, and outings in less well-known workhouse schools might well have gone unrecorded, except possibly in the provincial press. At this level, without much further research, it is difficult to penetrate the day-to-day life children led. Much depended on the personalities of the workhouse superintendent and matron, the teachers and other officials, and the chance factor of the interest taken by individual guardians and others in the children's welfare. Thus it is possible that children in small schools might have found life more varied and their treatment more humane than would have been the case in a large impersonal institution.[33]

Ill-prepared girls from workhouses, reformatories, and industrial schools were put to domestic service, an occupation they shared with 1,250,000 women in 1871. The practice of using poor and friendless girls as domestic drudges has a long history. To the impecunious employer they offered a cheap means of access to the respectability of the servant-keeping class: to the unscrupulous they were easy prey for economic and sexual exploitation, physical ill-treatment or sheer neglect. Guardians were encouraged to ensure that girls received a shilling a week, a wage that some were still earning as late as the 1890s. At the worst, girls found their money docked for months ostensibly to pay for their clothes and uniform. If they went to large households as 'between maids' or 'tweenies', at the beck and call of both the cook and the housemaid, the normal misery of such a post could be compounded by the added incubus of the workhouse taint. If girls who had known little love in their lives became pregnant, perhaps as a result of yielding to the blandishments of a member of the household, they faced instant dismissal without references. Whether they left a post from choice or were dismissed friendless and penniless, they had few means of support apart from temporary prostitution or returning to the workhouse, especially if they were pregnant. Yet returning to the workhouse in the knowledge that they might be set to oakum picking must have been an action of last resort.

To remedy this state of affairs a number of women decided to set up hostels in which to train ex-workhouse girls for domestic service. By the mid-1880s the Metropolitan Association for Befriending Young Servants was placing over 5,000 pauper girls a year in service. At the turn of the century 1,000 charities (600 of which exclusively dealt with girls in conjunction with the Reformatory and Refuge Union, founded in 1856) as well as larger institutions such as the Waifs and Strays Society, the Ragged School Union, and the Children's Aid Society, were involved. Apart from its eponymous function the Workhouse Visiting society acted in this other capacity as well. The total number so placed, it has been suggested, ran into tens of thousands annually. These servants, usually debarred from middle-class households, satisfied the demand for domestic servants at the bottom end of the market from those families unable to afford or not prepared to pay girls from a more respectable background.[34]

As well as finding a pauper girl employment, some voluntary agencies sent lady visitors to the girl's future place of employment to assess its suitability and avoid the more exploitative world of the public house, the common lodging house, or hostel. She also visited the girl while she settled down in what must have been a bewildering environment after a cloistered workhouse life. With the possible exception of Mrs Way's home at Brockham and a few other small agencies that might have placed respectable or orphaned girls in middle-class homes, it is difficult to sustain the argument that middle-class philanthropists were recruiting their own supply of cheap servants. Such households would not have employed workhouse girls, whose destination was rather that of a skivvy in a working-class home. The only possible benefit to the philanthropists would have been an indirect one, that by increasing the supply of servants as a whole they helped to depress the general wage level. Even then one needs much more quantitative evidence about the shifts of demand and supply in the different sectors of the domestic labour market to sustain such a hypothesis.

The new moves to assist pauper children in the 1860s met the opposition characteristic of all attempts to help the underprivileged, whether these were paupers, from reformatories, or destitute children living by their wits. They were seen as putting a premium on poverty and delinquency at the expense of the honest self-supporting labourer struggling to bring up his family. George Coode, assistant secretary to the Poor Law Commissioners, denounced Louisa Twining and her associates as 'irresponsible philanthropists' embarking on a 'paradisical arrangement', 'a pampering, coddling system, an eleemosynary travesty, a very pretty philanthropic romance'. He was 'wholly incredulous as to the benefit to be derived . . . from concealing from pauper children the fact that they are paupers'. Homes such as Miss Twining proposed as refuges between jobs were luxuries not enjoyed by other domestic servants. A job of drudgery was appropriate to those at the bottom of the social scale, for whom 'the lowest honest and independent work is moral promotion from the condition of pauperism.'[35]

The task of visiting children which was undertaken by the voluntary societies theoretically supplemented, but in practice virtually replaced, duties enjoined on guardians in 1851. An Act of that year required a relieving officer to visit pauper children under the age of 16 in their first place of employment twice a year. The Act soon became a dead letter. Not only did the Poor Law Board fail to issue any directive to its inspectorate to ensure that the Act was observed, but relieving officers had no authority to enter the abode of the child's employer. Thirty years later the Local Government Board, after drawing attention to the unavailability and uselessness of the registers which guardians were supposed to keep of these visits, attempted to tighten up the system. Nevertheless, the basic imperfections remained. Supervision applied only to the first place of employment. If a child worked more than five miles from his native union, visiting was the responsibility of the union within which the child worked, an arrangement that invited further disregard of the Act. However, the Poor Law Act, 1879, allowed guardians to subscribe towards the support of such agencies as the M.A.B.Y.S. and The Girls' and Young Men's Friendly Societies in an attempt to secure a better compliance with the Act.[36]

The Poor Law Act, 1879, was one of 98 other acts eventually consolidated into the Poor Law Act, 1927. Two years later the Local Government Act, which transferred the functions of the boards of guardians to the county borough councils, necessitated the passage of a further consolidating act in 1930.[37] Much of its language and intent remained essentially Elizabethan. Section 15, for instance, required county and county borough councils to 'set to work or put out as apprentices all children whose parents are not, in the opinion of the council, able to keep and maintain their children'. Again, despite the change of nomenclature from 'workhouse' to 'institution' in 1913 the earlier term still appeared in the Curtis Report after the Second World War.

Many children in 1946 would have found the confusion between the two terms excusable. Members of the Curtis Committee found many over the age of three who had spent more than the permitted six weeks in a workhouse, a period during which public assistance committees were supposed to find them alternative accommodation. 'It was clear', the Committee reported, 'that in some areas the workhouse served as a dumping ground for children who could not be readily disposed of elsewhere . . . and that older children . . . were looked after in the workhouse for a considerable length of time.' Workhouses still practised procedures condemned a century earlier. Because of staff and accommodation shortages exacerbated by the Second World War, children were still being left in the care of cleaners or aged inmates, or put in wards with senile old men and women and entrusted to the care of the duty nurse. In the 32 institutions visited the committee 'did not see any institution where the provision for occupation for children over the age of five could be regarded as satisfactory, there being no proper facilities either indoors or outdoors'. Moreover, many of the long-term residents had, for no apparent reason, not been sent to school. Although one must allow for changing social values the committee's comment, 'In many institutions although the physical care was fairly adequate, the staff, the buildings, and the equipment were such that it was impossible to provide an environment in which children could thrive, and it could certainly not be said that these children were being compensated for the lack of normal home care', might have been written in an earlier period. The bricks and mortar of the workhouse had survived, as had the flesh and blood of the guardians. In one particularly unsatisfactory instance 'the chairman of the Public Assistance Committee was 91 and the Vice Chairman over 80. The impression was left that they were maintaining the standards of 50 years ago'.[38]

Although there was still some use of large barrack buildings, children in local authority grouped and scattered homes physically fared better than those left in workhouses. There still remained a tendency to put the interests of the home before those of the children. Thus girls were kept on after reaching school leaving age ostensibly to train for domestic service, but in practice to carry out the routine work of the home. A number were found spending long hours at domestic work or tending younger children without adequate payment or fixed hours, and with little attention given to their training. The prospects for children on leaving the homes were almost as limited as they had been fifty years earlier. Remarkably few received any education after the age of 14. The majority went into unskilled occupations with little attempt at assessing their aptitude for a particular career. Almost as a matter of course girls went into domestic service. After-care, where it existed, remained a haphazard affair.[39]

The last category to be considered consists of those children in schools certified under the Education of Pauper Children Act, 1862. Although the Board of Education had assumed responsibility for the schools' inspection in 1904, they were slow to come under public scrutiny. By the early 1930s those recognized as elementary schools received visits from the schools inspectorate, while those taking children from the Public Assistance Committees were seen by officials of the Ministry of Health. Many of the remaining orphanages, preventive and rescue homes thus stayed uninspected until the passing of the Children Act, 1933. Until the thousand or so institutions had registered, as a preliminary to inspection under the Act, there was no information officially available about the number of children in them. Even then some schools evaded the intention of the Act by refusing to take young persons under the age of 17, while others failed to register either through ignorance of the Act or sheer defiance. A Home Office Report for 1938 indicates the – albeit partial – survival of conditions reminiscent of nineteenth-century institutions. 'The old system of repression, locked doors, silence at work, at meals, and even in the morning break, is much less frequently found.' There still remained homes in which girls were locked in their cubicles all night, and some with defective fire escapes, no lights in the bedrooms, or insufficient closet, lavatory, and bathroom accommodation. Others still relied on heavy, ugly uniforms, an insufficient dietary, and inadequate medical and dental care.[40]

Under the Children Act, 1933, the Home Office had no power to inspect schools whose accumulated funds made them independent of outside contributions. Only in 1944 did the Ministry of Education obtain the right to enter such premises. 'In these schools', the Curtis Report stated, 'the children may be shut away from any outside contact or advice for the whole of their childhood; they may be in the hands of untrained and narrow-minded staff with the result that they go into the world unprepared for ordinary life.' A recently published account of one such uninspected school describes how the boys had to march to a drill used by the Rifle Brigade for ceremonial purposes, be silent at all meals except Sunday tea and on Christmas Day, and be subject to frequent canings and other humiliating punishments.

The Curtis Committee found that those schools run as part of a larger organization had the advantages of a more enlightened central direction together with better opportunities for staff training. To some extent these advantages could be neutralized by the more conservative outlook of a local committee. Independent homes ranged from the 'very good to the definitely bad'. At worst religious obscurantism prevented the employment of outside teachers, at best one large organization ran a secondary school from which children could win scholarships to university. Treatment of the children showed a similar variety, as has already been suggested, ranging from one home where the children were so happily and busily occupied that they took no notice of the visiting committee's arrival, to another where the undue excitement displayed by the children on the official visitation suggested a lack of care and affection. Similarly, although 'corporal punishment with a cane was not often noted', a circumstance that the committee did not find surprising, the superintendent of one school had been successfully prosecuted for inflicting excessive punishment.[41]

To summarize, at the end of the Second World War some children deprived of a normal home life experienced conditions that had shown little change over the previous fifty years. It was after all the beating to death on a Shropshire farm of a boy who, at the age of 13, weighed less than 56 lb (25.5 kg) that had provided the immediate background to the appointment of the Curtis Committee. At best only a few children enjoyed a near substitute, physically and emotionally, to normal home life.

VAGRANT AND DELINQUENT CHILDREN

In 1882 or the following year John Watson, a boy of 13 with two previous convictions, was sentenced to 21 days' imprisonment and five years in a reformatory school for stealing five rabbits. He was one of 92 boys and girls, aged between 9 and 14, sent to prison that year for periods varying between ten days and a month, followed by two to five years in a reformatory. On the whole their crimes were petty – 83 cases of burglary or larceny, three of sleeping in the open air, two of absconding from industrial schools. Two cases might have had more serious consequences, one of causing wilful damage to property and one of arson. The two serious cases, out of 92, were of assaulting a female child and administering poison to a child.[1] A hundred years earlier most of these children would never have reached a court. The aggrieved individual would have dealt out summary justice himself, a box round the ears or a ducking under the nearest pump, to have taught the young delinquent a lesson. Would-be prosecutors in the 1780s were deterred by their knowledge of the harshness of contemporary judicial retribution, fears of reprisals, and the difficulties and expense of prosecuting in the absence of a regular police force. The reforms of the next century made punishment less severe but more certain.

In the absence of organized police forces, self-appointed vigilante groups took responsibility for maintaining law and order in their own hands from at least the sixteenth century onwards. Curbing lawlessness by removing indigent juveniles from the streets of London and elsewhere was a policy as old as British plantations and colonies overseas. A Poor Law Act of 1597 had legalized the deportation of incorrigible rogues. City of London merchants, concerned about the apparent rise in numbers of the unemployed in the Metropolis, thought Virginia would give a better return on their capital investment than Ulster. Virginia, England's first successful colony in the New World, became the export market for 'illdisposed' children from London of 'whom the City is especially desirous to be disburdened'. An unknown number of children sent illegally by unscrupulous agents, profiting from meeting the servant shortage in North America, joined political prisoners, criminals, and other undesirables on the westward voyage during the seventeenth century. Official and unofficial agencies continued to send orphaned and abandoned children to the colonies and Dominions until Barnardo's flew their last group of children to Australia in 1967.[2]

Antidotes of the 1690s for social unrest included the Society for the Reform of Manners and, specifically for juveniles, the charity school movement. Connected with the latter was the Society for Promoting Christian Knowledge, founded in 1698. As far as the charity school movement is concerned the Society's most active period was the first quarter of the eighteenth century. With the discovery of Bishop Atterbury's plot to restore the Jacobite dynasty in the early 1720s High Church influence within the Society waned as did its subscription list. Such charity schools as survived became largely fee-paying, catering not for indigent children but those of the respectable poor.

At this point it is convenient to show briefly how subsequent educational movements similarly failed to reach the class that their founders hoped to socialize. When Robert Raikes inserted his famous advertisement in the *Gloucester Journal* in 1783, he found a ready audience.

> Farmers and other inhabitants of the towns and villages, complain that they receive more injury to their property on the Sabbath than all the week besides; this, in a great measure, proceeds from the lawless state of the younger class, who are allowed to run wild on that day, free from every restraint,

Whatever the role played by working-class promoters may have been, Sunday schools were essentially conservative and evangelical institutions, espousing an ideology that attacked the allegedly depraved behaviour and radical inclinations of the poor. There can be little doubt that Sunday school scholars were members of the respectable poor and many working-class teachers espoused an essentially middle-class ideology. Robert Raikes's aphorism, 'Clean hands, clean face, and tidy combed hair, are better than fine clothes to wear', modest as were its requirements, must have excluded the very class he hoped to reach. Sarah Trimmer's regulations at her Old Brentford school acted as a similar social excluder. Children were to attend 'with their faces and hands washed, their hair combed, their shoes clean and their other apparel as neat and tidy as their parents can make them'. Pupils had 'to carry their Sunday gowns to the Mistress every Monday morning, well brushed and fuller's earth upon the spots, if there are any: to fetch them on Saturday and mend them if necessary'. In 1861 the remark of Patrick Cumin, later Secretary to the Education Department – 'The truth is that unless a mother can dress her child decently she will not send it to Sunday school' – seems to have been true of the nineteenth century as a whole. Indeed Cumin went so far as to argue that day schools had become socially inferior to Sunday ones which

> never contain so poor or so low a class as that which attends the week-day schools. The children in the dissenting Sunday schools are always from a higher class than those in Church schools, but even in the Church schools the really poor are fewer on Sundays than on the other days of the week.[3]

In similar fashion the voluntary day schools, whatever may have been the hopes of their founders, also failed to reach the destitute child. Both the British and Foreign School Society (1808) and the National Society for Promoting the Education of the Poor in the Principles of the Established Church (1811), despite the low unit costs that the monitorial system seemingly offered, soon found that when commitments began to outrun resources they had to start charging fees. Apart from other factors middle-class qualms about pauperizing the masses, together with the belief that parents would not value a free education, became so deeply entrenched that parents were unable to obtain free education as a right until a decade after school attendance became universally compulsory.

Meanwhile a series of agencies combining philanthropy with reformative, retributive, and custodial treatment in varying proportions tried to fill the gap left by charity, Sunday, day and workhouse schools. By the latter part of the eighteenth century a long period of political stability, combined with slow but steady economic growth, had nurtured a new middle-class elite whose wealth came from recently developed sources such as commerce, banking, and industry. Concerned to bring order to England's expanding cities and towns, the size of which now outstripped the resources that such earlier agencies of social control and order as still existed could muster, its members were actuated by motives of self-interest, humanitarian concern, and Evangelical fervour. At the same time they were staking out a claim, consciously or unconsciously, to a political and social leadership that was being vacated by the landed aristocracy in the urban areas.

A series of private institutions, varying from the primarily benevolent to those that were virtually vigilante, anticipated the central and local government bureaucracies of the nineteenth century. Amongst those intended mainly for welfare one can cite the numerous lying-in hospitals endowed in London and elsewhere, the establishment of Captain Thomas Coram's Foundling Hospital in 1739, and Jonas Hanway's legislation to reduce infantile mortality in the Metropolitan workhouses. Hanway, together with Sir John Fielding and the Duke of Bolton, was a founder member of the Marine Society for Educating Poor Destitute Boys to the Sea. In 1756, on the outbreak of war with France, they collected a number of poor boys, clothed them at the Duke's expense and sent them to his ship H.M.S. *Barfleur*, thereby neatly combining press-ganging with philanthropy. By 1815 the Society had sent nearly 31,000 boys into the Royal Navy. Before despatch Hanway cleaned up and kitted out children who had arrived at the Society's centre dressed in rags, covered in filth, and crowned with 'foul matted hair'. Here they stayed long enough to build up their strength to undertake the walk to Portsmouth, armed with a copy of *Christian Knowledge Made Easy*, and to face the spiritual and physical hazards of life below decks. After the defeat of Napoleon the Society sent a further 15,000 boys to sea, mainly to the ships of the East India Company, the deep-sea merchant ships and the fishing fleet. Another early institution was the Philanthropic Society, founded in 1788, whose 'great object was to unite the purposes of charity with those of industry and police'; it lodged and tried to reform the sons of felons sentenced to death or transportation as well as boys who had committed offences themselves. As its later acquisition of the prefix 'Royal' suggests it became one of the most famous of all reformatory schools.[4]

Anticipating the establishment of both the Metropolitan Police and the Charity Organization Society was the Society for the Suppression of Mendicity which began operating in 1818. This society took advantage of the Vagrancy Act, 1744, under which apprehenders of disorderly persons could receive 5s or 10s for each one caught. These fees enabled the Society to employ twelve constables who issued tickets to suspected mendicants to enable them to establish their credentials as members of the deserving poor, at the Society's central office. Edward Pelham Brenton, a member of the Society, on deciding that it did not do enough to provide employment, formed his own Society for the Suppression of Juvenile Vagrancy in 1834. After setting up a farm for boys at Hackney Wick and the Royal Victoria Asylum at Chiswick for girls, with Princess Victoria and her mother the Duchess of Kent as joint patronesses, he decided to send children to the Cape Colony to relieve the labour shortage expected there following the emancipation of slaves in the British Empire. By 1841 he had sent 700 poor, destitute children, including some who had been convicted. In many instances the children sent to South Africa did the kind of work previously performed by slave labour. Reports of their ill treatment reaching London led to the appointment of a committee of inquiry at the Cape. The subsequent decline in subscriptions to Brenton's Society brought about its dissolution in 1843 and that of the Cape agency five years later.[5]

Harsh though the treatment of these children might seem, it was mild compared with what the law had prescribed before the reform of the penal code. Until the 1820s children over the age of fourteen could be subject to capital punishment, between seven and fourteen they were held in principle to be *incapax doli* but could be sentenced to death if strong evidence of malice 'supplied age'. In practice it is difficult to substantiate a case of a child as young as this being hanged in the eighteenth century. For those over the age of fourteen the eighteenth century brought an extension of the number of capital offences, with little discrimination on the ground of age and none on that of sex. In 1785 Sir Archibald Macdonald, the Solicitor-General, stated that 18 out of 20 offenders executed in London were under the age of twenty-one. Since executions were public, they provided suitable object lessons for children. On one occasion Joseph Nollekens, the sculptor, took a neighbour's son aged eight to see an execution at Tyburn, his only regret being that they had not been able to enjoy the privilege of walking beside the cart all the way there.[6]

In practice imprisonment began to replace the earlier and more extreme forms of punishment, such as the death penalty, whipping, branding, and the use of the pillory, in the later part of the eighteenth century. In 1776 John Howard's prison census listed only 653 petty offenders, 15.9 per cent of the total in confinement. The incidence of the use of imprisonment at the Old Bailey increased from 1.2 per cent of all cases in the years 1760 to 1764 to 28.3 per cent thirty years later. Advocates of reform had to meet the charge that theirs was a soft option. Hence imprisonment in the new prisons involved such punitive features as the silent system, solitary confinement, a meagre diet, the treadmill, and hard and monotonous labour. These devices not only helped to reassure critics of the new penology but, in some instances, provided exemplars for the later reformatory, industrial and truant schools.[7]

With the greater availability of prison cells and the reform of the penal code, minor offenders accounted for more than half the prison population by the 1840s. As the treatment of children did not officially differ from that of adults, a number of those incarcerated were juveniles. In 1849 and 1850 there were 10,703 and 9,370 male juveniles in prison, of whom 214 and 167 in the respective years had been sentenced to transportation, a sentence sometimes commuted to imprisonment in England. The overwhelming majority, 8,024 and 6,801 in the years after discussion, had received sentences of less than two months' duration.[8] In practice few of those in prison were under the age of ten. Although three children under that age had been released from the House of Correction, Tothill Fields, Westminster, in 1838, following a protest in *The Times*, not all youngsters were equally fortunate. In 1847 this prison held one boy under the age of six whose misfortune it had been to appear before a short-sighted, deaf magistrate. Of the 600 in Tothill Fields that year, ten were aged less than eight, 36 under ten, another 54 under fourteen, and a further 100 were between fourteen and sixteen. At the top end of the scale there may well have been some understatement as boys claimed to be over sixteen to obtain a man's rations. Be the numbers as they may, the policy of sending boys and girls to prison, especially for short periods, raised misgivings on a number of grounds that brought both a reform of the judicial machinery and the passage of the Reformatory and Industrial Schools Acts in the 1850s and 1860s.[9]

One of the reformers' major concerns was that the harshness of the eighteenth-century penal code caused too many offenders to go scot-free. For instance, the first report of the Society for the Improvement of Prison Discipline and for the Reformation of Juvenile Offenders, founded in 1818 under the patronage of the Duke of Gloucester, drew attention to a general reluctance to prosecute young offenders because of the severity of the possible punishment. The consequence was impunity; crime and punishment, the society thought, should be inseparably connected in the minds of young offenders. A further deterrent to prosecution was the laborious procedure a prosecutor had to follow before the establishment of a nationwide police force. Until the late 1840s virtually all larcenies, however trivial the amount involved, were indictable offences. One of the few exceptions to this rule was provided by an act of 1826 that, *inter alia*, allowed justices of the peace to discharge first offenders if they made compensation for damages or costs, a provision intended for juvenile offenders.[10] Before 1847, generally a juvenile offender had to be brought by the aggrieved party before a magistrate who decided whether to discharge the prisoner or commit him to trial at Quarter Sessions or Assizes, if the offence was a serious one. Meanwhile the prosecutor and any witnesses were bound over to appear at the next stage of the proceedings by signing a recognisance to which was attached a financial penalty of £20 or £40 for failure to attend. The Clerk of the Peace or Clerk of Assize prepared a Bill of Indictment for the Grand Jury, who had the duty of determining whether or not there was a case to answer. With the development of the police force the importance of the Grand Jury's role gradually declined until its eventual abolition in 1933. When the case came up for hearing the prosecutor or his counsel presented the case against the defendant. At this stage the case might easily be thrown out for a technical reason such as the incorrect citation of a person's name or the place involved, or errors in the description of the property in the case. Again, if a witness or the prosecutor failed to appear the case suffered the same fate. Thus a prosecutor was faced with considerable expense, not all of which was necessarily returned to him. He had also to take part in a time-consuming procedure that involved travelling to the town where Quarter Sessions or Assizes were held and staying there with his witnesses until his case came up.[11] Two changes made the process simpler for the aggrieved party. Acts of 1829, 1835, 1839 and 1856 led to the eventual establishment of a nationwide police force. However, as the doubling of the Home Office grant from 25 per cent in 1856 to 50 per cent in 1874 indicates, some districts were reluctant to implement the Acts satisfactorily. Nevertheless, as the police forces grew in numbers and expertise they took on the labour and cost involved in preparing cases for the prosecution. The Juvenile Offenders Acts of 1847 and 1850, together with the Criminal Justice Act, 1855, provided the second means of simplifying procedure. Under these Acts certain minor larcenies, although technically still indictable offences, could be tried summarily. The 1847 Act had an age limit of fourteen, raised to sixteen three years later, and removed altogether in 1855. For the juvenile offender the first two Acts were a dubious blessing. On the one hand they appeared humanitarian by making a distinction between the treatment of juvenile and adult offenders. No longer did juveniles have to wait on remand in prison where they might be schooled in criminal lore by their elders. The Acts also offered the alternatives to imprisonment of a whipping or a fine not exceeding £3. On the other hand they satisfied the call for law and order by making prosecution and subsequent punishment more certain. For example, the number of larcenies tried under the Juvenile Offenders Acts rose from 17 in 1847 in the Black Country area of Staffordshire to 120 in 1860, peaking at 141 in 1857.[12] Until the passage of these Acts the treatment in prison of convicted juvenile offenders had not substantially differed from that of adults, the only concessions being the setting aside of the hulks, *Bellerophon* and *Euryalus*, from 1823 to 1844 and the building of Parkhurst prison, Isle of Wight, in 1837. Boys considered fit enough to withstand the rigours of convict life in Australia came to Parkhurst for two years' training, before setting out on the next stage of their sentence, a sealane 1,498 boys followed between 1842 and 1853, the year in which the abolition of transportation sentences for offenders under the age of fourteen virtually ended the transportation of juveniles.[13]

The Acts of 1847 and 1850 had reached the statute book as a result of growing concern about the incidence of juvenile lawlessness, a subject that had been under serious discussion since at least the end of the Napoleonic Wars. Connected with the Society for the Improvement of Prison Discipline and for the Reformation of Juvenile Offenders was the Society for Investigating the Causes of the Alarming Increase of Juvenile Delinquency in the Metropolis. Its members included the economist David Ricardo, Favell Buxton who assumed William Wilberforce's mantle as the leader of the anti-slavery party in the House of Commons in 1824, James Mill, philosopher, historian, and economist, Stephen Lushington, father of a future permanent under-secretary at the Home Office, William Crawford, one of the first two prison inspectors appointed in 1833, and the young banker Samuel Hoare. This group made what was probably the first systematic investigation of the causes of juvenile delinquency ever attempted. The evidence they subsequently gave the Select Committee on the State of the Police in the Metropolis anticipated much of the mid-nineteenth century debate on the causes of juvenile delinquency – and even that of today, if one allows for changes in terminology, with 'video nasties' and violence on television taking over in public imagination where 'flash houses' (brothels or thieves' kitchens) have left off.

> It appears that . . . there were several thousands of boys in the Metropolis who are daily engaged in the commission of crime; that the causes of this deplorable evil are to be traced to the improper and criminal conduct of parents, the want of education, – the deficiency of employment, – the violation of the Sabbath, – the prevailing habit of gambling in the streets. . . . All these may be considered as the principal incitements to crime. To these causes may be added the existence of Flash-houses and brothels, almost exclusively set apart for children of both sexes, and lastly to the bad management of prisons, which, instead of correcting the juvenile delinquent by discipline, are schools and academies of vice, which corrupt and vitiate their wretched inmates, and throw them back upon society, confirmed in every bad habit.[14]

After inspecting plans prepared by Samuel Hoare the Select Committee recommended the construction of a prison for the exclusive use of 400 boys. Although Hoare's plan was to cost only one-seventh of the prison then being built at Millwall, nothing came of the suggestion.

One factor that helped to create concern about the apparent increase in the incidence of juvenile crime was the sheer growth of the population. The under-twenty cohort, which had risen from 6,981,068 in 1821 to 14,422,801 thirty years later, had become increasingly concentrated in urban areas. Those who wished to confirm their general impression of growing lawlessness among the young could do so by turning to the statistical evidence of the committal returns that became available from 1834 onwards. The publication of details of the age, sex, and degree of instruction of offenders made possible the 'discovery' of the juvenile offender as a social problem. Thus contemporaries found 'juveniles "aged 15 and under 20", form not quite one-tenth of the population, but are guilty of nearly one-fourth of its crime.' At the same time criminal statistics showed an apparent rise in crime from under 5,000 indictable offences committed to trial per year in the quin-quennium 1806–10, to 20,000 and over by the 1840s.[15] This rise was, however, partly the result of changes in sentencing policy, the slow growth of police forces, and changing social attitudes towards crime and public disorder. During the years under discussion more than 190 Acts imposing capital punishment were abolished, leaving murder as the one crime on which capital sentences were passed. Some questioned whether the crime rate had risen at all and argued that the state of public order had actually been worse in the eighteenth century, a thesis put forward by Disraeli during the debates on the County Police Bill in 1839. In the same year W. Cooke Taylor had written:

> That crime has proportionally decreased is undeniable, . . . who now sleeps with pistols beneath his pillow or hangs a blunderbus within reach of his bolster. . . ?[16]

Four years earlier Francis Place, in giving evidence to the Select Committee on Education, had argued that London was a more law-abiding place than it had been fifty years earlier when he had been a young apprentice.

> It was within my recollection a rare thing for a pickpocket ever to be prosecuted, unless he was a very notorious person. A pickpocket when taken was ducked or pumped upon.

After referring to an incident when a gentleman had been ducked by mistake in Whitefriars Dock he averred:

> this was one of the cases which tended to put an end to that mode of summary and illegal punishment. Boys and young thieves were thrashed and sent about their business. Nobody ventures now to thrash a boy in the streets; he would be indicted for an assault if he did. . . . The number of commitments is no criterion of the number of crimes. There is the London police and the increasing vigilance of the magistrates. The present establishment of the magistrates, and the more recent establishment of the police, has made detection much more certain, and I have no doubt this vigilance will prevent crimes and that the number of persons committed will decrease.[17]

Allied to this concern about the possible rise in crime was uneasiness about the existing practice of sending young people to prison. Imprisoning children came under attack for both its inhumanity and its ineffectiveness. Unreformed prisons were held to corrupt the young by allowing them to associate with hardened criminals. Reorganized prisons, where children could spend long terms in solitary confinement, were condemned for their inhumanity. Common to both these charges was the belief that the committal of a young person to prison habituated him to it, so that he lost all fear of incarceration and would divide his future life between the workhouse and the prison. The suicide of a young prisoner at Winson Green Prison, Birmingham, a victim of the illegal and excessively punitive regime of Captain A. Maconochie, RN, already well known for his conduct while superintendent of the penal settlement at Norfolk Island, added to public disquiet at a time when the reformatory as an alternative to prison was being canvassed.[18]

The high cost of imprisonment made the search for an alternative attractive to those who might not have been swayed by humanitarian considerations. One estimate put the cost of a juvenile prisoner, together with his *pro rata* share of the upkeep of the police and judiciary, at £63 0s 0d, a year. Residence at Parkhurst cost £43 10s 5d a year. In contrast a boy could be accommodated at Mettrai, near Tours, built in 1842, for £42 a year, at the Warwick County Asylum, founded by local magistrates at Stretton-on-Dunstone in 1818, for £31 a year, while a mere £18 sufficed for his keep in an industrial school. Matthew Davenport Hill, the recorder for Birmingham, had operated an even cheaper variant to prison by handing youngsters over to guardians from 1841 onwards, if he thought that they were not wholly corrupted. He then arranged for the visitation of these wards of court. At the other extreme the Liverpool magistracy complained that fourteen offenders, of whom ten had been transported, had cost a total of £1,707 or £121 a head. The total cost of supporting the pauper and his near brothers, the vagrant and thief, through the poor rate, charitable funds, and the necessary judicial apparatus, was put by one essayist at £20,000,000 a year, nearly 5 per cent of the estimated national income.[19]

Contemporaries were concerned not only with the 'dangerous' child, one who had been convicted for committing a crime, but with the 'perishing' child whose near destitution might lead him into criminal ways. One unofficial body to tackle the problem of the unknown but large number of apparently abandoned and destitute children leading a precarious life in London was the City Mission, instituted in 1835. Two years later it opened its first ragged school in Westminster as part of its programme of bringing the Gospels to the poorest. In 1841 there appeared, on the site of Smithfield Market, Field Lane School, the first to receive the designation 'ragged', although other comparable institutions had been established earlier in London and elsewhere. With the advantage of the publicity given it by a visit from Charles Dickens, it became one of the most famous as well as one of the largest. The City Mission spawned a number of other evangelical organizations including the London Sunday School Society. Members of this society, together with others from the parent body, formed the Ragged School Union in 1844, thereby continuing the tradition of the earlier Society for Promoting Religious Knowledge among the Poor (1750). The RSU, with Lord Ashley, later the seventh earl of Shaftesbury, as its president, coordinated the work of existing ragged schools, encouraged the building of new ones, and supported refuges such as the Westminster Ragged Dormitory for those attending the New Pye Street Ragged

School in Westminster. The Day Industrial School in nearby Old Pye Street, founded in 1855 in a former thieves' public house, was credited with being the first to bring methods already developed in Aberdeen to London in a systematic manner.[20] In many ways the founders of the ragged schools, together with their teachers, undertook some of the hardest welfare work of the period, for the schools were situated in some of the poorest parts of the capital, receiving children whose dirty condition and ragged clothes made all other schools refuse them admission and caused the 'respectable' classes to shun them. The RSU also had to suffer the charge that it was offering vice a premium by treating vagabond and thieving children more kindly than those of honest labourers.

> 'Misery is the appointed punishment of sin', one critic argued, 'and . . . to attempt to rescue these children from the state into which their own and their parents' misdeeds have brought them, was detrimental to society by confounding the distinctions of right and wrong, lessening the divinely appointed penalty of crime, and thus weakening the deterring force of such examples of suffering.[21]

Censure of this nature hampered the RSU's migration policy. In a speech to the House of Commons in 1848 Ashley asked for £20,000 a year to take 1,000 children to South Australia. He received what proved to be a once-and-for-all grant of £1,500: when he renewed his request he met the charge that the support already given had tended to reward the undeserving and criminal and had encouraged parents to neglect their children. To qualify for migration children had to come regularly to a ragged school, attend an industrial class and meet certain minimal standards in the three Rs. Even when sending them abroad it was RSU policy to keep children away from such colonial fleshpots as the newly found Victoria goldfields or Sydney by sending them into the Australian bush.[22]

Similar reclamation work took place elsewhere. After the publication of H. A. Frégier, *Des Classes Dangereuses de la Population dans les Grandes Villes et des Moyens de les rendre meilleures* (Paris and Brussels, 1840) *salles d'aisles* for the reception of destitute and vagrant children were opened in Paris. In Aberdeen Sheriff Watson started a feeding and industrial training centre in 1841. Four years later he instructed the police to round up all children found begging and take them to his school, an action he justified on the grounds that the three meals a day the schools offered obviated any necessity for begging. The timetable for the Edinburgh Ragged School, opened in 1847, suggests that such children spent twelve hours a day at school, eleven in the winter, divided roughly equally between meals and play, lessons, and labour.[23] Although Aberdeen's success in clearing the streets of its juvenile beggars offered the rest of Great Britain a much quoted example, a policy that worked in an isolated city with a population of 63,288 in 1841 was one matter, while gathering in all the destitute children of London's teeming parishes was another. In practice the RSU's work touched no more than the fringe of the problem. The Educational Census of 1851 showed 132 schools with 26,000 pupils on the books. By 1870, the RSU's peak year, 250 schools claimed an average attendance of 30,000 with a further 100 provincial or un-affiliated schools. After allowing for double counting between day and Sunday school attendance some 40,000 children were in contact with ragged schools, of whom no more than a tenth to a quarter were in attendance at any one time. An analysis of children at one school in 1855 gives some idea of their social background. Of a total of 260 pupils, 42 were orphans, 21 had no fathers, 36 had run away from home, 19 were in lodging houses, 29 never slept in beds, and 41 lived by begging. In addition an indeterminate number supported themselves by mudlarking – gathering coal and other rummage from the river.[24]

Thus when Mary Carpenter's book, *Reformatory Schools for the Children of the Perishing and Dangerous Classes and for Juvenile Offenders*, appeared in the summer of 1851, it came after a long period of disquiet, some reform, and experiments at home and abroad. The following December a conference at Birmingham demanded an act of parliament to assist in the establishment of ragged, industrial, and reformatory schools. The government's response was to appoint the 1852 Select Committee on Criminal and Destitute Children to which Mary Carpenter gave evidence. Next year she published her *Juvenile Delinquents: their condition and treatment*, and the Select Committee published its report recommending a reformatory system, a view endorsed by a second Birmingham conference. A few months later, C. B. Adderley, MP for North Staffordshire, at that time a private member, introduced a bill implementing many of the Select Committee's recommendations, which the Aberdeen ministry adopted.

The Reformatory Schools' Act, more correctly the Act for the Better Care and Reformation of Youthful Offenders in Great Britain, was a compromise. The reformatory movement had provided common ground for humanitarians wanting to keep children out of prison, upholders of law and order looking for a cheaper and possibly more effective form of deterrence, punishment and rehabilitation, and those who saw the young offender, not as someone innately vicious, but as society's victim.

> There is no vicious child, as experience daily proves, who is prematurely wicked, that might not, under a well directed and religiously conducted system, still grow up an honest and industrious citizen. He was not born a vagrant; he was not born a thief. Our neglect made him a delinquent; our

pernicious interference hardened him for the gallows, the hulk, or Botany Bay.[25]

This was an essentially optimistic view of human nature. If one accepted John Locke's premise that a child's mind was *tabula rasa* then children were easily malleable for good or evil. Given the right kind of environment and the utilitarian and classical economist panacea of education the young offender could become a useful citizen. To accommodate the more widely held belief that the malefactor had to be punished, the new Act required convicted children to spend up to a month in prison as a punishment before going to a reformatory, which by definition though not in practice was not a place of punishment but of reform and rehabilitation. Imprisonment remained a mandatory preliminary to sojourn in a reformatory until 1893, when it became a discretionary one; six years later the requirement was abolished altogether.[26] Much of the resistance to the abolition of a preliminary spell in prison came from managers of reformatory schools who valued imprisonment, usually in solitary confinement, as a means of breaking the will of their future charges, thereby making them more docile on admission. The police and magistrates found it administratively convenient. As long as reformatories remained private institutions the authorities had to negotiate a child's admission with the management committees, a task that could take some time. If all efforts to find a child a place failed, they had no alternative but to let that child go, on his release from prison. Two provisions of the Act were especially valuable to the managers. They now had legal power to detain children, an authority they had lacked before. The Act also relieved them of their immediate financial problems through its system of certification and the offer of central government funds. Because of financial problems Stretton-on-Dunstone, for instance, had closed just before the new Act came into force.[27] Last, for fear that unscrupulous parents would exploit the Act by inciting their children to crime so as to relieve themselves of the cost of their maintenance, an amendment passed the next year required parents to contribute a maximum of five shillings a week towards their upkeep. This provision was valued not so much for its financial contribution to the Exchequer as for its perceived role in upholding parental responsibility.

In contrast to the child sent to a reformatory, who after serving his term of imprisonment had a criminal record, the industrial-school child initially was not a criminal. Scotland's experience provided England's example. In 1854 an Industrial Schools' Act for Scotland (Dunlop's Act) gave police power to bring before a magistrate

any young person apparently under the age of fourteen . . . found begging, or not having any home or settled place of abode, or guardianship, and having no lawful or visible means of subsistence, shall be found wandering, though not charged with any actual offence.

If nobody gave security for that child's future behaviour he could be sent to a reformatory or industrial school for a period not exceeding one year or beyond his fifteenth birthday. the Industrial Schools' Act (England), 1857 was restricted in scope to 'any child taken into custody on a charge of vagrancy'. Over the age of seven such a child could stay in an industrial school until he reached the age of fifteen. In contrast the Vagrancy Act, 1824, had made six months' imprisonment the punishment for an adult on his third conviction. Despite this the Act's supporters claimed detention was a deed of kindness as it rescued children from the streets, gave them food, shelter, and education, and prevented them from growing up as criminals. On the whole magistrates seem to have been reluctant to use the new Act and send children to industrial schools on the vague charge of vagrancy. The Newcastle Commissioners found the Act in danger of becoming a dead letter, for only 171 of the 1,193 children in the 18 schools certified by 1860 had been sent by magistrates. Moreover, the use of the Act had been geographically uneven. 154 were in three schools, 100 in one in Newcastle-on-Tyne, 35 in a Liverpool school, 19 in a Bristol school, with the remaining 15 schools holding 17 children between them. This bore no relationship to the location of the schools. Manchester, York, and Newcastle possessed one school each, Liverpool and Bristol had two each, while there were 11 near London. Declaring that 'the object which industrial schools are intended to promote is one which . . . should be accomplished at public expense and by public authority', the Newcastle Commissioners pressed for the wider terms of Dunlop's Act to be extended to England. As they did not think that sufficient industrial schools would be built to cope with the demand for places, they wanted workhouse and separate schools reclassified as industrial ones. Although this suggestion was not accepted the Industrial Schools Act, 1861, removed the lower age limit of seven, extended the scope of the earlier English one to include the categories covered by Dunlop's Act, and added children frequenting the company of reputed thieves. Such children could be brought before a magistrate by any person without the involvement of the police at all. The further inclusion of children under the age of twelve, guilty of minor offences, whom magistrates thought should be sent to an industrial school, blurred the distinction between the two types of institutions, a process carried still further by adding children under fourteen whom their parents found uncontrollable. A later act of 1866 extended this facility to poor law guardians who could also now send children whose parents were serving terms of imprisonment.

The Elementary Education Act, 1876, added the further offence of

truancy.[28] By 1882, the year in which the Royal Commission on
Reformatory and Industrial Schools began work, England and Wales
had 50 certified reformatories, 99 industrial schools, 10 day industrial or
day truant schools, and an industrial school built at Feltham, Middlesex,
under a local act of 1854, to which children could be sent without
undergoing a period of preliminary imprisonment. Reformatory
schools held 6,601 children that year while industrial schools contained
17,614. An analysis of the first 1,000 admitted to industrial schools in
1882 shows the extent to which offences under the Elementary
Education Act, 1876, had been responsible for this marked upsurge of
numbers, and also how certification had changed, their character from a
refuge for day scholars of the vagrant class to that of a quasi-
reformatory. As early as 1870, Sydney Turner, inspector of reformatory
and industrial schools, saw them as reformatories of a milder kind and
institutions of a corrective and not merely educational nature. Moreover, they had moved out of the crowded urban areas, where
absconding was easy, into the countryside and suburbs where inmates
worked the land. The two Elementary Education Acts, 1870 and 1876,

Table II

*Classification of the first thousand children admitted to industrial
schools, 1882*

Act of Parliament	Number of children	Offence
1861, Industrial Schools	403	*Found begging, wandering etc.*
"	184	*Charged with a criminal offence while under 12 years*
"	65	*Not under parental control*
"	6	*Sent by Boards of Guardians as refractory*
1876, Elementary Education	168	*Breach of attendance order cases*
	168	*Habitually wandering etc.*
1880, Brothels Act	6	*Found living in a brothel*

Source: *Report of the Royal Commission on Reformatory and Industrial Schools (Aberdare Report)*, P.P. 1884, XLV, H. Rogers' evidence,
Qs and As 1502–3.

carried the process of assimilation still further. From 1870 onwards school boards were able to contribute to industrial schools or build them for their direct use. Such schools – residential truant schools – were amongst the most repressive and punitive of all reformatory and industrial schools. The 1876 Act allowed school authorities to set up day feeding schools providing industrial training, elementary education, and one or more meals a day. This Act also allowed school authorities to commit persistent truants, together with children covered by the enlarged scope of the 1861 Act, as well as those beyond their parents' control or who had violated one school attendance order.

Children in both industrial and reformatory schools underwent a disciplined and oppressive routine of hard work, severe punishment, austere living conditions, and a spartan diet to eradicate the alleged defects of their characters, the evil influence of their previous environment, and the sins of their fathers. Indeed, in some respects there must have been little to choose between these schools and district workhouse ones. Within the physical and disciplinary constraints of the institution the child outwardly conformed, if only to come to terms with authority and enjoy as quiet a life as possible. Outward conformity, it was hoped, bred an inward conversion which would guide the inmate's way of life on release. In practice officialdom's faith in this principle was so attenuated that inspectors and managers alike believed that the best solution was to send children, on discharge, as far away as possible from their old haunts. Hence the armed forces, the merchant navy, and the colonies were thought to provide ideal outlets for boys, and domestic service within England and the colonies for girls.

The typical reformatory of the late 1850s had a single room, measuring 35' by 18', with walls of plain brick whitened with lime, and floors of concrete or tiles, at a time when the Education Department was trying to persuade school managers to put wooden floors in every elementary school. Heated by a single stove, this room served as schoolroom, meal room, and play room in wet weather. The dormitories were unplastered and ceiled roughly under the rafters of the roof. An outbuilding or shed contained a bath or trough for washing. The yard was open and unpaved. There was no hot air or hot water piping even in the cells, very few of which had gas. Children started their day at 6.00 a.m. and worked for eight hours, with three hours' instruction in basic school subjects. According to Turner many boys thought they had less work and more food in prison, and he was confident that few would think a reformatory a place of privilege. 'Their discipline, dietary, industrial occupation, lodging, habits of recreation, etc. must be made strict, and must have', he wrote, 'something of the hardness which St Paul prescribes as an essential element of the Christian's training'. The children 'should be really taught and required to work, their industrial training being as laborious as possible, and the Apostle's rule adhered to, "If a man will not work, neither shall he eat" '. 'A long sentence, an efficient and religious master, industrial training, and a conditional release under a ticket-of-leave whose conditions are carefully enforced', Turner saw as necessary preludes to setting the young criminal on the path of righteousness.[29]

In common with their workhouse contemporaries, children on leaving the reformatory or industrial school found their training for the world outside to be woefully inadequate. The Newcastle Commissioners guardedly reported that the schooling at the Philanthropic Society's school at Redhill was 'not first-rate'. As the chaplain, Turner's successor, explained, it was not their desire that schools for convicts should contain facilities for so good an education as that provided for honest children. Twenty years later Turner still subscribed to this school of thought. Reformatory schools offered 'a plain English education such as is considered sufficient preparation for the station which they are likely to occupy in after years'. In 1913, more than thirty years on, there was little evidence of change. The schools 'have the merits of the old type of elementary school. The work is accurate, careful and neat within a narrow range. . . . There is not the intelligence, the individuality, or the originality which are in the best of our schools today.' In other words, teaching methods were a generation behind the best of contemporary practice. Often there was only one classroom, in which all groups of children were taught together. In some cases it was impossible to arrange the room so that all the desks were properly lit. Frequently desks and other equipment were poor, the walls bare or hung with dingy maps. As late as 1905 the number of certificated teachers working in 37 reformatories was ten, a figure that had remained constant for the previous ten years. Because industrial work took preference over schooling, children received only three hours' classroom tuition a day, two hours less than in an elementary school. Moreover, the day's teaching took place at any time that suited the convenience of the institution. Yet these were the very children whose educational attainment lagged behind that of their peers in the first place, because of their deprived backgrounds, their previous truancy, and other related factors.[30]

The schools' record in industrial training was equally poor. The commonest occupations were chopping wood, picking hair, straightening nails, and working the land, none of which required a heavy capital outlay or specialist training, working the land being mainly confined to spade labour. Such tasks encouraged the formation of habits of work, application, and industry, qualities managers thought more important than gaining proficiency in any one handicraft. Schools relied on the sale of goods to supplement their income. For example, the Boys' Home,

Regent's Park Road, London, advertised large bundles of chopped firewood at 4s a hundred bundles, delivered free, as well as easily constricted items such as plate racks, clothes horses and boxes of bricks. More elaborate goods, made by older children, included folding tables and dwarf mahogany chests of drawers at 35s. Other schools sold boots, paper bags, and household brushes. As the example of the chest of drawers indicates, the longer a boy stayed in a school the more profitable became his services to the institution. Hence his chances of early release on licence were slight, however well behaved he might be. The Children Act, 1908, and pressure from the Home Office gradually brought some improvement. Shortly before the outbreak of the First World War one-third and one-sixth, respectively, of the children in reformatory and industrial schools were being released on licence more than a year before the expiry of their sentences. Girls, common with their sisters in workhouse schools, had a daily round of floor scrubbing, general cleaning and heavy laundry work; the heavier and more arduous the work the more reformative it was thought to be. Again, although their main outlet was into general service, they received none of the training they needed before entering small households. In neither case, at the turn of the century, did girls have much, if any, opportunity to learn such skills as dressmaking or the use of a sewing machine, or to prepare for a junior clerical post by learning typing, shorthand, the use of a telephone, or book-keeping.[31]

The financial problems of the schools affected the quality of training offered and of the staff employed, until after the Home Office increased grants just before and after the First World War. Despite the criticisms of the Aberdare Commission of 1884 and those of the Departmental Committee of 1896, one school was still producing a million bundles of firewood every six months in 1913, another ran a profitable paper-bag industry, while a third was making wooden bobbins on simple machinery.[32] A Board of Education report made five days after the Armistice condemned the farm schools, which instead of being places for training future farm workers, were still primarily places of detention striving to be self-supporting. If such schools were to train boys satisfactorily they needed more machinery than did ordinary farms, but in practice the opposite was usually the case. Farms were boy-labour intensive. One such school with 20 acres of heavy arable land and three acres of gardens did not even possess a plough, all digging being done by spade.[33]

Old traditions had died hard. As we have seen, the earliest reformatory had been provided by the local magistracy in a rural setting at Stretton-on-Dunstone, while the sudden growth of reformatories just before and after the 1854 Act also took place in the countryside. Indeed, Turner thought that every county should have its own reformatory while cities should arrange for their convicted children to go to distant rural ones. There can be no doubt that the motives of some of the early founders of reformatory schools were only partly altruistic. The landowner who gave land and buildings for a school, despite his subscription to the belief that agricultural labour was a character-cleansing therapy, was also providing the home farm and the land of his tenants with cheap, if not free, labour. The number of times the same land was turned over did not matter: fieldwork kept the mind from wandering as well as invigorating emaciated frames, while working in small groups was thought conducive to the elimination of immoral conversation. 'The most corrupt mind is kept comparatively healthy for a time, while the muscles are fully exercised by the use of a spade or a mattock, the thoughts cease to flow in their accustomed channel, and some preparation is made for a purer infusion.' In the case of girls 'the washing tub or churn will tranquilize the nervous system and quell excitability, a great deal better than needlework'.[34]

Given the paucity of industrial training in workhouse, reformatory and industrial schools, children on discharge mainly went into unskilled occupations or those in which there was a manpower shortage even in the nineteenth century. To cater for one such outlet, a seafaring life, poor law guardians, managers of industrial schools and reformatories established training ships. Under the Metropolitan Poor Act, 1867, the Metropolitan guardians used *Goliath* from 1870 until its destruction by fire with the loss of 21 lives in 1875, when *Exmouth* replaced it. There were three reformatory and nine industrial school ships, including the London School Board's *Shaftesbury* and *Mars* at Dundee in 1884, together with *Chichester* and *Arethusa* belonging to the National Refuges for Homeless and Destitute Children. In a ship's crowded quarters discipline was maintained with difficulty, as the attempted arson of *Clarence* in 1880, the successful firing of the same ship three years later, the equally successful firing of *Cumberland* in 1888 and the attempted arson of *Empress*, her successor, a few years later, indicate.[35] A complaint from a schoolmaster on *Wellesley* that boys thought guilty of masturbation had their genitals painted with a blistering liquid brought a Home Office enquiry which revealed a number of irregularities, including excessive corporal punishment, the unauthorized moving of the ship to a new berth near Liverpool's waterside brothels, and the use of boys to procure prostitutes and drink for the ship's crew during the master's absence. J. G. Legge, who carried out the enquiry, sharply criticized the personnel involved. The chairman, Hall, was virtually a one-man committee; 'he has secured the reputation of being a philanthropist, *Wellesley* has been a splendid advertisement for him – a shipowner.' He found the captain a weak man who did not command respect, while the chief officer did not create a very favourable impression either; the chief nautical instructor inspired no confidence at all: when he was in charge of the mess deck at dinner one day a boy had broken a bowl of soup on another's head. The bandmaster, Legge wrote, 'I feel very dubious about, I should not trust him,' and, 'I did not like the medical officer.' While the three schoolmasters and a new gunnery instructor were efficient, the cook, trade, and nautical instruct-ors were not up to the average of such officers on other ships.[36]

George Lushington, permanent secretary to the Home Office, pointed out the legal difficulties involved in removing either the ship's master or the chairman of the management committee, so tenuous was the control the Home Office exercised over reformatories and industrial schools. In raising the further issue of the heavier costs of maintaining training ships, and their poor standards of health and discipline, he questioned the wisdom of their use at all.[37] The ships, except for the privately controlled *Chichester* and *Arethusa* which sent over 90 per cent of their handpicked boys to sea, failed to fulfil their intended function. The Royal Navy, which refused to take boys from reformatories, was prepared to accept 'a boy of very good character . . . with the special permission of the Admiralty, notwithstanding his having been in an industrial school.' They later relented, by agreeing to accept a quota of 18 a year into the Navy or the Royal Marines, a limit lifted in 1948. Boys from workhouse and industrial schools, although eligible, usually failed to meet the Navy's height and chest measurement requirements. In the years 1890–5 nearly 60 per cent of the boys discharged from training ships went to sea. Some, however, made only one voyage, while others never sailed in a British-registered ship.[38]

One can hardly blame those who came ashore after one voyage. In 1881 the Board of Trade estimated that the 3,979 deaths of masters and seamen that year represented one in 56 of all who went to sea in British ships, a figure that Joseph Chamberlain compared with a death rate amongst miners of one in 315 in their worst year. Gradually the number of deaths fell to around 3,000 a year for the first decade of the new century and to 2,500 by 1914 except for 1911, the year of the loss of S.S. *Titanic*.[39] With a high death rate, low pay, and bad living conditions the merchant marine had difficulty in attracting enough British seamen. In 1866, following the loss of S.S. *London* in the Bay of Biscay with only 19 survivors out of 244 hands, E. Carleton Tufnell renewed his argument that pauper boys should receive a seaman's training. 'The deficiency of sailors is well known; many ships go to sea half manned, supplied with Lascars and foreigners, who often do not speak English, and generally fail in an emergency', a factor that was held to have contributed to the loss of S.S. *London*. More than thirty years later C. T. Ritchie, President of the Board of Trade, returned to the theme. No less than 30 per cent of the petty officers and seamen of the merchant marine were foreigners. In addition the recruitment of younger men, under twenty-five, was showing a marked decline. Between 1891 and 1896 the number of British sailors had fallen from 41,590 to 35,020, with the under twenty-fives accounting for 3,981 of this loss.[40]

As well as ocean-going ships, managers and guardians found the fishing fleets a convenient outlet for boys too small for the Navy and too young for the Army. 'For certain boys an apprenticeship to the fishing trade is their last chance', a committee reported in 1894. If a boy stuck to his dangerous trade long enough to become a master for the rising Grimsby Ice and North Sea Trawling Companies the rewards, the committee reported, were high: 'We know of no trade where so much money can be earned by men of average skill without capital.' Despite the lure of this apparent easily earned wealth boys preferred dry land. They readily stopped ship, especially at Grmsby where 42 per cent (1,778 of 4,237) of the apprentices registered between 1881 and 1893 were imprisoned for various offences, mainly for absconding from an apprenticeship involving conditions so arduous that they formed the subject matter of three enquiries between 1871 and 1894.[41]

Given the problem of manning the merchant fleets, patriotic guardians and managers were wont to impress on a boy that he could discharge his debt to the community that had maintained him over a number of years, by going to sea. The same considerations applied to joining the Army. 'Few social problems bedevilled the British army as persistently as those which attended the annual intake of recruits to the rank and file. Attracting men in sufficient numbers to offset the wastage . . . was a perennial problem.' In the 26 even dated years of the period 1862–1912, the Army's effective strength reached its establishment in only 11, despite a lowering of the minimum required height from 5′ 8″ in 1861 to 5′ 3″ by 1900, improvements in pay and conditions, and a reduction in the length of service. To augment recruitment the army took boys at the age of fifteen. Nearly three-quarters trained as drummers and buglers, while the rest became tailors and shoemakers. The Army, seeing poor law schools and reformatories as potential sources of recruits, urged them to include military training in their curriculum. Unlike the Royal Navy it did not require character references until 1903. Guardians and managers obliged. As one reformatory superintendent said, 'My experience is that all these boys become manageable and tractable, and acquire habits of industry; and I call it a shame that the country should permit them to be trained and taught and made efficient, and then that these wretched parents should be allowed to step in and take them back to their miserable homes and afterwards let them again become gutter Arabs.'[42]

Sending children to the colonies seemed an equally effective way of removing them from their 'wretched' parents and preventing a reversion to a gutter Arab's life-style. In the nineteenth century, the heyday of British migration, the Poor Law Amendment Acts of 1834, 1844, 1848, 1849 and 1850 provided a statutory basis for migration on the poor rate. Between 1868 and 1928 voluntary agencies alone sent 87,699 children to Canada to work under indentures as agricultural labourers and domestic servants. All were unaccompanied by their parents, although only one-third were orphans. Official agencies were less active. The Poor Law Guardians sent some 11,000 children to Canada between 1870 and 1914. Reformatory and industrial schools provided a further 5,877 up to the end of 1894, the most important single contributor being the Royal Philanthropic Society which had sent 1,302 by 1882. With a capital outlay of £10 to £15 for kitting out a child, paying his fares to Liverpool and then to Canada, together with some form of supervision, emigration was an expensive way of dealing with an inmate on discharge. Sending a child earlier in his sentence, however, could prove a useful economy as the Liverpool School Board discovered. By sending 633 children, whose average age was just under twelve, they saved a net £12,500 over the course of 14 years.[43]

At the end of 1884 Vernon Harcourt, Home Secretary, became concerned about the powers managers of reformatory and industrial schools possessed in their disposal of children: 'There is no created thing so barbarous as a philanthropist and world-betterer run mad. The greatest of all offenders in this respect are school board managers' (of truant schools).[44] Truant children prosecuted by school boards were apprenticed to fishing smacks in the North Sea, or transported to the colonies, 'and that where there was no complaint whatever to be made about the home'. He went on to state that if he had enough inspectors to carry out a 'regular goal and delivery and discharge from the clutches of the managers all children who had behaved well in school and who had good homes to return to', he would get three-quarters of them out of the schools. The managers of industrial schools, he continued, 'regard themselves as a sort of earthly providence and think the more children they can get and keep from the parents the better'. They failed to investigate the children's home conditions because they did not wish to do so, and the magistrates did not trouble to do so.

He accordingly drafted a circular requiring managers to obtain permission from the parents before sending children into the Army, to sea or to the colonies. In face of strong opposition from managers, who argued that the parents were a worthless lot, he modified his earlier instructions. Managers now had to attempt to give parents an opportunity of proving their fitness to control their children. A similar attempt to curb the powers of managers of training ships to send children to sea under licence without first seeking parental permission, also failed. Over the next few years the Home Office upheld the objections of parents whom it deemed respectable but overruled those thought disreputable.[45] An Act of 1891, passed to encourage managers to grant children early release, allowed them to dispose of a child, with his consent, in any trade, calling, or service, or by emigration. In emigration cases the Home Office required consent of both parent and child, 'unless it can be shown that such consent may, through parental neglect or misconduct, be dispensed with'. In making his decision the Home Secretary took into account the record of a parent's contributions to the upkeep of his child in detention, the character of the home, and whether the parents had the means of giving the child a start in life. If the alleged background of children sent to Manchester's industrial schools in 1883 is typical, parents had little chance of proving their worthiness. Of 122 children picked up that year, 52 came from families with an income of under 3s a head a week after allowing for rent, 26 families had 3s to 5s and a further seven had more than 5s. Thirty-seven had no regular income. Eighty-three children were from families classified as disreputable, 18 from families of doubtful character, while only 21 children came from well conducted homes. The dice were loaded against parents in another way, for officialdom was prejudiced against them. In looking at their objections sometimes' we cannot quite make out that the parent is bad enough to be absolutely ignored', lamented J. G. Legge, inspector of reformatories and industrial schools.

Legge also saw getting the child's consent as an unfortunate statutory obstacle. When asked the question, 'In some circumstances is not that rather a difficulty really?' he replied, 'Of course there is a difficulty, but *there* it is in the Act.'[46] To succeed he thought the subject should be broached some weeks ahead and not suddenly sprung on a child. If the statements of guardians and managers can be taken at face value, children were treated with every consideration when they were deciding whether or not to accept the offer of a passage to Canada. A surviving account suggests otherwise. A former pupil of Swinton Workhouse School, Swinton, near Manchester, described in 1969 how she left for Canada in 1906.

> A man came in the school that day in my room and said all who belong to the Prestwich Union and would like to go to Canada put up your hands so I put my hand up. . . . I must say if I had known what I was doing I would never have put my hand up. I never saw my sister or brother again and I spent many a day weeping. . . . I had a very bad time for years earning my living working on farms, the people were very cruel to me. I was 12 when I arrived here, weight 61 lbs, when I got up in my teens I began to fight back and from then I made a go of it.[47]

The writer of this letter and her brother had been put into Swinton School at the age of two following their mother's desertion of them on the day of her husband's funeral. The brother, sent into the army at the age of fourteen, was killed at Gallipoli.

As this letter suggests the care given both to the selection of children for emigration and their welfare on arrival in Canada varied considerably. The best agencies in these respects were Dr Barnardo's and Miss Macpherson's, the two largest involved in this work, who sent 26,790 and 14,578 respectively to Canada between 1868 and 1928. Dr Barnardo's children, for example, might be visited three times a year by one of their Canadian workers. At the other end of the scale were smaller organizations, sending a handful of children annually and lacking the resources necessary for adequate supervision. There was also at least one professional exporter of workhouse children who went round workhouses contracting to take children to Canada, and sending them inadequately kitted out for a prairie winter at a profit of £4 to £5 a head. The legal requirement that a child should give his consent before the justices of the peace seems to have afforded little protection. All that one boy 'could remember of the *modus operandi* of his coming out was that they took him with 40 other boys before magistrates, and then he was handed over.' Workhouses, if not other institutions as well, at times paid no more than lip-service to the principle of sending only those children best suited to life on the prairies. For example, they were happy to use the businessman referred to above to offload their social, psychological, and physical misfits. Although poor law children were supposed to receive two visits annually, one from a Canadian agent acting for the Poor Law Board and one from the agency that had handled the passage, tracing the children was another matter. Major Gretton, Honorary Secretary to the East End Emigration Fund, who gave evidence to the 1896 Departmental Committee, had been unable to find any of the children whose addresses the Canadian authorities gave him in 1891, 1892, or 1893.[48]

As well as being the cheapest overseas outlet for Britain's undesirables, Canada's great merit was its predominantly agricultural economy. Boys trained *in* industry rather than *for* industry, and girls trained in household drudgery rather than in housewifery, provided suitable child labour for conditions that even adult immigrants found harsh. There can be no doubt that children were exploited and harshly treated in remote homesteads, especially if they carried the stigma of pauperism, by employers whose own children had grown up and left home, a matter well known to the Home Office. As late as 1928 one official admitted, 'I strongly suspect that a close investigation of much of the emigration to Canada would reveal a great deal of exploitation of young people.' The Home Office, despite legislation passed by the Dominion of Canada and the Provinces of Manitoba and Ontario restricting emigration to those considered acceptable, managed to send

57 ex-reformatory inmates in 1910 and 1911 alone.[49] Managers of schools either failed to disclose relevant information about the boys' origins or used private agencies. Before going to the Home Office as Inspector of Reformatory and Industrial Schools, C. E. B. Russell had 'never found any difficulty in emigrating young fellows . . . who, in certain cases, have been more than once in prison'. As a shipping agent explained to him, 'When a private gentleman, such as yourself, pays the fare for a young man without any express declaration, I am under no obligation to enquire into his past history. Your status has made it previously unnecessary to ask anything further than the recommendation given by your name and interest.' In the far west, British Columbia offered a further potential outlet. The British Columbian Development Association Ltd wrote to the Home Office in 1912 explaining its scheme for developing the province by settling 'a highly desirable class of Public School boys from England . . . of good family who have limited means and [of] retired officers, both naval and military' to start apple orchards. An official minuted, 'I believe that ex-Reformatory inmates would be just the right sort of people to work under English Public School boys.'[50]

With the ending of the First World War the new Ministry of Health once again turned its attention to the Empire as a means of disposal of pauper children. Between 1909 and 1913 only 850 persons had been emigrated on the rates, following objections made by the Canadian Government to receiving paupers in the late 1880s. In contrast 1,426 children were sent in the single year 1920. A Ministry circular pointed out that the United Kingdom's population was now a million greater, despite wartime casualties, than it would have been if emigration had been able to continue during the recent hostilities at its immediate pre-war level. Meanwhile, the circular added, unemployment and poor relief were on an unprecedented scale. With the Empire Settlement Act, 1922, providing a means of restoring emigration to its pre-war levels, the Ministry looked to an annual rate of overseas settlement of 10,000 to 15,000 children a year, using the eleven agencies in operation, and once the prejudices of parents had been overcome, for emigration still remained one of the cheapest ways of dealing with the orphan or deserted child.

Although little came of this grandiose scheme, emigration to the white Dominions continued to receive official blessing. In 1927 the Duke of York, later George VI, with Leo Amery, Secretary of State for the Dominions, visited Kingsley Fairbridge's farm school at Pinjarra, near Perth, Western Australia, which took pauper children under the age of twelve. Nine years later the Prince of Wales launched an appeal through the Child Emigration Society for £100,000 to establish more schools on Fairbridge lines. Meanwhile the Home Office had met opposition from both Canada and Australia to the idea of receiving ex-reformatory or industrial school children. In addition Canada banned the immigration of children under the age of fourteen, unaccompanied by their parents, in 1925. Yet when the Home Office received details of a Toc H scheme for assisting young men going overseas for the first time, an official wrote, 'Overseas emigration from approved schools has been in abeyance for several years. . . . When it does revive, it would be well to bear Toc H in mind with a possibility of providing overseas local friends. Our principal avenues of emigration are Canada, New Zealand, and the Australian Commonwealth.' Yet the latter two, partly in reaction to their early origins, whether as convict stations or as free colonies, had never accepted Home Office children.[51]

Meanwhile reformatory and industrial schools had ceased to be private institutions and had become Home Office approved schools. Until the change their position had been anomalous. The upsurge of interest in reforming the young offender collapsed shortly after the passage of the 1854 Act. Private subscriptions to reformatory schools fell from a peak of £24,903 6s 7d a year in 1860 to a quarter of that figure, £5,956 6s 3d, by 1882, and to £2,014 by 1899. Whereas private donations had accounted for more than a quarter of all expenditure in 1860, the proportion had fallen to 2.2 per cent by 1911. In the case of industrial schools it was then less than seven per cent as compared with 33 per cent fifty years earlier. Treasury grants did not make good the shortcomings of the philanthropic. They had mainly stayed at the same levels since the 1860s; the few changes that took place were usually downward. With little more than a fifth of their income coming from the rates, the financial plight of reformatory schools was particularly parlous. By 1905 they were running at an annual deficit of nearly £10,000 with an expenditure of £111,769 14s 0d. Industrial schools, drawing around 46 per cent of their income from the rates, had a deficit of £8,332 13s 5d with an expenditure of £324,957 6s 9d. Reformatories, in particular, were finding it increasingly difficult to meet the higher educational, sanitary, and medical standards expected of them by the early twentieth century.[52]

Although central and local government sources provided over 90 per cent of the income of both reformatory and industrial schools at the turn of the century, the majority were privately owned. In 1900, out of 227 schools, public bodies controlled only 19, all of which were industrial or truant schools.[53] Whether owned privately or by a local authority the Home Office's control over their day-to-day activities remained slight until at least the 1930s. Model rules issued by the Home Office lacked the force of law. Hence, when it tried to curb the excessive use of corporal punishment in the 1880s by requesting superintendents to display monthly lists of punishments inflicted, it could take no effective action when schools refused to comply. Similarly, the Home Secretary could not veto the appointment of a superintendent, demand his dismissal, nor exercise any power over the appointment and constitution of the managing bodies until after the First World War. In contrast, the poor law authorities had been granted powers in comparable fields in 1834. As the Treasury did not make any capital loans until the early 1900s, and then with reluctance, the Home Secretary could do little to persuade managers to improve unsuitable buildings, his only weapon being his power to withhold his certificate, the passport to an annual grant.

The chequered history of the Mount St Bernard's Reformatory, Leicestershire, highlights the system's weaknesses. Opened in 1856 for Roman Catholic children, it had a debt of £6,000 two years later. The following year three of the lay brothers committed sex offences with some of the boys. The school received an adverse report from Sydney Turner in 1862. Following disturbances in 1863 and 1864 that required police intervention, standards improved under a strong superintendent until 1873. Break-outs in 1874 preceded a mass escape in 1878 when over fifty boys absconded, eight of whom were never recaptured. At this stage the Home Office demanded improved buildings, a condition the Catholic authorities were unable to meet. When the Home Office withdrew its certificate in 1881, 96 boys had to be set free as no other reformatory, Catholic or Protestant, would take them.[54]

The status of the inspectorate added to the problems of exercising effective supervision. It was the Home Office's poor relation, forming the only department housed outside the main office, firstly in Delahay Street and then in Scotland Yard, a site thought morally detrimental to visiting parents as the entrance lay between two public houses. As well as being paid less than the Home Office's other inspectors, the reformatory inspectorate was understaffed. By the mid-1880s Colonel Inglis and his assistant had to inspect over 200 schools containing more than 20,000 children in mainland Britain. They made an annual visit, of which prior notice was given, together with an occasional extra one to some of the schools. By 1913 an inspectorate of seven made a minimum of one formal visit, after giving warning, together with at least one surprise inspection of the 219 schools then in existence. Despite the increase of staff there still remained the time-consuming problem of reaching schools in remote areas, some far from any railway station, as well as coping with absences from sickness and bureaucratic tardiness in filling vacant posts. In contrast the prison inspectorate had the less demanding task of visiting roughly the same number of charges, in approximately 70 prisons situated mainly in urban areas.

The publicizing of reports of excessive cruelty at Heswell Reformatory School's training ship *Akbar*, berthed at Liverpool, led to a Home Office enquiry whose report was debated in the House of Commons in

February 1911, and followed by the appointment of a Departmental Committee which in turn reported in 1913. A few months later the Home Office formed the Children's Branch to deal with certified schools, juvenile courts, probation, cruelty to children, and street trading. In 1921 the Board of Education recognized service in reformatory, industrial, and workhouse schools. Staff now qualified for increments on the Burnham Scale and service became pensionable. Before the war schools had tended to get young newly qualified teachers, if they were fortunate enough to obtain qualified teachers at all, tempted by the prospect of free accommodation. Such teachers had had to take locally negotiated salaries. In 1914 annual salaries for superintendents of boys' schools had ranged between £88 (40 boys) and £375 (300 boys), although there was one head on £300 for 80 boys. More typical was the range of £130 to £175 for 100 to 150 boys. Girls' schools of 50 to 80 inmates offered £50 to £75. Out of 33 examples of salaries of technical staff, five were in the £100 to £130 range, with the median salary at £78, the lowest of £30 a year being earned by a domestic science teacher.[55]

With more generous funding by central and local government, certified schools improved during the inter-war years. A fall in numbers of children admitted, from 6,602 in 1916 to 1,831 in 1922, partly the result of the development of the probation service after 1907,[56] virtually halved their pre-war total of 18,976. This allowed the closure of some forty schools, thereby enabling the Home Office to dispense with some of those whose premises and management were the least satisfactory. The Chief Inspector issued a circular looking for higher standards of training: 'The view that inferior forms of training are good enough for undeserving boys and girls is now, I hope, quite dead . . . the more difficult the children the greater the need for uplifting their minds.' Although the restrictions on employment contained in the Education Act 1918 did not apply to children in reformatory and industrial schools, it became incumbent on managers to see that they were not worse off than other children. In other words, the excessive hours spent on industrial training under conditions that would have been illegal outside were to cease. Children under the age of fourteen were to receive the normal ten sessions of classroom instruction a week in which swimming lessons, outside visits, and nature rambles could be included. All such instruction was to take place in normal school hours. Children under the age of twelve were to be employed only on light personal work such as making their beds, those between twelve and fourteen were to work for not more than an hour a day. Over that age there was to be a combination of school and vocational work, with more school work for the educationally backward. The circular looked to the cessation of the nineteenth-century practice of putting children on outwork, the hiring out of boys to farmers to perform some simple task no longer being justified. Last, the Home Office hoped that children would spend at least a fortnight a year at camp or by the sea, and that classes would be suspended for a week or more at other times.

By 1923 the Home Office reported that the earlier grotesque uniforms, serving the double purpose of reminding inmates of their convict status and facilitating their recognition if they absconded, had *virtually* disappeared, as had the cropping of children's hair, the barring of windows and the locking of dormitories. Shortly afterwards the Home Office issued new model rules under which every school committee was to have a minimum of two women members. Clothing was to be 'similar to that worn by boys and girls in every day life', the few schools still using the old style clothing being recommended to pass it on to museums or scarecrows (*sic!*). A further proviso at last gave the Home Secretary the right to approve the appointment of super-intendents. Thus, after a decade, many of the recommendations of the 1913 Departmental Committee had been implemented.[57]

The beginnings of the study of adolescent psychology, the psychology of the individual, and of delinquency, brought a questioning of the earlier explanations for the causation of delinquency. Professor Cyril Burt, in the preface to his *The Young Delinquent* (1925), rejected the widely held earlier notion that juvenile offenders were necessarily incipient criminals. 'Delinquency I regard,' he wrote, 'as nothing but an outstanding sample – dangerous and extreme, but none the less typical – of common childish naughtiness.' This book, perhaps the most widely read of all his publications, was based on material he had collected in his capacity as the London County Council's educational psychologist, from 1913 onwards.[58] The *Third Report of the Children's Branch* (1925) reflected these new attitudes.

> It would be wrong to take too stern a view of acts of delinquency at fourteen or even fifteen years of age. Delinquency at this age frequently, if not generally, is due to bad training leading to a lack of self-control or to the illegitimate use of normal instincts. In no small proportion of the cases a predisposing cause is mental instability . . . of the great problems of adolescence.[59]

Hence the task of managers, the Home Office counselled, was that of training the neglected mind, together with the development of character from material that was often excellent. Although there was a need for discipline and firm treatment, rigid routine and dull monotony had no place in the modern reformatory. Industrial schools were homes for neglected children, who even if they had robbed an orchard were not necessarily criminals. Thus 'efforts have been made to remove every aspect of the punitive character of these schools – they have become residential schools with exceptional opportunities.'[60]

The Children and Young Persons Act, 1933, the main provisions of which were based on the recommendations of the *Report of the Departmental Committee on the Treatment of Young Offenders* (1927), abolished the largely artificial distinction between industrial and reformatory schools. They became Home Office Approved Schools, a step that made possible the classification of children according to their age, religion, ability, and the whereabouts of their homes. The 1933 Act also required children to be medically examined before admission to approved schools for training. Over the next five years, 17 girls were found to be pregnant and 31 suffering from diseases that made them unfit for training, while a further 77 had been committed under the Mental Deficiency Act.[61]

How far the reforms the Home Office instituted were carried out in the spirit and in the letter is difficult to assess. Members of the Curtis Committee, who visited 52 approved schools, were generally satisfied with what they saw. Despite the artificial situation in which such visitations are conducted they found one instance of excessive regiment-ation, described in a passage that hints at others:

> The mealtime behaviour of these boys was one of the most depressing sights we have seen in any school. The boys were lined up and marched in and out. Signals were given by the member of staff in charge to 'sit down', 'pour tea', 'stop pouring tea', 'begin eat'. . . . The boys looked strained and unhappy.

Again, despite the iceberg nature of evidence provided in punishment books, it was clear that some schools inflicted corporal punishment thought excessive by the standards of the time. Similarly the amount of 'spit and polish', and the enforcement of military style bed and kit layouts in large dormitories where personal possessions had to be kept to a minimum, drew comment from the Committee. On the other hand 'at most schools' the diet was very good, medical care 'seemed excellent in almost every case', clothing was 'usually satisfactory . . . sometimes in the girls' schools very good', and the provision of group activities in leisure time 'was nearly always good and very often excellent'. As the careful qualifications made by the Committee and the findings of the enquiries into troubles at the Standon Farm Approved Schools and Carlton Approved School indicate, however, not all managers and staff of approved schools met the standards the Home Office now demanded of its approved schools.[62]

THE EDUCATION OF
BLIND AND DEAF CHILDREN
BEFORE 1893

The children forming the subject matter of this chapter no more constitute a neatly formed group than do those of the previous three. Because their condition was not always diagnosed, understood, or provided for, workhouses, reformatory and industrial schools held an indeterminate number of mentally and physically handicapped children throughout the nineteenth century and later. For most of the century the state's concern was to make special provision for those children labouring under social and familial handicaps in the types of institutions already discussed. From the closing decades of the century, with the gradual spread of free, universal, compulsory education, school authorities gradually became aware of the need to provide for children suffering from educational difficulties and handicaps. It is to these children that we must now turn our attention.

Of the handicaps now being considered, blindness, deafness, and dumbness attracted the sympathy and attention of philanthropic individuals and the state earlier, and to a greater extent, than did other impediments to the receipt of a normal education. Blind, deaf, and dumb children received special consideration in the Poor Law Amendment Act, 1834, under which parents seeking relief in respect of such children did not suffer disfranchisement, the political-social penalty imposed on all other recipients of relief at that time (although, with an English and Welsh electorate of only 650,000 immediately after the extension of the franchise in 1832, it is easy to exaggerate the importance of this penalty). As well as the powers guardians possessed under the Education of Pauper Children Act, 1862, and modified in 1868 and 1882, legislation of 1879 allowed them to support institutions and societies caring for blind, deaf and dumb children. Generally guardians used these powers, either through design or ignorance, charily. In September 1887 there were 336 blind children, aged five to fifteen, receiving relief. Of these 286 were in special schools for the blind, five in workhouse schools, and ten in public elementary ones. The remaining 35, most of whom were thought to be mentally incapable of benefiting from education, received indoor or outdoor relief. 672 deaf and dumb children also received poor relief, 575 in special schools, 33 in workhouse schools, and eight in public elementary ones. The remaining 56 had no instruction as they were considered too young, or mentally incapable of profiting from any, or because of the lack of suitable facilities. The fees guardians paid special schools for both groups of children were usually 4s to 5s a week, but could be as high as 8s or as low as 1s a week. Yet the census return for 1881 shows 1,710 children between the ages of five and fifteen returned as blind, and 5,129 deaf and dumb. In both instances the figures probably underestimated the real state of affairs.[1]

Helping the blind had been a charitable and religious duty undertaken from the earliest days of the spread of Christianity, one of the first recorded instances being the hospital St Basil established at Caesarea in the fourth century. The first important moves affecting modern developments came in the latter part of the eighteenth century. An article published in the *Edinburgh Review* in 1774 set out many of the themes that were influential for at least the next century. In discussing the teaching of the blind the pseudonymous Demodocus wrote

> The most important view, therefore, which we can entertain in the education of a person deprived of sight is to redress as effectually as possible the natural disadvantages with which he is encumbered, or, in other words, to enlarge as far as possible his sphere of knowledge, and activity. This can only be done by the improvement of his intellectual imagination and mechanical powers. . . .

In their training music was 'their easiest and most obvious province'. As well as being persons particularly worthy of sympathy, they offered a more effective field for investment in education than did other groups of handicapped persons.

> There is no rank of persons more meritorious of public compassion, or better qualified to repay its generous exertions than the blind.
> They are meritorious of compassion; for their sphere of action and observation is infinitely more limited than that of the deaf, the lame, or those who labour under any other corporal infirmity consistent with health.
> They are better qualified to repay any friendly interposition . . . because they are free from the distraction which attends that multiplicity of objects and pursuits that are continuously obvious to the sight, they are more attentive to their own internal economy.[2]

The will to educate a particular handicapped group can only be translated into practice if there are also the means. In pre-revolutionary Paris both were present. One of the first influential figures in the training of the blind was Valentin Haüy who founded *L'Institution des Jeunes Aveugles* in Paris in 1784. His interest in working with the blind is said to have been aroused by hearing a discordant performance by some blind musicians at the *Café des Aveugles*, an experience that led him to consider how they might be helped. To Europe's first school for the blind, Haüy brought materials developed earlier elsewhere. Nicholas Saunderson, the blind professor of mathematics who succeeded to Newton's Chair at Cambridge, had already invented an apparatus for working at mathematical problems. Weissembourg's tutor improved this device when teaching a blind pupil, and prepared maps using devices for indicating coastlines, rivers, and other features. He also helped to train Mme Paradis, a god-daughter of Maria Theresa, who used relief musical characters developed by Lamoroux to give concerts in Paris. As well as using and improving extant material, Haüy evolved methods of teaching handicrafts such as net-making, sewing, and book-binding.[3]

Two important developments took place at *L'Institution des Jeunes Aveugles*. In 1819 Charles Barbier, a French artillery officer, had invented a form of secret writing, *écriture nocturnal*, for passing messages. Louis Braille, a pupil of *L'Institution des Jeunes Aveugles*, changed Barbier's arrangement of two vertical lines of six points into a six-dot form ten years later. This gave a possible 64 combinations and permutations with which to represent the alphabet, punctuation signs, and common combinations and contractions of letters. Braille also adapted his system for musical notation. Two years after his death in 1852, his *alma mater* adopted braille as a teaching medium. Despite competition from other systems of notation it has now become universally used. Another student, Claude Montal, with the assistance of a companion, taught himself to strip, repair, reassemble, and tune pianos, accomplishments that enabled him to establish a pianoforte manufactory. His success led to the training of blind pupils as piano tuners both in France and England, an accomplishment more highly regarded in the former than the latter. Parisian piano tuners in the 1880s were reputed to be earning £80 to £150 a year, while blind tuners in England were averaging only 14s 6d a week.[4]

Whereas the early institutions on the Continent and in the USA were partly supported by public money, the initiative in the United Kingdom came entirely from private individuals. England's first school for the blind opened at Liverpool in 1791. By 1811 five other schools, in London, Dublin, Edinburgh, Bristol, and Norwich, had been founded on the lines of the Liverpool model. The names of some of them, the Society for the Relief of the Indigent Blind, Edinburgh (1793), the School for the Indigent Blind, Southwark, London (1799), and the Richmond Institute for the Instruction and Employment of the Industrious Blind, Dublin (1810), suggest both the principles on which they were founded and the social group they were attempting to help. The Abbé Carton, who conducted a survey of the English schools for the blind in 1837, found that their purpose was to instruct inmates 'in manual labour – to make artisans of them', whereas in France it was to give them an intellectual instruction. The buildings, though, impressed him: 'An inexhaustible philanthropy and lavish subscriptions have permitted of palaces being built. . . . But people have had the good feeling not to make lords of this class of unfortunate beings. . . . The rank of all is shown by their appearance. Their work is unremitting and well regulated; their clothes are very common and their food whole-some and plentiful . . .'[5]

Although indigent, early inmates had to be respectable. Applicants for the Liverpool school underwent careful vetting, their sponsors having to answer questions such as:

> Has the blind person been a common beggar, wandering minstrel, a player upon any instrument at ale-houses, within two years before application for admission, such persons being entirely excluded?

Despite the general realization that applicants for privately endowed pensions would not deliberately induce blindness, the elderly were equally carefully scrutinized. Hetherington's Charity to the Blind (1774), excluded those who had ever begged, received alms or been deemed objects for parish relief; or had been day labourers, soldiers, sailors, servants, journeymen, or persons living by turning a mangle. At the same time it set applicants an upper income limit of £20 a year from other sources. The Painters' and Stainers' Company, with an upper income limit of £10 a year, excluded common beggars, and required applicants to be of 'sober habits and conversation'. The London Society for Teaching the Blind to Read and Training Them in Industrial Occupations normally only took inmates of a grade superior to that of the indigent classes On the other hand, middle-class fathers had to await the opening of the Worcester College for Blind Sons of Gentlemen in 1869 before their offspring could be trained for the professions and universities rather than for basket-making.[6]

The founders of the early schools concentrated on training their inmates in a number of manual crafts, thereby setting the pattern of what was deemed suitable training for the blind for many generations to come. Work at Liverpool included spinning, making hampers, baskets, floor cloths, sacks, list shoes and pack thread, and weaving worsted rugs. A record of the school's sales for 1836 gives some idea of the relative importance of the various items. Out of a total gross revenue of £1,818 18s 0d, the sale of ropes contributed £754 11s 10d; rope matting, carpets, and mats made of old tarred rope provided £502 11s 10d, while baskets brought £368 18s 8d. With the average cost of maintaining a pupil ranging between £29 at Glasgow to over £60 at the newly opened school at York, schools depended heavily on private contributions, fees paid by friends on behalf of the pupils at around 3s 6d a week, and the product of their pupils' labour. With no generally accepted method of teaching the blind to read and write yet available, little attempt was made, apart from offering tuition in music at some schools, to supplement the industrial training.[7]

The industrial occupations for which the blind were trained required little capital for entry. Hence blind workers suffered intense competition from small-scale sighted competitors who had great difficulty in earning more than subsistence wages. The plight of the blind naturally was worse. Young people, who found that the existing institutions could not often keep them beyond the age of sixteen, faced the world inadequately trained to earn a living, a problem that the shortage of suitable workshops only exacerbated. As the Royal Commission on the Blind, Deaf and Dumb, etc., disapprovingly reported, 'they take to begging, playing musical instruments in the streets, or in public houses, or sitting reading the Bible to passers by and asking for alms', practices that the Commissioners hoped to eradicate by a series of measures aimed at improving the existing educational and training facilities then available. Enquiries made on behalf of the Commission showed that 58 per cent (734 of 1,267) of the blind men followed the trade they had learnt in an institution. Around 15 per cent earned less than 5s a week, about 25 per cent claimed 5s to 10s a week, a further 16 per cent earned 10s to 15s, while around 10 per cent earned over 15s a week. On the other hand the 42 per cent not following a trade they had been taught fared less well than the 58 per cent who capitalized on their training. Out of 5,846, 4,605 stated they were unable to maintain themselves without recourse to charity, with 3,282 declaring they earned nothing, and only 959 claiming to be self-sufficient. The occupations followed closely matched the training offered. The largest group were basket makers, 21.5 per cent of those in employment, music and piano tuning accounted for a further 8.5 per cent, brush making 7.5 per cent, chair caning and other cane work, 6.5 per cent, while mat and mattress making, rope and twine spinning, and weaving, all attracted less than 3 per cent. The most affluent were missionaries, Scripture readers, visitors and others employed to minister to the spiritual and physical needs of the blind, who had a weekly average income of 17s 4d. Music offered the best career, with piano tuners and instrumentalists earning 14s 6d, more than double the 7s 1d declared by those following the various handicraft trades.[8]

In possible anticipation of this state of affairs the early training institutions had taken precautions aimed at preventing their inmates relapsing into the ways of pauperism on their discharge. Religious instruction at Liverpool, where the chaplain's stipend took £500 of the annual wages bill of £1313 12s 5d, was obviously a matter of importance. The superintendent and his wife had to be content with £283 10s, while the craft teachers earned £70 5s or £58 5s. The masters of music and singing were on £90 10s and £70 respectively. At Edinburgh those living out had to attend classes in religious instruction twice a week on pain of dismissal. They had to be in their homes by 9.00 p.m. each night, with the least sign of drunkenness attracting severe punishment. To discourage drunkenness at the weekend workers received their pay on Monday nights. The wage structure at Glasgow was designed to encourage industry. Those exceeding their norm received pay for their additional output plus one shilling. This gave workers the prospect of earning 8s to 11s a week. As might be expected in the mother country of the savings bank movement, both institutions ran a savings bank to which workers were expected to contribute.[9]

The production of religious literature for the blind was one matter on which the inventors of different scripts could agree, however bitter their rivalry to secure the acceptance of their particular system might have been. By the early 1850s there were at least five arbitrary systems – Braille, Carton, Frere, Lucas, and Moon – with a further five based on the alphabet – Alston, Alston modified, the American, the French, and Gall. With each institution using its chosen type – Alston at Glasgow, Moon at his institute for the Blind, Brighton, (1847), the American system at the Perkins Institution, Boston, Massachusetts (1832), and the London Society for Teaching the Blind to Read (1839) using Lucas, to give a few examples – a blind person learnt only one system. The systems using raised characters based on the alphabet were of greater assistance to the teachers, spared the task of having to learn an arbitrary system, than they were to the blind who had difficulty in distinguishing the raised letters. The London Society for Teaching the Blind to Read admitted that it took three months to learn to read a Gospel moderately well in Lucas's raised script. As one critic of the system pointed out, they could have learnt it off by heart in the same time. Only when a blind person had surmounted this hurdle did the London Society allow him to move on to secular literature. Two factors compounded the confusion the multiplicity of systems had caused. In some instances, in Lucas, Frere, and Moon, closely similar characters stood for different letters. At least one system ran from left to right on one line and then from right to left on the second without reversing the characters on the second line or indicating that a word ran over more than one line. Because there were so many systems in use at various stages of development, the Society for Printing and Distributing Books for the Blind was handling parts of the Bible in five different types in the late 1850s. The first of these had been St John's Gospel whose publication by James Gall in 1834 was prompted by his belief that the evil effects of not being able to read the Bible were apparent 'in that morbid self-opinionativeness and metaphysical distortion of mind, which would be corrected by the enlightening influence of reading'. The Glasgow Institute had published 13,460 copies of books, 8,960 of which were of religious works, in the Alston system by 1842. In 1839 the institute had sent a copy of parts of the Bible to Queen Victoria who had granted £400 from the Royal Bounty. Encouraged by this gift it then sent the whole of the Bible two years later, reminding her of her grandfather's desire that every child in his kingdom should learn to read the Bible. Unfortunately this initiative went unrewarded. By the 1850s the New Testament cost between £4 10s, using Moon's script, and 16s, using the American system. In the middle price range were New Testaments produced by the Alston and Frere systems at £2 and £2 10s respectively. As well as books from the Bible other works available to the blind were of a spiritually uplifting nature such as *Five Addresses to Those Who Wish to go to Heaven*, *The Baptismal Vow*, and *Sunlight in the Clouds*. *Robinson Crusoe* provided secular relief, while some of the Books of Euclid gave secular instruction. With this heavy concentration on works of religious instruction England lagged behind France and Germany in two respects. First, *L'Institution des Jeunes Aveugles* had been publishing grammars, dictionaries, and collections from various authors from 1832 onwards. Second, England had failed to produce books on methods of training the blind apart from primers setting out the various scripts. The one work available in England was the translation made in 1819 of Dr Guillee's *Essai sur l'Instruction des Aveugles*, which was reprinted as late as 1894.[10]

In 1868 the British and Foreign Blind Association, now the Royal National Institute for the Blind, was formed by Dr T. R. Armitage, whose sight was gradually fading. Its objects were to provide employment, education, and literature for the blind. To end the confusion resulting from the existence of various scripts, it consulted the blind on their suitability. It decided to use Braille at a time when not a single institution in the United Kingdom did so. By 1885 all made some use of it. The Institute evolved mass-production techniques, employing sighted workers to emboss books in Braille for copying by forty blind ones. By this means their output of books in Braille exceeded that of all systems put together by the 1880s. However, when the Royal Commission took evidence in the late 1880s, the battle of the types had not yet been decided. Societies that possessed considerable stocks in other systems defended their vested interests. Although the Report came down heavily in favour of Braille, 'For those blind from birth, or from early childhood, Braille seems to be, without doubt, the most suitable, as it can be read more quickly and can be printed in a much smaller bulk than any other [type] . . . and is the only one well adapted to musical notation', the Commissioners felt a need to compromise: 'It is useful to the blind to know all the leading types.' Yet they had admitted that two, Lucas and Frere, were gradually dying out. Apart from Braille the only other survivor is Moon's script, still in use to a limited extent.[11]

The deaf and dumb did not attract either as much sympathy or as much attention as the blind. The Egerton Report gave details of 45 missions to the blind but of only 19 to the deaf and dumb. Blindness is obvious to the onlooker, while deafness is not. Children born deaf, until the development of means of teaching them to speak, remained dumb as well. Consequently the prelingually deaf were written off as ineducable and of no account until comparatively recent times, notwithstanding a few isolated examples demonstrating the falsity of the assumption. Early pioneers included the sixteenth-century monk, Ponce do Leon, Juan Pablo Bonet, whose *Simplification of the Alphabet and the Method of Teaching Deaf Mutes to Speak* (1620) contains the first recorded comment on lip reading, and Professor John Wallis of Oxford. These and others during the period 1500–1750 accumulated piecemeal an understanding of how a knowledge of speech mechanism, of hearing, and of language could be applied to teaching the deaf. Such men had worked in isolation with just a few pupils. In the middle of the eighteenth century two influential figures, the Abbé de l'Epée (1712– 89) and the German, Samuel Heinecke (1729–90), founded schools that became the first two state-supported ones for teaching the deaf. The Abbé de l'Epée developed a method of teaching the deaf and dumb a sign language so sophisticated that pupils could, in theory but not necessarily in practice, distinguish such closely associated words as *aimer*, *l'amitié*, and *l'amour*. The second volume of his work, *Institutions des Sourds et Muets*, was translated into English in 1819. De l'Epée's successor at the Paris Institute, the Abbé Sicard, wrote *Cours d'Instruction d'un Sourd Muet* describing a means of teaching the deaf and dumb to write simple sentences, held in the 1830s to be 'one of the best books an instructor can have'.

Meanwhile Heinicke had taken a different route after realizing that because deaf children could cry, laugh, and shout, they must possess vocal chords. He was also aware that part deaf children could hear loud noises and distinguish certain speech sounds. As he thought it erroneous to teach deaf children their letters first, he introduced functional words, followed by syllables, leaving individual letters to the last. The oral method he developed was based on the earlier work of Johann Konrad Amman (1669–1724) who had taught deaf children to speak by making them feel the vibrations of his own throat and watch their mouths in a mirror when trying to speak. In contrast De l'Epée had decided that articulation and lip-reading, while within the competence of the deaf, were not worth the time and trouble involved. Within the field of the education of the deaf, they were uncompromising proponents of differing methodologies, generating a deep professional schism. The de l'Epée/Heinicke methodological dichotomy has plagued the profession from their time to the present.[12]

In Great Britain the duel between the proponents of the two methods was as bitter as that between the factions supporting rival reading schemes for the blind. Thomas Braidwood, who had started teaching deaf children in Edinburgh, moved to Hackney, then still outside London, in 1783. Throughout his life he kept his methods secret; only after his death did his nephew, Thomas Watson, publish *Instruction of the Deaf and Dumb, a Theoretical and Practical View of the Means by which they are Taught to Speak and Understand* (1809). This manual advocated beginning with articulation but included a two-handed alphabet, still in use, as a means of communication until the deaf pupil had mastered articulation. Although the Birmingham Institution for the Instruction of the Deaf and Dumb was established at Edgbaston using Braidwood's system in 1813, it adopted the sign system in 1825 when Louis du Puget, one of de l'Epée's pupils, was made superintendent. Another early school at Doncaster, opened in 1829, also used the French method under Charles Baker, headmaster 1829–74, who considered articulation a 'specious accomplishment'. By the 1850s the use of oralism in Great Britain had largely died out except at a school in Margate belonging to the Asylum For the Support and Education of Deaf and Dumb Children (1792), where Richard Elliott found Joseph Watson's picture dictionary of 1806 in use nearly sixty years later.[13]

The physical isolation of British institutions, together with their overcrowding, led to a stagnation which was compounded by their use of the sign system, at a time when other European countries were developing oral teaching. The late 1850s and early 1860s saw the revival of the oral method in England when Susannah Hull, in London, and Gerrit van Asch, in Manchester, began teaching small groups of children. Van Asch, and William van Praagh, came to England in 1867 from David Hirsch's school in Rotterdam. Hirsch, in turn, was a follower of Victor Augst Jäger and Friedrich Maritz Hill. Hill's influence on the German system has been described as being without doubt greater than that of any other single person. In turn Hirsch's two acolytes were largely responsible for the revival of the oral method in England. Baroness Mayer de Rothschild, whose concern over the plight of deaf Jewish children in London had induced her to bring van Praagh to England, was instrumental in founding the Association for the Oral Instruction of the Deaf and Dumb and a small training college in Fitzroy Square, London, in 1871. Seven years later the Society for Training Teachers of the Deaf and Dumb and the Diffusion of the German system, founded by B.St John Ackers, MP, father of a deaf daughter, established a second college at Ealing. By this time a third advocate of the oral method had achieved some prominence. Thomas Arnold, founder of the Northampton High School for the Deaf, published *Aures Surdis; The Education of the Deaf and Dumb; a review of the French and German Systems* (1872). In this he attacked the arbitrary nature of the French system under which, for example, the use of the thumb indicated 'bad' and the little finger 'good'. He also made a distinction between arbitrary signs such as those quoted and natural or pantomimic ones. He went on to produce *A Method of Teaching the Deaf and Dumb Lipreading and Language* (1881) and *Education of Deaf-Mutes: a manual for teachers* (1888). This manual was revised in 1901 by A. Farrar, who in 1881 as Watson's pupil had been the first deaf boy in the United Kingdom to have passed a public examination, when he obtained his London University Matriculation certificate. Arnold's school at Northampton remained the only school in England offering an academic secondary education for the deaf until the opening of Mary Hare Grammar School in 1946.[14]

Mrs Dancy, first one of Van Praagh's students, then his assistant, joined the London School Board in 1879 to provide classes for London's deaf and dumb children using the oral method. The following year an International Congress at Milan endorsed, with the English delegates dissenting, the superiority of the oral over the sign system. With the subsequent abandonment of the sign system in France the oral method became almost universal throughout Europe. In England and Scotland, the example of the London School Board, followed by other school boards and the growth of the colleges in Fitzroy Square and at Ealing, enabled the oral method to make headway. Thus deaf children learnt to communicate with people other than those who knew the manual system, thereby widening their social horizons. By 1888 just over half the deaf and dumb children being taught in some kind of an educational institution, 1,563 out of 3,138, were following the oral method; 545 followed a course combining the two methods, 1,026 remained confined to the restriction of the sign method, while the remaining four were classified as 'special cases'. It is probable that another 2,000 deaf and dumb children received no education at all or sat virtually uselessly in classrooms. Parents were reluctant to return their children as deaf and dumb to census enumerators, partly because they believed that any deafness caused by scarlatina would prove to be temporary. Hence the census figure for 1881, of 5,129 children aged five to fifteen, was an estimate based on the proportion between the deaf and dumb and the whole population. This state of affairs created problems for school-board officials. Leicester School Board, for example, thought it had no deaf and dumb children until a private survey unearthed twelve.[15]

In making use of the two devices, Braille for the blind and the oral method for deaf and dumb children, school boards had taken an important initiative. As new educational bodies they had been able to enter these fields of special education free of the prejudices and vested interests of the founders of existing institutions. In addition school boards provided access to special education for a social group previously largely neglected. Before 1870, except for such assistance as the poor law guardians offered under the 1862 Act, provision for blind, deaf and dumb children had been confined to those whose parents not only met contemporary canons of respectability but could also afford the fees, usually around £20 a year, demanded by private specialist institutions. Yet children of the poor seem to have been particularly susceptible to purulent ophthalmia, a complaint that led to blindness from near birth. As various simple remedies were available and were used on the Continent, the Ophthalmological Society had sent a deputation to the President of the Local Government Board in 1884 urging him to send instruction cards to those in charge of newly-born babies giving appropriate advice, a request he had refused as it would have cost an estimated £7,300 a year. In turn the Egerton Commission recommended the circulation of such information through the sanitary authorities or by the Post Office. Not until 1914 did ophthalmia neonatorum, defined as 'purulent discharge from the eyes of an infant commencing within twenty-one days of birth', become a compulsorily notifiable disease throughout England and Wales. In the meantime children of the poor, unless their parents lived in one of the hundred local authority areas that had made ophthalmia neonatorum a notifiable disease by 1911, remained at hazard.[16]

The campaign to secure elementary education for all blind children began in 1869 when it became apparent that an Act to lay the foundations of universal elementary education was imminent. In that year Elizabeth Gilbert, the blind daughter of the Bishop of Chichester, had organized a petition praying that children blind from birth should be brought within the orbit of any educational legislation that might be enacted in the near future. Early the following year she arranged for a deputation, representing 29 institutions for the blind, to wait on Earl de Grey and Ripon, Lord President of the Council, and W. E. Forster, Vice-President of the Committee of the Privy Council on Education, to urge them to consider the petition presented the previous summer. Apart from an expression of sympathy, nothing came of the meeting, one possible hurdle mentioned by the Lord President being that bodies representing deaf and dumb children would want equal treatment for their protégés. Moreover, the deputation's request had raised the question of the nature and extent of the state's responsibility for the welfare of its people at a time when this was still primarily seen as confined to the relief of destitution. Thus, even when the Egerton

Commission was sitting, Elizabeth Gilbert's biographer could write 'probably no special action on behalf of a class, however afflicted, can be expected from the Government of a country'. W. St James Wheelhouse, MP for Leeds, was more optimistic. He introduced a succession of bills during the 1870s under which the powers guardians enjoyed under the Education of Pauper Children Act, 1862, would have become duties in respect of blind and deaf and dumb children.[17]

Conferences of teachers of the blind, held in Indianapolis and Vienna in 1871 and 1873, showed that Great Britain was lagging behind the Continent and the USA in the provision it made for training the blind. Accordingly, the Charity Organization Society (1869) appointed a committee to investigate the problem. Its report, published in 1876, called for the appointment of a Royal Commission on the blind to secure reforms in their training and education. The report showed that, while there were 800 or 900 blind persons capable of working in the Metropolis, there were only 150 workshop employees in London, the majority of whom were connected in some capacity with the Association for Promoting the General Welfare of the Blind, founded by Elizabeth Gilbert in 1856. The Committee accordingly recommended that, with nearly 300 children in the Metropolis thought to be educable, provision should be made for their elementary education between the ages of five and fifteen, to give them two years more schooling than the sighted. Part of the time should be spent in an ordinary elementary school to enable them to develop their other faculties to the fullest and to become self-reliant. Such a policy, the Committee pointed out, had already been adopted in parts of Scotland with success for the previous seven years, while blind children were now attending more than twenty London schools. After the age of fifteen 'arrangements should be made for continuing their education and teaching them trades, and . . . the training should be such as thoroughly to fit them for the trade or calling by which they are most likely to support themselves.'[18]

During the course of the next decade, despite the absence of any specific legislation, blind, deaf and dumb, and feeble-minded children made their way into the new classrooms. However, the precise legal obligations of school authorities, as well as those of their parents to send them in the first place, remained obscure. Both parties could shelter behind the clause in the 1870 Act exempting children from attending school if there was 'some reasonable cause'. Where there was a sympathetic school attendance officer London parents exploited this legal ambiguity. 'Unfortunately it is often the case that parents wilfully or ignorantly neglect the opportunities afforded', the London School Board reported in 1890, 'and either let such children run the streets or nurse the babies at home, the visitors for years accepting the excuse of "very nearsighted" or bad eyes.' When attendance had been insisted on and the parents' bluff called, in a few instances the child miraculously 'had developed entirely satisfactory sight for the remaining school years' after attending a class for blind children for a short time.[19] On the other hand the Act required boards to provide sufficient accommodation in public elementary schools, to be 'available for all children resident in such districts for whose elementary education efficient and suitable provision is not made.' The Elementary Education Act, 1876, did little to clarify the situation. Parents now had a duty to cause their children to receive an efficient education in reading, writing, and arithmetic. Excuses for non-attendance included being 'prevented from attending school by sickness or any unavoidable cause'. During these years the Education Department sidestepped the issue. When the Leeds School Board asked W. E. Forster in 1872 if the Act passed two years previously gave them power to provide for the education of blind, deaf and dumb children, his equivocal draft reply stated that he personally was of the opinion that the Act did not prevent school boards from making provision for the education of such children, providing regard was paid to the definition of an elementary school in the Act. In 1885 Sunderland School Board's petition for a legislative amendment to the 1870 Act to make being blind, deaf or dumb no longer a 'reasonable excuse' for non-attendance was turned down, the Education Department having no intention of introducing such a measure. Not until the passage of the relevant legislation in 1893, 1899, and 1914 were these legal ambiguities removed. Nevertheless, by the late 1880s five school boards in England and Scotland were providing education for 194 blind children, 133 of whom were at one of the London School Board's 23 centres, the first having been opened in 1879. The L.S.B. was educating just under half the 289 children in its area known to be blind, yet there was probably twice that number, 578, of partially-sighted children for whom no special provision was being made, public sympathy being almost totally confined to the completely blind. Between them the five boards employed eight blind and two sighted teachers. In addition ten school boards were teaching 577 deaf and dumb children, of whom 313 were in the L.S.B.'s 13 centres, with a further 47 being sent for education elsewhere. There were probably 140 others for whom no provision was made. Relatively the London child fared better than his Welsh counterpart where 70 received instruction, 50 in Swansea and 20 in Llandaff, out of 197 deaf and dumb children in Wales. Between them the boards employed 55 hearing teachers and one deaf one.[20]

Drafting difficulties, the lapsing of the bill in two sessions, and the fall of Lord Salisbury's government when the third bill was before Parliament, delayed the passage of legislation implementing some of the Egerton Commission's recommendations until 1893. Although called the Elementary Education (Blind and Deaf Children) Act, its provisions also covered those who were partially blind or deaf. The definition of a blind child as 'too blind to be able to read the ordinary school books used by children' was wider in scope than that contained in the Blind Persons' Act, 1920, which entitled a person 'so blind as to be unable to perform any work for which eyesight is essential', to receive an old age pension at fifty, instead of seventy. Similarly a deaf child was one 'too deaf to be taught in a class of hearing children in an elementary school'. The Act left parents in no doubt about their responsibilities. Blind children were to be subject to compulsory education from the age of five to sixteen. Deaf ones started two years later, at seven, in accordance with the Egerton Commission's finding that

> that the systematic teaching of language cannot be profitably begun with children before seven as they are not so forward then as other children of four or five, and the prepondering weight of evidence is in favour of commencing at seven.

Not until after the passage of the Deaf Children Act, 1937, did deaf children start their education at the same age as blind ones. There was some parental opposition to this extended period of education. In the same year, 1893, while another Act had raised the minimum school-leaving age for other children to eleven, such children could still escape from school five years before their blind or deaf siblings. In addition the 1893 Act removed the 'distance excuse', whereas other children were exempted from school attendance if they lived more than three miles from the nearest public elementary school. School authorities now had to make suitable provision for the education of children covered by the Act or contribute towards some other school in which blind and deaf children could be educated. Such an arrangement could require the boarding out of a child, and a school authority to contribute thereto – a provision that encouraged collusion between parents unwilling to see their children sent away from home, and school authorities reluctant to foot the bill, to neglect the child's education.

Other factors militated against the successful operation of the Act. Magistrates were understandably hesitant to enforce it, especially when children would have been required to leave home to attend some distant school. The level of grants offered – £3 3s 0d a year for a child attending a certified school, whether residential or not, for elementary education without manual instruction, and a further £2 2s 0d with its inclusion – constituted a financial disincentive to any liberal implementation of the Act. In negotiating the rates the Education Department had got off to a bad start with the Treasury, who complained that the Blind and Deaf Bill 'will cost the taxpayer from £16,000 to £20,000 a year. . . . My Lords cannot but feel surprised that Their Lordships of the Committee of Council should have introduced and carried through Parliament a measure, which may involve such an addition to the Public expenditure, without any previous intimation of their intentions to this Board.'[21] In the event the total grant available, £5 5s 0d, a year compared unfavourably with the figures provided by the Egerton Commission. The annual cost of educating a blind child under the London School Board had been put at £9 10s 5d, while classes under the boards at Cardiff, Bradford, and Sunderland averaged £7 3s 1d a child. Similarly, the average cost to the rates of educating deaf children at ten board schools in England and Scotland was £7 11s 6d a head. The level of the grant discouraged school authorities from searching out blind, deaf and dumb children, while it penalized those that did so. Urban school boards with large populations could generally use day centres for their children, to which guides could conduct them if necessary. Rural authorities and smaller towns, with only a few children requiring special education, had to use residential schools costing £12 to £20 a year.[22] Despite all these difficulties, education authorities made proportionately better provision for children brought into the mainstream of elementary education by the 1893 Act than they did for the next group to be considered, the mentally handicapped.

THE FEEBLE-MINDED CHILD
BEFORE 1890

To avoid lengthy circumlocutions this and subsequent chapters use the terminology of the period without qualification. Thus the phrase 'idiot children' does not imply any acceptance of the validity of the concept but is used instead of the lengthier 'children deemed to be idiotic in the 1850s' or whatever period is under discussion. However offensive the stark use of terms such as 'idiot', 'imbecile', 'lunatic asylum' – to take just a few examples – may seem today, they are valuable pointers to the attitudes, beliefs, and knowledge of those who used them. Indeed, in attempting to write about the past in any meaningful way it is as impossible to avoid their use as it would be for the medievalist to avoid the technical terminology peculiar to the feudal system.

Feeble-minded children, the 'et cetera' of the Egerton Report's short title, were aggregated with deaf and dumb children following the reconstitution of the Royal Commission in January 1886. They were the Cross Commission's cast-offs, 'the Royal Commission on the Elementary Education Acts having suggested that the case of feeble-minded children would come more appropriately within our terms of reference'.[1] Despite their inclusion in the Egerton's extended remit, they had to wait six years longer than blind, deaf and dumb children, and be the subject of a departmental committee report, before legislation gave school authorities the power, but not the duty, of making special educational provision for them.

With the study of mental health and handicap still emerging from a welter of superstition, prejudice and primordial shame, the feeble-minded child had remained one of the most neglected of all groups considered in this book. The formulation of the concept of feeble-mindedness, together with the realization that such children were trainable and possibly educable, were products of a greater understanding of the nature of mental defect. In medieval times the *Statute De Praerogativa Regis* (17 Ed. II, cc. 9, 10) had recognized two categories of mentally defective persons, the idiot – '*fatuus naturalis*' – and the lunatic who, though '*non compos mentis sicut quidam sunt per lucida intervalla*', had periods of lucidity. This distinction had been important in feudal law for the propertied classes as it determined the conditions under which the Crown could enjoy the profitable business of administering a lunatic's or idiot's estate. In the sixteenth century the *Natura Brevium* offered a rudimentary intelligence test, that made certain cultural assumptions, by which an idiot could be set apart from a 'normal' person. An idiot was 'one who cannot count or number twenty pence, nor tell who was his father or mother, nor how old he is . . . if he has sufficient understanding to know and understand his letters, and to read by teaching and information, then it seems he is not an idiot.'[2]

John Locke's *An Essay Concerning Human Understanding* (1690) made two important contributions to an understanding of insanity. Unlike the *Natura Brevium* it hinted at a gradation of idiocy. After discussing the ability to distinguish between ideas, and the power of abstraction, Locke wrote, 'How far *idiots* are concerned in the want or weakness of any or all of the foregoing faculties, an exact observation of their several ways of faltering would no doubt discover.' As for the difference between madmen and idiots he wrote

> In fine the defect in *naturals* seems to proceed from want of quickness, activity, and motion in the intellectual faculties, whereby they are deprived of reason; whereas *madmen*, on the other side, seem to suffer by the other extreme. For they do not appear to me to have lost the faculty of reasoning, but having joined together some ideas very wrongly, they mistake them for truths, and they err as men do that argue right from wrong principles. For, the violence of their imaginations, having taken their fancies for realities, they make right deductions from them. . . . In short, herein seems to lie the difference between idiots and madmen, that madmen put wrong ideas together and reason from them, but idiots make very few or no propositions and reason scarce at all.[3]

If then madmen had not lost the faculty of reasoning they might be susceptible to treatment, training, or education. However, the belief that the madman had lost his reason, the faculty that distinguished him from an animal, died only slowly. Bethlem remained a place of entertainment until 1770. Not for another two decades did Philippe Pinel, who taught his followers that madness was a disease rather than a demoniacal possession, release the mad from their chains in the Bicêtre and La Saltpêtrière in Paris, some forty years before John Conolly did so at the Hanwell Asylum, Middlesex. Early in the next century the eminent mad-doctor Joseph Cox could still write, 'If the possession of reason be the proud attribute of humanity, its diseases must be ranked among our greatest afflictions, since they sink us from our preeminence to a level with animal creatures.'[4]

However, the appointment of Select Committees in 1742 and 1763 and the passage of legislation in 1744 and 1774 suggest a new concern for the lot of the inmates of madhouses. The opening of St Luke's hospital in 1751, London's second hospital for the mad, followed by other asylums in the provinces, gave doctors opportunities to practise a new branch of medicine that received a measure of prestige with the appointment of the Rev Dr F. Willis to treat George III in 1788. Willis's claim that he had cured nine out of every ten patients over the previous 22 years, however exaggerated his self-advertisement might have been, contrasted sharply with the previously prevailing therapeutic pessimism.[5] The greater understanding of mental illness and allied disorders that began to develop from the latter part of the eighteenth century, together with the provision of asylums, both public and private, were part of a new humanitarianism encompassing prisoners, slaves, and other underprivileged groups. Without this new humanitarianism, the product of a desire for social order and of changing behavioural norms, more enlightened methods of treating the insane would have made little headway. At the same time as economic growth nurtured the philanthropy that made possible the building of new asylums, the growth of scientific rationalism provided a new understanding of mental derangement at the expense of the one based on superstition covered by a religious gloss.

Against this background the first sustained attempt at training an idiot boy can be seen more as a contribution to the late eighteenth-century debate on the nature of man than to the training of idiots. Carl von Linnaeus in his *Systema Natura* (1735) had placed man and primates in the same order. By so doing he had raised profound issues about the nature of man. How, for example, did he differ from animals? Were any differences a matter of degree or of kind? Hence the *philosophes* of the Enlightenment were interested in searching for animals such as the orang-outang, the closest to man, for primitive peoples, and for feral or wild children untouched by social conditioning, to determine the respective influences of nature and nurture. Thus the final capture in 1800 of *l'enfant sauvage*, the wild boy of Aveyron, and Jean-Marc Itard's subsequent attempts to train him, conducted under the auspices of the *Société des Observateurs de l'homme*, aroused considerable scientific interest given the rarity and scanty documentation of earlier cases. Moreover, as some naturalists were now arguing that man had originally been a quadruped, a mode of locomotion Linnaeus had seen as defining *homo ferus*, the Aveyron boy's tendency to run on all-fours was seized upon by commentators. A further issue that contemporaries wanted to resolve was whether wild children and deaf-mutes possessed innate ideas. Did they, for instance, have some idea of the existence of God or was such an idea acquired through socialization? Thirdly, what did man owe to society? – a question that could be answered, it was hoped, by studying a wild child to determine 'what he is and deduce from what he lacks the hitherto uncalculable sum of knowledge and ideas which man owes to his education'.

In the training of the boy and the resolution of these questions Itard, a disciple of associationist psychology who believed that experience was the sole factor that had to be taken into account, predicted success. It was a prognosis that Philippe Pinel did not share. Meeting the boy shortly before the publication of his *Traité médico-philosophique sur l'aliénation mentale ou la manie* (Paris, 1801), Pinel thought the boy shared many of the idiot's characteristics, 'destitute of speech or confined to the utterance of some inarticulate sounds. Their looks are without animation; their senses stupefied; and their motions heavy and mechanical.' In his estimation the boy had been abandoned because he was an idiot: he was not an idiot because he had been abandoned. The limited progress Itard made with his pupil before the abandonment of the training programme in 1808 was sufficient to encourage his student, Edouard Séguin, to set out to prove that idiots were trainable. The programme he devised of training in motor control, sensory education, and speech owed much to Itard's work with the deaf and dumb. In turn, Maria Montessori applied the techniques of Itard and Séguin first to idiot children and then to normal ones. During his work at the Bicêtre and La Saltpêtrière Séguin published *Traitement Moral, Hygiène et Education des Idiots* (Paris, 1846) which soon secured him an international reputation. Finding the political climate of the Third Empire unhealthy for a follower of Saint-Simon he went to the USA, where he eventually founded the Séguin Physiological School for Feeble-Minded Children.[6]

Meanwhile, in England, the idea that there were gradations between idiocy on the one hand and 'normality' on the other enjoyed sufficient acceptance for Sir John Nicholl to declare in the case of *Ingram* v. *Wyatt* (1828, 1, Hag. E.R. 401), 'imbecility and weakness of mind may exist in different degrees between the limits of idiocy on the one hand and perfect capacity on the other'. Two years later John Conolly, who is credited with coining the term 'feeble-minded', published his *An Inquiry Concerning the Indications of Insanity*. In a chapter entitled 'Inequalities, weaknesses, and peculiarities of the Human Understanding, which do not amount to insanity' he contrasted the 'man of feeble mind' with the 'man of sound mind'. Feeble-mindedness he defined as 'A general weakness of all the faculties; a state of cerebral organization permitting no alacrity of sense, or depth of emotion; no strength of attention, or vigour of memory, or force of imagination; a state in which the power of comparing is limited and feeble, and the judgement necessarily weak.' He continued, 'The question of their sanity turns wholly upon the degree of their imbecility. These cases are never proper cases for confinement.'[7] In 1838 Jean-Etienne-Dominique Esquirol published *Des Maladies Mentales* (Paris) in which he used the term 'imbecile'. With the development of intelligence testing the term 'imbecile', in common with 'moron' – coined by H. H. Goddard from a Greek word meaning 'foolish' – took on a precise meaning when used by alienists. High-grade defectives with a mental age of between eight and twelve were morons, those with a mental age between three and seven imbeciles, while idiots were those below the latter band.

The growing interest and expertise amongst medical men on the nature of mental maladies and handicaps received little statutory recognition in England. The most important exception was the passage of the Safe Custody of Insane Persons Act, 1800, which was first used retrospectively to confine Charles Hadfield to Bethlem after he shot at George III. In a few earlier cases, such as that of Mary Lamb who after stabbing her mother in 1796 had been confined to a Hoxton madhouse, action seems to have been taken unofficially.[8] Much of the Poor Law Amendment Act, 1834, was in the same vein as the earlier vagrancy laws. Those who could not work were seen as those who would not work and were now offered workhouses, unlike their forebears who went to Bridewells. The Act, however, made an exception of dangerous lunatics, insane persons, or idiots. After fourteen days in the workhouse they were to be transferred to county lunatic asylums. As counties were not required to build asylums for another decade, guardians allowed many of their dangerous inmates to languish in workhouses rather than face the high charges imposed by existing asylums. The Factory Act, 1833, had also done little to safeguard the interests of the feeble-minded child. Under it the surgeon had to certify that any prospective employee was 'of ordinary strength and appearance of a child of at least nine years of age.'[9] In theory the surgeon could have refused to pass children suffering from Down's syndrome, cretinism, and other abnormalities such as hydrocephaly and microcephaly. Normal-looking aments, however, would have passed his scrutiny only to fail to meet the factory-owner's satisfaction.

In England, unlike the continent of Europe where schools and asylums for the handicapped owed something to state support, private individuals and philanthropists took the initiative, following the public-ation of a number of articles on the training of idiots abroad. Information about Dr Guggenbühl's work with cretins became more readily available in England following William Twining's visit to his establishment on the Abendberg, near Interlaken, in Switzerland which led to the publication of his *Some Account of Cretinism, and the Institution for Its Cure* (1843). A few years later the *Westminster Review* and Chambers's *Edinburgh Review* ran a series of articles on the Bicêtre and the education of idiots.[10] Inspired by these reports the Misses White started a 'school' for four children near Bath in 1846, which as the Rock Hall House School eventually amalgamated with the Magdalen Hospital. In 1847 the Rev Dr Reed, an eminent nonconformist divine and accomplished fundraiser, made a grand tour of European institutions, visiting Dr Guggenbühl at Abendberg, Carl Saegert the director of the Institute for Deaf-Mutes in Berlin, and Edouard Séguin in Paris. With the support of John Conolly and Samuel Gaskell, a Commissioner in Lunacy, he collaborated with the Lord Mayor of London to launch an appeal to raise funds for a training institution for idiots. The following year he opened a small asylum, which enjoyed the sponsorship of the Duke of Cambridge, at Highgate, then a small village north of London. Here a number of children received 'pictorial teaching', learnt to march and sing to an inmates' band, and developed their motor movements through exercise on playground swings and poles. In 1850 Reed bought Essex Hall, near Colchester, later the Eastern Counties Idiot Asylum, to which he transferred his children from Highgate. He subsequently undertook the purchase of Earlswood, whose grounds abutted those of the Royal Philanthropic Society's Reform School at Redhill. This new venture was sufficiently prestigious for him to be able to induce the Prince to lay the foundation stone and perform the opening ceremony. Earlswood, with its schools for idiots and imbeciles, became the first large-scale asylum undertaking work of this nature in England. By 1869 it held 291 children, most of whom returned to their families after a five-year course which included learning to articulate, some attempt at the three Rs, and learning such basic skills as dressing and having 'shop lessons'. Boys helped with the laundry work, baking, and gardening. Girls assisted with cooking, bed-making, scrubbing, and other kindred duties. The range of inmates, socially and intellectually, was wide. A large number of adults were entirely supported by their relatives, others were partly paid for by philanthropic individuals, the balance were admitted by a subscribers' election. Paupers were excluded. A small proportion would later have probably been classified as 'feeble minded'. Twenty-four of a group of 164 knew all their coins and weights and could make simple calculations, 20 could read fairly well, eight could tell the time to within a minute and a further eight were accurate to within five minutes. On the other hand 51 knew none of their letters and 90 could not tell the time at all. However, the comparative success of the few helped to show the unreality of any clear-cut division between idiocy and 'normality' and demonstrated that some previously thought ineducable could be taught.[11]

In 1854 the Rev E. Sidney, who had worked with children at Highgate and Earlswood, gave a lecture to the Society of Arts in which he showed how far some educators had moved from the earlier idea that idiots were without reason.

> The experience of the present day tends to show that there is no malady incident to man, which is not capable of some compensation, palliative, or remedy. We can not only instruct the dumb and the blind, but we can sooth the insane and teach the idiot and the cretin.

The idiot, he asserted, 'does possess in every case a mind like that of men in a normal condition, but all its faculties are obscured or deterred by a defective bodily envelope'. Accordingly the teachers had to proceed on the assumption that 'idiots are not only endowed with animal instincts and propensities, but with the feeble germs of those better qualities which are superadded to our physical nature. . . .'[12]

The training of idiots received further publicity with the publication of P. M. Duncan, *The Method of Drill, and the Manner of Teaching Speaking to Idiots etc.* (1861). Five years later P. M. Duncan and W. Millard, respectively the honorary consulting surgeon and the superintendent of the Eastern Counties Asylum for Idiots and Imbeciles, published *A Manual for the Classification, Training and Education of the Feeble-Minded, Imbecile and Idiotic* which postulated a four-stage continuum from the 'true and profound idiot', the *idios* or solitary, to the feeble-minded. All groups were to learn 'regularity of habits', eating, walking, dressing, and obedience. The top grade, the feeble-minded, were to learn propriety of behaviour at meals and religious worship, reading, counting and drawing, a knowledge of form and colour, telling the time, simple weights and measures, and elementary geography. Games were to include football, cricket, bagatelle, and draughts. They were to have excursions to the seaside and elsewhere. Their schoolroom was to contain bagatelle boards, marbles, balls, the *Illustrated London News*, scrap books, magnets, models of machinery, ships, and similar articles. Finger lessons were to be given to develop fine motor and other skills by sorting and stringing beads, taking apart and reconstructing simple toys, and tying and untying parcels.[13] With experiments of this nature in progress the Lunacy Commissioners had good reason to complain about the failure to make any effort to train idiot children in lunatic asylums. To remedy this neglect they wanted existing legislation simplified so that the children could go to idiot asylums for training.

> It has long been our opinion, as the result of extended experience and observation, that the association of idiot children with lunatics is very objectionable and injurious to them, and upon our visits to county asylums we have frequently suggested arrangements for their separate treatment and instruction. It is always a painful thing to see idiot children, whose mental faculties and physical powers and habits are capable of much development

and improvement, wandering, without object or special care, about the wards of a lunatic asylum. To facilitate the operation of such institutions [idiot asylums] . . . we think it desirable that the requirements of the Lunacy Acts . . . should be as much as possible simplified; and we hope shortly to see these objects achieved by legislation. The benefits to be derived, even in idiot cases apparently hopeless, from a distinctive system, and from persevering endeavours to develop the dormant powers, physical and intellectual, are now so fully established, that any argument upon the subject would be superfluous.[14]

Unfortunately their wish remained ungranted until the Idiots Act, 1886, facilitated the admission of idiots and imbeciles certified by a doctor as being capable of receiving improvement in an institution. The Act also made it clear that idiot asylums came within the jurisdiction of the Lunacy Commissioners, as previously their right to visit had been in doubt. In short, the law now admitted the principle that idiots were educable, as did the earlier Poor Law Amendment Act, 1868.

Furthermore, the growth of public asylums assisted the professionalization of the study of the mentally afflicted, albeit on a limited scale. The Association of Medical Officers of Asylums and Hospitals for the Insane (1841) founded the *Journal of Psychological Medicine and Mental Pathology* (1848–60), later the *Medical Critic and Psychological Journal* (1861–3) and, after a hiatus, the *Journal of Psychological Medicine and Mental Pathology* (1875–83). There was also the *Asylum Journal* (1853) which appeared later under the titles *Asylum Journal of Mental Science* (1858) and the *Journal of Mental Science* (1859). The first modern published work in English was Dr, later Sir, Alexander Morison's *Outlines of Lectures on Medical Diseases* (1825). For a long time J. C. Bucknill and D. H. Tuke, *A Manual of Psychological Medicine* (1858), which reached its fourth edition in 1879, was the main textbook, until the publication of T. S. Clouston, *Clinical Lectures On Medical Disease* (1883).

The study of insanity received little attention in the medical student's curriculum. The first lectures on mental diseases were given by William Battie at the newly-formed St Luke's Hospital from 1753 until his retirement. Morison gave his lectures at Edinburgh in 1823 and in London in 1826. He also made an unsuccessful attempt to induce the University of Edinburgh to establish a chair in the discipline, an appointment he hoped to secure for himself, but without success. When Dr John Conolly became the first professor of medicine in the newly established University of London in 1828 he was unable to include lectures on mental diseases in his lecture courses because of the opposition of his colleagues. Only in 1842 when he was at the Middlesex County Pauper Lunatic Asylum, Hanwell, was he able to hold clinical classes for students from the London hospitals and walk the wards with them. Twenty years later Dr P. M. Duncan could still say of idiocy, 'As yet it has not received great attention from any one who has had the advantage of that education which qualifies the alienist physician for his career.' Literature, he stated, was scanty apart from 'an admirable volume by Séguin, many reports of American origin by Dr Howe, of English [origin] by the projectors of idiot asylums, and pamphlets and speeches.' Séguin's earlier works, *Hygiène et éducation des idiots* (Paris, 1843) and *Traitement moral, hygiène et education des idiots* (Paris, 1846) received wider publicity with the appearance of his *Idiocy and Its Treatment by the Physiological Method* (New York, 1866) but no English publisher thought it commercially worthwhile to enter this field until extracts of Séguin's works appeared in H. Holman, *Séguin and His Physiological Method of Education* (1914). Psychiatry only came of age as a medical discipline when Shaw Bolton accepted a Chair in Psychiatry at Leeds University in 1918, the first such chair in Great Britain. For much of the nineteenth century doctors working in pauper lunatic asylums, anxious though they were to develop a corporate identity, found their status in the medical profession as a whole coloured both by the social status of their patients, and by the moral disrepute attaching to the maladies they treated. In the middle of the century asylum doctors could not achieve recognition, as could those in general hospitals, by being appointed in an honorary capacity to public medical charities and other institutions. They had no chance of becoming consultants. As general and teaching hospitals did not treat the mentally ill, their staffing establishments had no place for alienists. When hospitals eventually appointed consultants in psychological medicine, they recruited them from the ranks of their own medical super-intendents. Unlike doctors in other hospitals, asylum doctors had no control over whom they admitted. Patients came via the parish doctor, who initially declared them insane, and the justices of the peace who issued the necessary admission orders. With the medical superintendent all-powerful within his asylum, prospects for assistant medical officers were even less attractive. Poor pay, the need to live in, a ban on early marriage, poor promotion prospects, and few opportunities for research, must have deterred all except the most altruistic or those desperate for a job.[15]

Despite the limited medical environment in which many of the pioneer teachers-cum-physicians worked with the mentally afflicted, classification initially was more in terms of a person's educability than in terms of the aetiology or nature of that person's mental disability, a shortcoming that reflects the slow progress of psychiatric knowledge. Thus even Guggenbühl, dealing with one of the first disabilities to be classified, could write 'we may consider as mentally weak, and therefore on the road to cretinism, all children, who neither at home nor in school can be made accessible to the ordinary means of education and instruction'. Although Abendberg catered specifically for cretins it received other mental defectives. As well as receiving an undifferentiated intake of idiot children, the early schools and their programmes generally shared certain other characteristics. They were usually small institutions run by men such as Guggenbühl, Séguin, and Itard, who possessed medical qualifications and had a strong belief in the efficacy of a physiological approach. Acting on the premise that organ function and structure were interrelated, they believed that the teacher had to take 'hold' of that organ. Since the organs of sensation were the most easily within the educator's reach, instruction was to be accomplished by perceptual training, not by an appeal to reason and ideas.[16] In Séguin's words,

> Some idiots are more afflicted in their minds, even to the verge of insanity, and others in their motor and sensory functions, even to the point of paralysis or of anaesthesia, but in either form their treatment must proceed more from the training of the senses, in order to improve the mind, than from the education of the mind in view of developing the sensory aptitudes.[17]

Many early workers shared a strong sense of humanitarianism and religious commitment. In Séguin's case, as we have seen, it was his adherence to the teaching of Saint-Simon that had made it prudent for him to leave France after 1848. Guggenbühl's conviction that God intended him to devote his life to cretins is traditionally dated from the day he saw one saying the Lord's Prayer in front of a wayside shrine.[18] Although the etymological origin of the word 'cretin' is open to dispute, one suggestion has a strong religious connotation. The Savoyard peasantry, seeing cretins as part of the great family of Christ, called them 'Chrétiens'. In similar vein is the use of the term 'innocents', to denote that the mentally afflicted were *les enfants du bon Dieu*. Born irresponsible, they were incapable of displeasing Him. Again, to Séguin the indigent and infirm were the chosen friends of the Lord Jesus. There was also a school of thought that saw the mentally deranged as proper objects of Christian charity, a belief that extended to the blind and deaf and dumb who suffered disabilities that one would not deliberately cultivate merely to sponge on the philanthropic. Yet, as we have seen, charity was given only to the respectable. Moreover the charitable, despite seeing the blind and deaf as deserving, saw also the need to guard against those who might exploit their handicap. The blind, the secretary to the Home Teaching Society for the Blind averred, had a strong inducement 'to make a profit out of what they consider a piece of personal property, namely, the sympathy of the sighted for the blind man. It is a stock in trade to them'.[19]

Many early schools had been established in the hope of largely overcoming, if not actually curing, idiocy by the application of the physiological method. However, as it gradually became clear that cure was not as easily achieved as originally thought, these initially educational institutions became custodial ones, a characteristic especially marked in the large lunatic asylums built under the permissive act of 1828 and the mandatory one of 1845. In an attempt to reduce unit costs the average size of county and borough asylums grew from 116.0 in 1827 to 802.1 in 1890. This shift of emphasis stemmed as much from the slow growth of psychiatric knowledge as from a lack of human resources to cope with large numbers of inmates. In at least one case, however, the argument that the care of the individual patient was more important than any financial savings accruing from economies of scale won the day. When the Middlesex justices wanted to double the size of Hanwell, already capable of accommodating a thousand patients, the medical superintendent and the Commissioners in Lunacy successfully opposed the scheme. Colney Hatch Lunatic Asylum, in the eastern part of the county, opened in 1851. At a cost of £232 a bed it was the most expensive asylum yet built. Yet the floors were of uncovered brick, Yorkshire flagstone, or asphalt, while the walls were unplastered. On this latter feature the advice of William Ellis, superintendent of Hanwell, may have prevailed: 'In asylums designated for paupers only, it is unnecessary to have any plaster on the walls; limestone on the bricks is all that is required.'[20]

Children, though, normally remained in the workhouse where they received little in the way of treatment or attention. For example, of the 745 admissions to the Hook Norton and Witney Asylum between 1828 and 1857, the youngest were two sixteen-year-old boys. Before the advent of large asylums the average annual cost of £40 in 1844 for custody in the workhouse was lower than for that in an asylum where it could be as high as £350. The Poor Law Guardians' other remedy was to use a private madhouse controlled by the Lord Chancellor's Office, under the Madhouses Acts of 1828 and 1832. By 1843 their average charge was 8s 11d a week. Proprietors had to keep down their charges if they were to attract the guardians' custom. The lower the charge, the more likely was the use of restraint to keep down labour costs. Dr T. Monro had explained the economics of the madhouse business in 1815.

> If a gentleman was put in irons, he would not like it. . . . The more keepers there are, the less the necessity I should think for restraint [and] the less the number of irons. . . . In Bethlem the restraint is by chains . . . there is no such thing as chains in my [private] house.

The new asylums built after 1845 were cheaper. Two years after its opening, Colney Hatch Lunatic Asylum housed its patients for 8s 2d a week. The cost of feeding a patient, around 4s 4d a week, was comparable to that of providing fodder for one of the asylum's cows, 'not less than 4s a week'. However, the large asylums became convenient dumping grounds not only for a workhouse's mentally ill patients, but for cases of advanced senility and other incurable cases that strained its meagre human resources. At times such inmates, if not sent to an asylum, were put under some form of restraint in the workhouses. In such circumstances guardians must have been more concerned about ridding themselves of troublesome or intractable adults than they were to remove mentally defective children. Even if one leaves aside the problem of attempting to judge how effectively or conscientiously workhouse medical officers examined children, it remains difficult to determine how many mentally defective children were in workhouses or asylums. For instance, in 1866, London's 43 workhouses held 51 children classified as insane. Yet 14 years later the Metropolitan Asylums Board thought it necessary to provide accommodation for a thousand pupils when it opened a school for subnormal children at Darenth, Kent. Unfortunately, with the Metropolitan Asylum Board's new asylums at Leavesden, Herts., and Caterham, Surrey, soon filled to capacity, Darenth had to make some of its accommodation over to adult imbeciles, so that in 1890 this fruit 'of the first attempt by a statutory body to develop the potentialities of subnormal children' housed only 300 boys and 168 girls. In addition to Darenth there were by this time the Starcross Asylum, Exeter, opened in 1864 which the Poor Law Board certified under the 1862 Act the following year, and the Northern Counties Asylum for Idiots and Imbeciles at Lancaster opened in 1868. The latter institution charged fees of between 50 and 200 guineas a year, but admitted a few children of straitened circumstances at 20 guineas.[21]

In contrast to the optimism a few committed educators showed over the potentialities of the feeble-minded and other mentally handicapped children, the weight of medical opinion offered a pessimistic prognosis, an aetiology tinged with moral opprobrium and, later in the century, grounds for believing that there would be a progressive degeneration of the British stock unless the numbers of such children were checked. Attitudes and beliefs such as these help to explain not only the slow progress of psychiatric knowledge and the low status of the alienist, but also why educational provision for the feeble-minded child failed to attract pressure groups comparable to those urging the cause of the blind or deaf-mute child.

A medley of such factors is discernible in two of the mental conditions, cretinism and Down's Syndrome or trisomy-21, to be distinguished at an early date from the previously undifferentiated concept of madness. Guggenbühl's treatment of cretins, which involved the removal of children from low-lying places, and attention to diet, suggests some understanding of the possibility of environmental factors playing a part in the incidence of the malady. By the 1850s practitioners were advocating the use of iodized salt or iodine. Forty years later subcutaneous injections were used, before the prescription of a similar treatment in tablet form. Yet a medical student's handbook of the 1870s, while mentioning an enlarged thyroid as a possible cause of cretinism, also suggested miasma, overcrowding in badly-ventilated houses, and ill-assorted marriages. As late as 1911 a standard reference work on medical matters said of cretinism, 'It is generally supposed that coitus during intoxication is a cause of this condition.'[22]

The term 'Mongolian Idiocy', nowadays superseded by 'Down's syndrome' and 'trisomy-21', reveals atavistic fears aroused by the debate on the origins of mankind taking place at the time Dr Langdon Down gave his lecture. The studies of embryology, comparative anatomy, palaeontology, and prehistoric archaeology had led scholars to question the accuracy of Bishop Ussher's chronology based on Biblical evidence. Two schools of thought flourished, the monogenists who believed that all human beings had developed from one primary stock, and the polygenists, who saw the different races as separate biological species. Both schools saw the coloured races as inferior to the white. Monogenists ascribed racial differences and inferiorities to a degeneration of the original stock of Adam and Eve; thus Shem, Ham, and Japheth, the sons of Noah, had fathered the white, black, and yellow races respectively. Some degenerationists also subscribed to the theory of recapitulation, under which the white embryo in its journey to adulthood passed through successive stages equivalent to the adult status of inferior races. Thus the white embryo represented the Negro state in the development of mankind and a white infant the Mongol stage. Charles Darwin gave both monogenists and polygenists a better rationale for their racism. After 1859, the year of publication of *Origin of Species*, there was 'a comprehensive evolutionism which was at once monogenist and racist, which affirmed human variety even as it relegated the dark-skinned savage to a status very near the ape'.[23] Dr Down, encouraged by Dr John Conolly, a founder member of the Ethnological Society (1843), produced his classification of idiots 'based upon the best biological theory (and pervasive racism) of the age'. Using the theory of recapitulation he argued that some Caucasian (white-skinned) idiots represented developmental arrests that made them analogous to adults of inferior races. Taking the fivefold division of mankind attributed to the anthropologist Johann Blumenbach (1752–1840), he claimed that at Earlswood and the London Hospital he had seen idiots and imbeciles who could 'fairly be referred to one of the great divisions of the human family other than the class from which they have sprung'. Hence there were 'several well-marked examples of the

Ethiopian variety', and 'the Malay variety', as well as those analogous to the aboriginal inhabitants of the American continent. The greater part of the paper he devoted to 'the Mongolian type of idiocy . . . for the most part instances of degeneracy arising from tuberculosis in the parents'. After describing some of the Mongolian idiot's attributed characteristics, he continued, 'The boy's aspect is such that it is difficult to realize that he is the child of Europeans [the fifth division of mankind], but so frequently are these characters presented, that there can be no doubt that these ethnic features are the result of degeneration.' From this lecture there probably dates the idea that Down's children 'have considerable powers of imitation, even bordering on being mimics'. Yet, as S. J. Gould has argued, this concept can be seen as one of the devices that helped to reconcile white racial supremacy with the obvious fact that Oriental culture was complex and sophisticated. To resolve the dilemma white-skinned Caucasians, while admitting the intellectual powers of the oriental, limited them to a facility for imitative copying rather than conceding the possession of innovative genius, a limitation that has continued to be voiced down to the present day. In making his ethnic classification Down's interest was more than a purely medical one: 'Apart from the practical bearing of this attempt at an ethnic classification, considerable philosophical interest attaches to it.' Rejecting the polygenist argument he concluded:

> If these great racial divisions are fixed and finite, how comes it that disease is able to break down the barrier, and to simulate so closely the features of the members of another division. I cannot but think that the observations which I have recorded, are indications that the differences in the races are not specific but variable.

Five years later Charles Darwin wrote in *The Descent of Man*, 'man is the co-descendant with other mammals of some unknown or lower form'. Although Down was a racial 'liberal' in that he argued that all mankind came from a common stock, his assumption that there was a racial hierarchy put idiots on a lower level than other white Caucasians. His other important contribution to the debate on idiocy was to produce a threefold classification based on an aetiology of congenital, developmental, and accidental idiocy, within which he distinguished a number of sub-groups. The term 'Mongol', which survived until after the Second World War when Sir Peter Medawar persuaded *The Times* to use 'Down's syndrome' instead, received a boost with the publication of F. G. Crookshank's *The Mongol in Our Midst: a study of man and his three faces* which went through three editions between 1924 and 1930. The idea still heard today that the Down's child is an unfinished child is perhaps the last vestige of the early-Victorian recapitulation theory.[24]

Despite the development of a more humane treatment of those

afflicted with mental illness or handicap the nineteenth-century work ethic predisposed society against the unfortunate sufferer, the possession of the necessary personal discipline and moral fibre being regarded as an important factor in determining whether or not an individual could overcome the vicissitudes of unemployment without lapsing into pauperism. Moreover, 'The strong or well-formed character which a well-fashioned will implies is the result of good training applied to a well-constituted original nature; and the character is not determined directly by the will, but in any particular act determines the will.'[25] Given beliefs such as these, the mentally afflicted failed to meet the social norms of an entrepreneurial competitive society that put a premium on individual effort and equated success with character.

Sufferers were also seen as objects of divine retribution by those given to quoting *Deuteronomy* VI, 5: 'the Lord will smite thee with madness'. Even those who no longer believed in demons could still postulate the existence of a supernatural agency that was possibly visiting the sins of previous generations on some unfortunate. The implications of Hippocrates' denial made two millenia earlier that epilepsy, the sacred disease, was no more sacred than any other, had yet to be fully accepted. On a par with belief in the evidence of divine displeasure was concern over whether or not the lunatic possessed a conscience and could comprehend the existence of a revealed God. Those who thought the idiot lacked a moral sense believed he was unable to blush, the ability to do so being the outward sign of the possession of moral power and conscience.[26]

Closely allied to these ideas was the conviction that conscience, held to be the last mental faculty to be acquired, was also the first to be lost. Henry Maudsley the distinguished physiologist of the mid- and later-nineteenth century (whose *Physiology and Pathology of Mind* (1867) has been described as a turning point in English psychiatry), had written that one of the first symptoms of insanity was a deadening or a complete perversion of the moral sense. Even when a person recovered his reason, and his intellectual faculties were as acute as before, he was no longer the moral man he had been. For the feeble-minded, suffering less mental impairment, not all was lost. 'A large number', the Charity Organization Society reported, 'are able to take in elementary ideas of the Deity and of their duty to their neighbour', a view endorsed by A. F. Tredgold, the author of *Mental Deficiency (Amentia)* (1909). Although imbeciles and idiots lacked all moral, ethical, or social sense, he thought the feeble-minded could 'develop hazy, anthropomorphic ideas of a Supreme Being . . . understand Bible stories . . . and tell that the good people go to Heaven and the bad ones to Hell'.[27]

From the middle of the nineteenth century onwards physicians, influenced especially by Maudsley's writings, began taking a more pessimistic and alarmist attitude towards mental derangement. One aspect of the therapeutic optimism of the turn of the eighteenth century had been the belief that man's self-control offered the way forward, a proposition advanced by William Tuke and others, who discontinued physical restraint as 'Insane persons generally possess a degree of control over their wayward propensities.' Thirty years later, in 1843, John Barlow wrote: 'Nothing . . . but an extent of disease which destroys at once all possibility of reasoning, by annihilating, or entirely changing the structure of the organ [the brain], can make a man necessarily mad. In all other cases, the being sane or otherwise . . . depends on the individual himself'. Maudsley, while conceding that 'a man has, or might have, some power over himself to prevent insanity', saw him as the victim of his inheritance. 'There is a destiny made for man by his ancestors, and no one can elude, were he able to attempt it, the tyranny of his organization.'

Similarly, education could only play a limited role in a patient's rehabilitation and improvement: 'Men are in much alike, but each individual differs in some respects from any other individual who now exists. . . . And this is not a difference which is due to education or circumstances, but a fundamental difference of nature which neither education nor circumstances can eradicate.' Accordingly, 'Great as is the power of education, it is yet a strictly limited power. . . . No training in the world will avail to elicit grapes from thorns or figs from thistles.' Improvement, possible for some, could only come after a long sustained effort:

> Striking examples of the gradual development of the power of will over both movements and ideas under most unfavourable conditions are witnessed in our idiot asylums; the records of these establishments showing that there is hardly an idiot so low that he cannot be improved by patient and laborious culture as to acquire some power of self-government both in regard to his body and his mind.

Yet there remained an irremediable core: 'It is an undisputable though extreme fact that certain human beings are born with such a deficiency of mind that all the training and education in the world will not raise them to the level of brutes. . . .'

Maudsley furthermore saw a connection between criminal conduct and mental deficiency. Criminals, he declared, constituted 'a degenerate or morbid variety of mankind, marked by peculiar low physical and mental characteristics'. They are 'stupid, sullen, sluggish, deficient in vital energy, and sometimes afflicted with epilepsy . . . and not a few of them are weak-minded and imbecile'. They are 'true moral imbeciles'. Investigation of their familiy histories showed that 'a considerable proportion of them are weak-minded, or epileptic, or become insane, or that they spring from families in which insanity, epilepsy, or some other neurosis exists'.

With his belief in the hereditary nature of criminality and mental deficiency and the limited extent to which education could assist a man in overcoming the 'tyranny of his organization', he was probably the first to raise the issue of the desirability of restricting the propagation of degenerates. After referring to the care taken in breeding racehorses and hounds he asked, 'Is it right then to sanction the propagation of his kind by an individual who is wanting in that which is the highest attribute of man – a sound and stable mental constitution?' The alternative was 'to permit degeneracy to go on increasing from generation to generation and end finally in the extreme degeneracy of idiocy'. Ducking the issue, unlike some eugenists later, he added, 'I note this as a question to be seriously faced and sincerely answered, although not expecting that mankind, in the present state of their development, will either seriously face it or sincerely answer it.' Fortunately nature had the ultimate answer: 'With the general occurrence of idiocy there is happily the extinction of the degenerate variety, for with it come impotence and sterility.'[28] As will be seen, many of the attitudes first given wide publicity by the influential Maudsley towards the mentally disturbed and deficient were elaborated during the course of the next half-century, when the problem of feeble-minded children received prominence following the introduction of compulsory education.

Before 1870 the idea that children could progress from year to year through the syllabus of the Revised Code may have worked reasonably well in practice. With no compulsion for children to be kept at school those who did not 'get on well' would have been quietly withdrawn by parents who saw other uses in the home for money laid out in school pence that did not seem to be yielding a worthwhile result. The gradual enforcement of compulsory education revealed the illusory nature of the Code's basic premise. For a variety of reasons many children failed to keep pace. Allegations of over-pressure led to the appointment of Dr Crichton-Browne in the early 1880s to investigate the matter. His finding that 20 per cent of London school children were backward corresponded with an estimate one teacher put to the Cross Commission that 40 to 50 per cent were in the wrong standard. Twenty per cent were in one too low while the balance were in a class or two too high. The Education Department, recognizing that all was not well, issued the Revised Code of 1882 which allowed children to be examined in the same standard as the previous year and others to be exempted altogether. Two years later the Code required the inspector to satisfy himself that teachers had neither improperly withheld candidates from examination nor unduly pressed those who were dull or delicate in preparation for it at any time during the year. In addition he had to satisfy himself that due attention had been paid, *inter alia*, to the child's mental capacity. Reasonable excuses for withholding children now included 'obvious dulness or defective intellect', delicate health or protracted illness, and 'the temporary deprivation, by accident or otherwise, of the use of eye or hand'.

In common with other sections of the Revised Code, the exemptions granted in 1882 gave inspectors wide latitude in their interpretation. One inspector saw three possible explanations for children's slow progress: the natural dulness of English children, their irregular attendance, and inefficient teaching. The first explanation he dismissed out of hand: 'English boys and girls are bright, teachable, and under favourable circumstances well taught.' The remaining two causes accounted for all the deficiencies in a school's results. Another inspector largely supported this view. After claiming that he was gradually learning to discern 'the difference between the "obvious dulness" of the child and that of the teacher' he continued, 'When many such exceptions are presented to me, I find, generally, the dulness on the teacher's part.' A further inspector attempted a rudimentary intelligence test by asking such questions as 'How far do you live from school?', or 'How old are you?' Yet another claimed that although obvious dullards were easily protected by the Code too much discretion was left to the inspectorate who were becoming 'pretty good physiognomists', yet the problem still remained of dull children who looked bright, and those who looked bright but were of delicate and nervous temperament. Only one inspector openly welcomed the new regulations allowing dull, delicate, and very ill-fed children to be withdrawn: 'I rejoice at this, and have acted freely upon it.' To counter the charge that inspectors interpreted the Code's provisions too rigidly the Cross Commissioners were able to point out that no more than 200 of the 81,000 London children for whom teachers had claimed exemption had had their names disallowed.[29]

When the Egerton Commissioners sat shortly afterwards they found that idiot and imbecilic childen were excluded as much, if not more, than any other handicapped group from ordinary elementary schools. Major General F. J. Moberley of the London School Board, for instance, stated that only 20 out of 455 known idiots attended school, while of those children under the age of thirteen who were permanently disabled in some way 596 of the 2,854 known cases were in school. There was little other provision for those suffering from severe amentia. Although the Education of Pauper Children Act, 1862, had implicitly recognized the possibility of training or instructing idiot persons in suitable institutions, an unknown number of severely mentally handicapped children remained in workhouses. Whatever the institution, be it a workhouse where people of unsound mind were detained, an asylum, or an institution for the reception and training of idiots, and whether or not it was certified by the Local Government Board – if it was registered or licensed under the Lunacy Acts, the Lunacy Commissioners visited it. Unfortunately neither they nor any other government body possessed any supervisory power over the education of idiots in the seven specialist idiot asylums (that is, ones that did not house the insane as well), until the passage of the Idiots Act, 1886.[30]

On their visits to some of the asylums the Egerton Commission found that a 'substantial percentage of the idiot class are capable of improvement'. In support of their general impression they quoted the evidence of Dr G. E. Shuttleworth, superintendent of the Royal Albert Asylum, Lancaster, who rated 40 per cent as being able to benefit in a minor degree from school instruction and discipline, while the remainder would not improve much. As at Earlswood, admission procedures may have played their part in providing Lancaster with inmates of a wide range of ability. Surprisingly, Shuttleworth described pauper patients, for whom the guardians paid £26 to £35 a year, as 'of a higher grade as far as intellect goes than the elect cases'. Whether pauper or elect, with few exceptions pupils had to leave at the age of thirteen, unless they could find sponsors to pay for their upkeep. Whatever the cause of the mixture of ability found at Lancaster, Shuttleworth's evidence, together with the impressions the Commissioners gained from their own observations at idiot asylums they visited, led them to enunciate a principle as valid in the 1880s as it is today: 'To develop the capacity of imbeciles in every way, either for education, happiness, or industrial employment, is an object worthy of attainment'; but they added a cautionary note, that 'such training can never qualify imbeciles to compete on equal terms with those who possess the "*mens sana in corpore sano*" '. After setting out a training programme based on Séguin's principles and containing many of the features earlier advocated by Millard and Duncan, they recommended that it should continue until the recipients reached the age of twenty-one, a length of training that many severely mentally handicapped have yet to experience. Moreover, children were not to be left to languish in asylums or workhouses but transferred to these new educational institutions, which were to be inspected by the Lunacy Commissioners, to receive long-term training. Despite these far-reaching recommendations an unknown number of 'idiotic' children remained without any education until after the Education (Mentally Handicapped Children) Act, 1970, came into effect.[31]

Despite Shuttleworth's evidence about the educability of some of the children in idiot asylums, the Report's recommendations for the education of feeble-minded children were cautious. Although they found that large numbers did not attend school, they did not put them on a par with blind, deaf and dumb children by recommending their compulsory education. They went no further than recommending that 'they should be separated from scholars in public elementary schools in order that they may receive special instruction, and that the attention of school authorities be particularly directed towards this object'.[32]

The legacy of the Report was considerable. School authorities were to be given the power to require imbecile children to be sent to an institution, which local authorities were to have the power to provide. School authorities were to have their attention 'particularly directed', as we have seen, to providing special classes for the feeble-minded. Thus the question of the compulsory education of all grades of mentally handicapped children was left unresolved. However, the Report envisaged separate pathways for the two main groups of children, one through the elementary school following much of the ordinary school curriculum, the second through a programme predominantly of training in an institution. Also left unresolved was the fate of the child, declared imbecile, whose parents did not want him institutionalized. Last, as the wide spectrum of abilities discovered in the idiot asylums reveals, there was the problem of assessment and classification. The destination of an idiot or feeble-minded child in the 1880s was largely fortuitous. Depending on parental predilection, the availability of suitable provision either within the Poor Law or without, and the attitude of school boards, school attendance officers, or particular teachers, a child might be in an idiot asylum, abandoned by his parents at a workhouse, in a school of some kind, or at home. Apart from treating one practitioner with scepticism, 'Dr Warner thinks that these feeble-minded children can be recognized by certain outward and visible signs . . . Dr Warner's views are not at present generally accepted', it offered no solution to the problem of diagnosing feeble-mindedness, only the further complication of a reference to the multiply-handicapped child: 'Though the three classes of blind, deaf and dumb, and idiots differ among each other, both as regards their character and educability, yet there are among the idiot class many deaf and dumb, and partially or completely blind.'[33]

THE DEFECTIVE CHILD,
1888 to 1918

In response to the Egerton Commission's promptings a number of school boards began making provision for feeble-minded children. By the end of 1897 seven school boards, those of Birmingham, Bradford, Brighton, Bristol, Leicester, London, and Nottingham had formed classes, while Plymouth was about to do so. Just over a thousand of the 1,300 children being taught were in one of London's 27 centres or classes, where the policy was to admit 'those capable of learning elementary subjects at some rate, however slow' but to exclude idiot children. The decision to receive some children who might have bordered on idiocy received the guarded support of Sir George Kekewich, the Permanent Secretary, when a London School Board delegation met him to press for a higher grant for mentally-defective children in June 1896. Although Kekewich thought that 'Imbeciles properly so called' ought not to be admitted to London School Board schools, the Board might properly be inclined to admit rather than exclude doubtful cases, as the only other place for them was Darenth, where the 'pauper taint' was upon them. At the same time it was admitted that some Darenth children were brighter than some in the Metropolis's schools. As children, whatever their affliction, were sent to the nearest available class the centres contained an unclassified mixture; the resulting strains in one case were held to have contributed 'largely to the absolute breakdown in the case of one very capable head mistress'. At one extreme Dr A. Eichholz, then HMI for West Lambeth, found children of pronounced mental deficiency bordering on imbecility, exhibiting depravity of morals and conduct, and with no sense of responsibility and a minimum of intelligent response. Apart from parents' objecting to sending their children to Darenth, there was a lack of accommodation there. At the other extreme were physically and mentally healthy but backward children, many of whom soon became fit to return to their original schools. In between were epileptic children and those suffering from some form of physical defect, the result of constitutional disease or malnutrition.[1]

Boards that ran special classes were usually able to claim the grant paid under the Revised Code for infants and teach them for shorter periods, concessions that did little to help them meet the heavy extra expense teaching such children involved. To remedy this state of affairs the London School Board had first approached the Education Department at the time of the passage of the Elementary Education (Blind and Deaf Children) Act, 1893, to have defective children included in the new legislation so that they would become eligible for the higher grant payable under the new legislation. Eastbourne School Board similarly asked for idiots and imbeciles to be included, an initiative that caused Kekewich to minute, 'So far as children of somewhat deficient intellect are eligible they may for the most part, I should think, be dealt with in public elementary schools.' Two years later the Education Department wrote to 19 of the largest school boards asking if they had considered how education of defective and epileptic children might be provided. Surprisingly the Department admitted in this letter that the London School Board, to whose prodding the letter owed its origins, had asked for legislation to provide for the education of such children on the lines of the 1893 Act. A year later in 1896 Kekewich agreed, when he met a delegation from the London School Board that 'the claim for a special grant was quite reasonable'. However, he dampened any hope they might have had of speedy action when he stated that legislation was not imminent and that 'a departmental committee might be appointed to consider the whole subject'.[2]

Meanwhile the Report of the Poor Law Schools Commission, which had recommended the formation of separate classes for feeble-minded children, showed that opinion was hardening. The Report singled out a comment from Dr Tait, the medical officer for a home run by the Metropolitan Association for Befriending Young Servants: as feeble-minded girls 'grow up they are subject to particular dangers as regards tendencies to immorality, and . . . they have a strange kind of foolish simplicity which is apt to make them the dupe of any unscrupulous person into whose hands they fall'. Late Victorian England saw feeble-minded, ex-workhouse, or delinquent girls as particularly liable to become the slaves of their 'animal' spirits. This heightened fear of their promiscuity had helped to generate the financing of seven homes for 127 girls but none for boys. Another witness to the Poor Law Schools Commission started the hereditarian hare: 'These children should be put away altogether, and their lives made as happy as possible, but they should not be allowed to produce other lives.' A decade earlier the Egerton Commissioners had made no such recommendation. The nearest they had got to endorsing the hereditarian ticket was that, while asserting the causes of idiocy to be various, they had given pride of place to Dr Shuttleworth's statement, 'The most frequent cause of idiocy is, no doubt, ill-assorted marriages; marriages of persons of the same morbid tendencies.' On the other hand they had also shown concern for the possible hereditary nature of blindness and mutism. Intermarriage within each category was to be discouraged. Presumably because the deaf had sight, they were to be taught in single sex classes, and the mixture of the sexes in later life was thought 'inadvisable'. Although the intermarriage of the blind was to be discouraged no such precautions were recommended for them, sexual attraction being, one assumes, thought to be an entirely visual matter.[3]

The general tenor of the 1898 Departmental Committee's Report on the Education of Defective and Epileptic Children was equally alarmist. Idiots and imbeciles formed a distinct class 'whose seclusion for life in institutions is highly to be desired in the interests of society as well as in their own.' The distinction between educable and trainable children made in the Egerton Report was repeated. On low-grade feeble-minded children education would be wasted, thus institutional life was not to prepare them for taking their place in the outside world but to make them as happy as their condition would permit. Other feeble-minded children, not constituting a menace to the rest of society, faced a brighter future. Although those that stayed in ordinary elementary schools had learned little or nothing more than the acquisition of certain habits of discipline, the prognosis was guardedly optimistic for those who attended special classes. 'By the age of thirteen or fourteen they may sometimes arrive at a stage of elementary instruction equal, perhaps, to that attained by ordinary children of eight or nine years of age, and they often show themselves capable of being trained in some manual occupation. Thus there is a fair chance that with favourable surroundings, they may take their place in the world, and may not become inmates of workhouses, asylums, or prisons.' In common with the education of blind, deaf and dumb children, that of defective children, the term preferred by the 1898 Report since it could be used to exclude idiots and imbeciles, could be made politically acceptable as offering a means of reducing future social costs.[4]

While the Report had no difficulty in recognizing three broad categories – the idiots and imbeciles, the feeble-minded or defective children, and those who could cope with the ordinary curriculum of an elementary school – the problem still remained of deciding which designation suited a particular child, an issue that had exercised the Egerton Commissioners. Although Dr Warner's reliance on the presence of physical signs may seem naive and simplistic today, one must remember that medical men had only limited means of diagnosis at their disposal, while psychiatry and any form of mental testing were still in their infancy. Furthermore, some of the earliest forms of mental defect to be diagnosed, such as cretinism, Down's syndrome, and hydrocephalus, to take just a few examples, were readily apparent even to lay observers. A standard textbook of the late nineteenth century, W. W. Ireland's *The Mental Affections of Children, Idiocy, Imbecility, and Insanity* (1898) for instance, gives illustrations of many of the twelve major conditions discussed therein. Given the role played by doctors, who often had no specialist knowledge of mental illness or handicap, and justices of the peace, with no medical training at all, in the certification process, one suspects that the majority of asylum inmates showed some outward sign of their mental malady. However, some witnesses to the Departmental Committee pointed out that not all mentally defective children showed outward signs of their inward disability, while others stated that the signs Warner relied on could be present in normal children:

> 'Nerve signs' . . . appear amongst children who are naturally incapable, and amongst children who are incapable through faulty nurture. But a slouching slovely child of the latter kind may be made smart and tidy by drill, food, and care, for he has it in him to be so, just as loutish recruits are soon turned into smart soldiers.[5]
>
> I find that many of the signs are not constant, being present in a child without the mental impairment; and that they are also inconstant in the same individual, so that when the child is in feeble health, the nerve signs may be very prominent, and a little time after, when he is in better health or is perhaps less nervous in coming to see one, . . . the signs have disappeared.[6]

Evidence of this nature, coupled with the realization that Warner had not invented a new system of diagnosis but had only collated a number of signs already known, counselled the Departmental Committee to be cautious.

'Feeble-minded children are, in the great majority of cases, marked by some physical defect or defects discernible by the trained observer, and to some extent also by the untrained.' Furthermore, 'A child may be abnormal in one or more of these respects without being necessarily feeble-minded.' The identification of a feeble-minded child was 'a matter which requires not only medical knowledge, but some special study. . . .' Given the imperfect state of medical knowledge on the subject and the perceived need to protect the public purse against the heavier costs of special classes, the selection process of children had to be rigorous. Just as there were teachers alleged to be eager to offload dull or backward children on other schools, so there were children in other schools whose cretinism or Down's syndrome had not been recognized by their teachers.[7] Clearly the HMI was a key figure, not only to prevent possible abuse but also to see that schools set about the preliminary selection of children as efficiently as possible. Since this was to take place at the minimum age of seven, the two years in an infants' class providing a period for a preliminary assessment, the second person involved was the child's teacher. Equity demanded the presence of the teacher of the special class to which the child might be sent. The fourth person whose presence was needed was a medical officer, a requirement marking an important step in the development of a school medical service. Lastly, the presence of a parent was thought desirable, 'for it often turns out that the child who is believed to be feeble-minded really suffers from curable defects in eyesight or hearing. In such cases the medical officer is able to impress upon the parent the desirability of having the child treated for the defects in question ' – but he was unable to offer treatment through any official channels. In making his assessment the doctor was to be assisted by having a record of the child's progress in the infant's class. If admitted to a special class a further record was to be made about the child's family history. The one used in London, containing questions such as 'What is the bodily and mental condition of the parents?', 'Are they temperate or otherwise?' and 'Has any near relative, dead or living, suffered from insanity, Fits, Consumption, Scrofula, or any other hereditary disease?', shows the current hereditarian and moralistic assumptions underlying the aetiology of mental defect.[8]

The Departmental Committee dealt with two further groups of children, the physically defective, and the epileptic. Since most, if not all, feeble-minded children were thought to suffer from some form of physical defect, the only ones requiring special consideration were the unquantified number of mentally normal children who had some form of physical disability. Unless they were ill enough to miss so much schooling as to be backward, they were to attend ordinary schools, while backward ones were to go to special classes.[9] Partially blind or partially deaf children, if also feeble-minded, were to attend special classes in blind or deaf schools. The last group, epileptic children, caused more difficulty despite the advances that had been made in understanding and treating the condition in the fifty years before the Departmental Committee sat.

From about 1850 British physicians began entering a field that previously, as the terms *grand mal* and *petit mal* indicate, had been largely a French preserve. In 1857 the use of bromide salts as an anticonvulsant therapy, a palliative that remained in use until at least the outbreak of the First World War, was advocated at a meeting of the Royal Chirurgical Society in London. Two years earlier the founding of the National Hospital for the Relief of Paralysis, Epilepsy, and Allied Disorders had given the world its first neurological centre. Here Hughling Jackson, often described as the father of English neurology, 'reconstructed the subject of epilepsy and introduced with the highest genius and with hardly an error which has since needed correction, our present day [1934] conception of epilepsy'. In the same decade Sir J. J. Reynold's *Epilepsy* (1861) distinguished between idiopathic epilepsy, that is those cases of epilepsy in which one other disease was discernible, from the symptomatic variety which included every kind of brain lesion. He also gave an analysis of 62 cases in which 24, his largest group, showed no sign of mental failure and only nine exhibited a notable degree of mental incapacity, a far cry from Esquirol's classification of four-fifths of the Saltpêtrière's female epileptic cases as insane.[10]

Despite these developments Dr F. H. Walmsley, medical officer of the Darenth School for Imbecile Children, told the Departmental Committee:

> Many epileptics in the earlier years are very bright, intelligent, and exceedingly sharp; but of course, the history of epilepsy, unfortunately, is that with the recurrence of fits their mental powers become blunted and dulled, and they would have, say, attacks of acute mania, finally lapsing into dementia.

He transferred his epileptic children at the age of sixteen to county asylums where 'finally they become utterly and absolutely demented in time'. He ended on an incongruous note: 'Some of our ablest men, as we know, have been epileptic.' Aetiological studies placed a heavy emphasis on the hereditary nature of epilepsy, thus linking it in both contemporary medical judgement and popular opinion with feeble-mindedness, idiocy, and imbecility. Ireland, for instance, asserted that 'The children of epileptics are frequently insane, idiotic, or hysterical, and the descendants of an insane person are often epileptic, idiotic or insane or their epilepsy passes into insanity, or epilepsy supervenes upon the idiocy . . . deafness, chorea, locomotor ataxia, hysteria, and other disorders of the nervous system now and then occur in the descendants, apparently as the result of an inherent neurotic tendency in the same stock.' A survey in which 39 per cent of those examined were classified as hereditary cases and a further 17 per cent were attributed to drunkenness gave added currency to his belief.[11] Ireland's views showed how little attitudes had changed since Maudsley had written:

> There is a kinship between nervous diseases by virtue of which it comes to pass that they undergo transformation through generations. The two diseases most closely related in this way are insanity and epilepsy; the descendant of an epileptic parent being almost if not quite as likely to become insane as to become epileptic, and one or other of the descendants of an insane parent not unfrequently suffering from epilepsy.[12]

However, G. Penn Gaskell, secretary of the National Society for the Employment of Epileptics, argued that epileptic children should not be educated with defective children in special classes as, apart from their epilepsy, they were not mentally defective. They simply required a place where they could be educated without danger to themselves or others. Faced with conflicting evidence the Departmental Committee guardedly concluded, 'Many epileptic children are feeble minded. . . . Children with severe epilepsy tend to become insane; but there remain the small number (estimated at one-sixth of the total) who are afflicted with severe epilepsy and are not insane.' The Report went on to recommend that local education authorities should be required to provide residential schools for those too severely afflicted to attend ordinary schools. Sufferers with *petit mal* if of normal intelligence could attend ordinary schools, if feeble-minded as well, special schools. With scant regard for the susceptibilities of other feeble-minded children the Report added that there was little reason to 'suppose that the sight of ordinary epileptic fits are [sic] specially alarming to defective children'.[13]

The Report also set out details of the kind of teaching that should be provided for mentally defective children. In a school week, varying between 15 and 22½ hours, at least six were to be devoted to manual skills. The greater part of the time, in lessons not normally exceeding half an hour, was to be devoted to basic elementary school work, reading, writing, arithmetic, drawing, singing, and object lessons. As the goal of diagnosing mental defect was essentially an educational one, that of discovering children who could not benefit from instruction in an ordinary school, the remedy was seen to lie largely through the conventional school syllabus taken more slowly and aiming less ambitiously. Although this was a far cry from a physiological approach, Séguin would have welcomed the range of handicrafts proposed for young children – knitting, macramé work, basket- and mat-making, clay modelling, as well as painting and colouring. Older boys and girls were to earn schools an extra grant if their occupational training occupied at least six hours a week, certain approved subjects were taught, and mentally-defective children were not taught alongside others. The use of nearby training centres was also approved. As the Technical Instruction Acts did not apply to the existing schools for blind and deaf children, nor to the ones proposed for defective children, pupils could be taught a trade that would enable them to earn a livelihood later. Boys were to follow a wide variety of courses including basket-making, cane-seating, wood carving, fretwork, joinery, gardening, and farming. The proposed girls' syllabus was equally sex-stereotyped, with a mandatory two hours spent on needlework and two hours each, where possible, on cookery and laundry work, and such other domestic crafts as the Department might approve.[14]

The proposal to make education compulsory between the ages of seven and sixteen for all defective children, estimated to total one per cent of the school-age population, (apart from one-sixth who might not use the provided system because they could afford private schools) raised the problem of teacher supply. All existing teachers in London, Brighton, Leicester, Bradford, and Bristol were certificated women, Birmingham alone employing uncertificated mistresses. Most had come from infants' schools and had spent some time with special classes before taking one on their own. Faced with the problem of finding more teachers for whom no suitable training courses existed, and for which no teachers' manual had yet been written, the Report could do little but let current staff remain in their posts, allow Froebel-trained teachers to be responsible for classes of under ten pupils, and require certificated teachers for classes that were not normally to exceed 20. Having received evidence of the 'repulsive and immoral habits' of some children, the Report set a minimum age of twenty-one for all teachers, thereby ruling out the use of pupil teachers.[15]

Unlike the earlier act dealing with blind and deaf children, the Elementary Education (Defective and Epileptic Children) Act, 1899, was not mandatory on local authorities. Apart from the difficulties of determining whether an individual child was merely backward, mentally defective, or an imbecile, other considerations must have included the poor prognosis usually offered for all forms of mental defect and, in particular, epilepsy. The social obloquy attaching to sufferers, the lack of suitably trained teachers, the sheer numbers of children involved, and doubts about the cost-effectiveness of teaching mentally defective children, also militated against compulsory legislation. Even when a school authority had determined the presence of mentally-defective children, it was under no obligation to make separate provision for them. It could, however, establish classes, provide day or residential schools, or board out children near such facilities. On the other hand, once a school authority started making provision, the attendance of defective and epileptic children became compulsory between the ages of seven and sixteen. The extensive leakage between the ages of twelve and sixteen suggests that the enforcement of this part of the Act was both difficult and lax. The numbers on the rolls at special classes in the London County Council area in 1914 fell from 994 to 216 over the age span in question, yet this authority's record in special education was probably the best in the country. Undoubtedly school attendance officers had still to struggle against the shame, ignorance, and social snobbery that had made parents reluctant to use the London School Board's facilities in the 1890s. To facilitate attendance school authorities could provide guides, transport, and meals for children at special classes and require parents to contribute to the costs incurred, a power they also possessed in relation to classes for blind or deaf children. In dealing with epileptic children school authorities could establish schools, certified by the Education Department, but could not provide special classes or board out such children. The restriction on the size of schools for physically defective or epileptic children, to 15 places in any one building and to four such buildings in all, was later removed in 1903.[16]

In negotiating the size of the school grant the Education Department had got off to a bad start by not consulting the Treasury early enough. When it asked for an average grant of £4 5s a head, the Treasury pointed out that Birmingham School Board ran its two classes at a yearly average cost of £4 3s 6d and £4 8s 10d a head. However, the Education Department's argument that Birmingham did not employ certificated teachers or provide manual instruction, and that the London School Board was spending nearly £8 10s, prevailed. As with the grant fixed for blind and deaf children, that for defective children of £2 10s, plus £1 10s for simple manual instruction, and £2 for more advanced work, acted as a brake on a school authority's readiness to make suitable provision for handicapped children. By the year 1902–3, the average net cost of educating a defective child was £10 5s 2d a year, of which £4 3s 3d came from the government grant. Whereas local authorities were finding over £6 for defective children, they only had to find £1 15s for normal children. Similarly, the offer of a grant of 7s a month for each defective or epileptic child in a residential home did little to encourage LEAs to use this facility when the average yearly cost was between £20 and £30.[17]

A further barrier to the implementation of the Act, the first to give doctors statutory powers in connection with educational administration, was the absence of a nationwide school medical service and of any means of securing the medical inspection of children. Consequently, until the Education (Administrative Provisions) Act, 1907, required medical examinations as part of the school routine, the nomination of children as candidates for special education, whatever their handicap, depended largely on the classroom teacher's initiative. To implement the 1907 Act the Board of Education created a Medical Department, with George Newman as chief medical officer and Alfred Eichholz as his assistant, and required local education authorities to appoint school medical officers, actions that led to a considerable expansion of the special schools and their functions.

The passage of the Mental Deficiency Act, 1913, marks an important stage in the development of a national policy towards the feeble-minded child. This act implemented a number of recommendations made by the Royal Commission on the Care and Control of the Feeble Minded (the Radnor Commission) whose report appeared in 1908, four years after its appointment. The campaigns to provide education for handicapped children, whether their disability was physical or mental, owed much to a compound of humanitarian considerations and to a realization that handicapped adults could be a liability for the rest of the community, a liability that appropriate training and education might well reduce. Outside the world of educational bureaucracy the Charity Organization Society (1869) had pressed the case for educating the mentally handicapped in its report *The Feeble Minded Child and Adult* (1893), by advocating special classes and a system of grants similar to those recommended by the Egerton Commissioners for blind and deaf children.[18] Doubts about the United Kingdom's ability to maintain its imperial role while meeting the demographic, political, and economic challenge posed by possible rivals, expressed with increasing force after early military reverses in South Africa following the outbreak of war, had led to the appointment of the question-beggingly entitled Inter-Departmental Committee on Physical Deterioration, which reported in 1904. In an increasingly competitive world a falling birth-rate pointed to the need to conserve the nation's human capital. Thus, in one sense, the expansion in special education in the years before 1914 was part of a greater whole that included the provision of school meals, of medical inspection, and the teaching of housewifery and other domestic subjects. However, the feeble-minded child, unlike the hungry or rickety child, posed a double threat. From him or her there might stem both a physically and a morally degenerate stock.

A series of publications gave further life to the views expressed earlier by Maudsley, which were endorsed by the new school of Social Darwinism and, by members of that essentially professional middle-class organization, encompassing a wide spectrum of beliefs and opinions, the Eugenics Society (1907). An early work reflecting the language of Social Darwinism is S. A. K. Strahan's *Marriage and Disease: a study of heredity and the more important family degenerations* (1892) in which he quoted from Sir W. Aitken's *The Science and Practice of Medicine*, which appeared in the same year as Sir Francis Galton's *Hereditary Genius* (1st edition, 1869):

> Legislative enactments regarding the inter-marriage of persons tainted by disordered intellect are greatly to be desired; and the concealment of such disorder, with a view to marriage, ought to render marriages null and void which are concluded under such arrangements.

A quotation from Maudsley, without attribution to its context, shows how prejudice could kill scientific method:

> The more exact and scrupulous the researches made, the more distinctly is displayed the influence of the hereditary taint in the production of insanity. It is unfortunately impossible to get exact or accurate information on this subject. So strong is the foolish feeling of disgrace attaching to the occurrence of insanity in a family, that people . . . will disclaim or deny most earnestly the existence of any hereditary taint. . . .

Parents who defied social norms by marrying early or late in life when the 'vital forces' were at a low ebb were thought equally culpable. Early marriages produced feeble, degenerate children who, if they did not die in infancy, ended up in workhouses, infirmaries, asylums or prisons. On the authority of Macbeth's speech to Banquo's ghost such children also lacked physical courage.[19]

A brief examination of the *Radnor Report* (1908), written after making the most comprehensive survey of the extent of feeble-mindedness that had so far taken place, reveals the state of expert opinion of the day. Its short title, *Report of the Royal Commission on the Care and Control of the Feeble Minded*, highlights the main pre-occupation of a Royal Commission appointed to 'consider the existing methods of dealing with idiots, epileptics, and with imbecile, feeble-minded or defective persons not certified under the Lunacy Laws. . . .' Thus the first principle enunciated in the Report was that special provision should be extended to all mentally defective persons lying outside the orbit of existing legislation, in effect the feeble-minded.[20]

In a number of areas the Commission found proof for the beliefs of the day. Thus, on the causation of mental defect, the Report came down on the side of the hereditarians. Twenty-five of the thirty-five witnesses who gave substantial evidence on the issue attached 'supreme import-ance to the fact that in a very large proportion of cases there is a history of mental defect in the parents or near ancestors'. The non-hereditarian minority received short shrift. Few of the dissenting ten had the experience of working with large numbers of congenitally defective persons or of seeing many of the parents of the children in their care, while the hereditarians were 'experienced witnesses' who cited 'a large number of weighty instances in support' of their thesis. In contrast non-hereditarians were theorists, some of whom included cases of mental dulness within the category of mental defect. Guilty of this misjudgment was Dr Eichholz, now the HMI for Special Schools, who maintained that feeble-mindedness was largely bound up with 'general physical degeneracy', the 40 to 50 per cent of children whom he had found to improve in special classes being merely backward. Despite careful caveats such as, 'owing to the absence of necessary statistics, an absolutely conclusive reply based on facts alone, cannot be given to the question whether a parent or parents who are mentally defective from birth are more likely to have mentally defective children than are mentally normal parents' and 'inadequacy of data is, indeed, a difficulty which at present militates against any absolutely final statement',[21] the Report concluded:

both on grounds of fact and of theory there is the highest degree of probability that 'feeble mindedness' is usually spontaneous in origin – that it is not due to influences acting on the parent – and tends strongly to be inherited.[22]

Similarly, the Report admitted, 'It appears to be generally asserted that the number of children born to mentally defective children is abnormally high. . . . But with one or two exceptions, sifted and precise statements on the subject are wanting.'[23] However, after giving weight to the evidence of Miss Mary Denby, honorary secretary of the Lancashire and Cheshire Association for the Care of the Feeble Minded, who produced evidence to show that 'the higher grades of feeble-minded persons (who are the most numerous and dangerous) tend to have very large families', the Report concluded:

> especially in view of the evidence concerning fertility, the prevention of mentally defective persons from becoming parents would tend largely to diminish the numbers of such persons in the population.[24]

In sum it was more important to protect society from the mentally defective than to protect the mentally defective from society:

> the evidence . . . strongly supports measures, . . ., for placing mentally defective persons, men and women, who are living at large and uncontrolled, in institutions where they will be employed and detained; and in this, and in other ways, kept under effectual supervision so long as may be necessary.[25]

By extension, such would be the fate of some feeble-minded children when they reached adulthood. For the feeble-minded were now defined as 'persons who may be capable of earning a living under favourable circumstances, but who are incapable from mental defect existing from an early age (a): of competing on equal terms with their normal fellows; or (b) of managing themselves and their affairs with ordinary prudence'. Earlier, the idea of being unable to manage one's affairs had related principally to the question of testatory capacity. Now it was being extended, essentially as a social judgment, from the particular to the general. Yet the criteria for selecting children for special education were essentially educational, a capacity or otherwise to profit from instruction in an ordinary public elementary school, not social ones. The feeble-minded child had also to be distinguished from the moral imbecile, a group first defined by Isaac N. Kerlin in 1887, and now described as 'persons who from an early age display some mental defect coupled with strong vicious or criminal propensities on which punishment has little or no deterrent effect'.[26]

In examining the operation of the 1899 permissive Act the Radnor Commission found much to criticize. Up to September 1906, 87 local education authorities had adopted the Act. No school had been established in a rural area, all were in towns, usually with a large industrial population and a high rateable value. In Wales, for example, the only two special schools were at Cardiff and Barry, while Lancashire had five in Liverpool, three in Manchester, two in both Bolton and Burnley, and one in Blackburn and Oldham. In addition there were a number of voluntary schools of which the most important were at Sandlebridge, Cheshire, and Sandwell Hall, West Bromwich. Taking England and Wales as a whole, the schools were few in number and very unevenly distributed.[27]

The Commission considered the results of such special education as was provided to be equally unsatisfactory. Here their yardstick was a non-educational one, reflecting the social fears of the day: the extent to which children on leaving their special classes became self-supporting. In making such an assessment one problem was the lack of any common, nationwide standard of mental defect for admission to special classes. As H. F. Pooley, Assistant Secretary to the Board of Education, had explained:

> In some cases they like to get the children they think will do credit to the schools, and they leave the imbeciles out in the cold. In other cases they think more of the good of the children, taking in all who are not absolutely excluded.[28]

After examining the records of a school in Southwark, London, where 58 children had stayed until the age of sixteen, the Report concluded: '86.2 per cent of the 58 children – the classes entered . . . as "not earning at all", "occasional small earnings" and "at fairly unskilled work" – stand very close together, while those earning good wages come mainly from the "dull and backward" ' children admitted when the school was first formed and the demand for places was not so great as later. Yet this school was in an area where 'the homes are of a very low class' and the 'ignorance and want of foresight of the parents' were very great, a genuflection to the hereditarian school of thought and equally to the environmentalists. One is left wondering how successful the children from ordinary public elementary schools were in obtaining regular employment in a district beset with social problems. After considering evidence from other schools in London and the provinces the Report demoted special schools to a subordinate role: 'the special school should serve as a place for the education of those likely to be able to look after themselves and to be employed under supervision, and for testing and observing the children, and should be treated rather as an introduction to a wider system of training and occupation than as an educational institution by itself.'[29] The Report suggested that committees at the local government level, subordinate to the new proposed central government authority, the Board of Control, should supervise new and existing schools run by the Local Education Authorities acting as agents of the local bodies. In turn the LEAs would lose their power of controlling pupil access to the schools to the new local Mental Deficiency Authorities, who would be able to move children between schools, institutions and homes, or board them out, as they felt necessary. These recommendations ran contrary to the first thoughts of a Home Office departmental committee which met in March 1904 and whose recommendations formed the basis of Pooley's evidence to the Commission. Under this plan the Board of Education would have assumed responsibility for all improvable mentally defective children who were not within the remit of the Lunacy Laws, while the 1899 Act would have become compulsory. [30]

During the subsequent tussle between the Board of Education and the Home Office over the fate of the feeble-minded child, the publication of a number of studies temporarily strengthened the hereditarian school of thought and the case for lifelong control. In 1900 the botanists De Vries, Correns, and Tsvhermark had independently verified, and thus made more widely known, the Mendelian theory of heredity. Sir Francis Galton, coiner of the term 'eugenics' in his *Inquiries into Human Faculty and Its Development* (1883) published his paper 'Possible Improvement of the Human Breed' in *Nature* in 1901. Around the same time W. L. Johannsen identified the gene as the physical embodiment of Mendel's determinant 'factors' in heredity. The way now lay open for scientific study of the importance of heredity as a factor in the causation of mental deficiency. Despite this, some of the early genealogical studies of supposedly defective stock sacrificed scientific rigour in the cause of confirming current social beliefs. One of the first fruits of this new interest was the republication of R. L. Dugdale's *The Jukes* (1877), a study of the offspring of five notorious sisters, in which Dugdale had placed considerable stress on environmental influences in determining the intellectual and moral traits of the family. Moreover, he had noted only 'one case of outright deficiency, one of mental disease and one of epilepsy'. The reworking of the evidence in A. H. Estabrook's *The Jukes in 1915* (1916) showed a significant shift of concern from the problem of criminal degeneracy to that of mental deficiency. Estabrook concluded: 'one-half of the Jukes were and are feeble minded, mentally incapable of responding normally to the expectations of society', and 'all of the Jukes' criminals were feeble minded'. H. H. Goddard's *The Kallikak Family* (1912) traced the descendants of the illicit union of a young man in the American Revolutionary army with a supposedly feeble-minded tavern girl (the *kakos* line) and those of his later marriage with a Quakeress (the *kallos* line), the compound word kallikak amalgamating the Greek words for 'beauty' and 'bad'. Needless to say all 496 descendants of the 'good' stock turned out to be normal, while the two alcoholics and the one sexually immature person were held not to be mentally deficient.

Despite the common forebear only 46 of the 480 members of the other line were considered normal. To reinforce his point Goddard's photographs of the non-institutionalized *kakos* were 'phonied by inserting heavy dark lines to give eyes and mouths their diabolical appearance'. A number of similar studies were made in the decade before 1918 to support the thesis that mental deficiency was transmitted substantially in accordance with Mendel's findings.[31]

In the USA these studies, the intelligence testing of recruits for the army in the First World War, which seemed to show that recent immigrants of a southern or eastern European stock were intellectually inferior, and the increasing popularity of a hereditarian theory of intelligence, helped to confirm the belief that the post-1890 immigrants were posing a social threat to the older-established America drawn from British, German, and Scandinavian stock. One result was the restriction of immigration from the suspect countries by the passing of the Immigration Restriction Act, 1924, which laid down national quotas based on the 1890 census. A second response was the passage of sterilization laws in a number of states, a course of action Indiana pioneered in 1907. By 1955, 28 states had passed such laws, and 31,038 operations, of which 7,518 were in California, had been performed. At most risk were the 'moron' class, sexually capable and attractive, while idiots and imbeciles were unlikely to be either sexually attractive or potent.[32]

Some English authorities saw the one-to-one hereditarian causal theory of mental deficiency as the exception to the rule. In his second edition to his *Mental Deficiency (Amentia)* of 1912, A. F. Tredgold wrote:

> In a certain proportion of cases the mental defect of the individual has been preceded by a similar defect in his ancestors, and it may then be regarded as a definite instance of 'heredity' in the strict meaning of the word. But this is by no means always the case; indeed, it is not even the rule, and in my experience it is commoner for the ancestors of defectives to suffer from such conditions as insanity, epilepsy, dementia, and allied psychopathological states, than it is for them to be actually mentally deficient.[33]

In Tredgold's opinion environmental factors played no more than a precipitating role, thereby enabling him to question the idea that a neuropathic constitution was transmitted as a recessive trait according to the Mendelian formula: 'It may well be that in a family characterized by neuropathic diathesis there will be several members whose circumstances and mode of life are such that the necessary excitement does not occur with the consequences that they pass muster as normal individuals.' It only needed 'some exciting cause in the shape of ill-health, intoxication, severe stress or strain . . . to determine the attack'.[34]

Whereas Tredgold had found evidence of a neuropathic inheritance in 80 per cent of his cases C. P. Lapage, in a book written for the guidance of school medical officers, teachers, and social workers who had to deal with feeble-minded children, put the figure at 90 per cent. However, he agreed with Tredgold about the nature of the neuropathic inheritance:

> There is no doubt whatever that by far the most importance cause of feeble mindedness is an inherited taint of certain affections of the nervous system, . . . The *Neuropathic Inheritance*. These affections of the nervous system, which have a far reaching effect, are mental deficiency, insanity and epilepsy. They seem to be quite interchangeable as far as heredity is concerned. . . .

Lapage, writing after the publication of the Radnor Report but before the 1913 Act, argued the need for controlling the feeble-minded. The purpose of his book was essentially twofold. He wanted to warn of the danger of allowing unrestrained sufferers transmitting the taint and thereby affecting tens of thousands in future generations. From this premise stemmed the need to demonstrate that the only effective way of dealing with the problems was through lifelong supervision and control of the feeble-minded individual. A comparison of the first and second editions of Tredgold's standard textbook shows how he also moved towards perceiving the need for some form of control over the feeble-minded. Whereas in 1908 he had been content to describe the feeble-minded person as one who is 'unable to perform his duties as a member of society in the position of life to which he is born', by 1914 he was writing that such a person is 'incapable at maturity of so adapting himself to his environment or to the requirements of the community as to maintain existence independent of external support'.[35]

Much of the Board of Education's response to the criticism made in the Radnor Report of the special schools' record was devoted to improving their success in placing former pupils in jobs. One means of doing this was by excluding lower-grade mentally defectives, thereby confining admission to those likely to become semi-skilled or unskilled workers. To encourage local education authorities who might not have shared the view that 'it is now generally admitted that defective children of low grade have no place in a day school, and after probation it is usual to exclude them', the Board reminded them that such children were not eligible for the grant. By pursuing this policy the LCC was able to report that 212 of the children who had left school in 1908 had found employment, a far higher success rate than any reported by the Radnor Commission. In the same year the Liverpool Education Committee was commended for the energetic steps it had taken to exclude those who failed 'to respond readily to education'. The *Annual Reports of the Chief Medical Officer to the Board of Education* over the next years contain examples of local authority practices that Dr George Newman wished to be seen generally adopted to obtain administrative uniformity. Unable to offer specific grants to improve standards in particular areas, Newman could do little except cajole by example. In the particular case of selecting children for special education, the inauguration of medical inspection for all school children gave him another opportunity. Whereas the 1907 regulations had required doctors to examine children in special schools 'from time to time' those of 1909 required an annual assessment, not only to see whether or not a child could attend an ordinary school but also to weed out those thought too defective to profit from education of any kind.[36]

Another development was the provision of special schools for older boys. Here the LCC, the authority with the largest number of children in special schools, was able to take the initiative. At the end of the decade the Board claimed that the LCC's system of classification was so successful that there were only eight imbecile boys in the six schools whose results were analysed. 208 of the remaining 449 were 'in good or promising work', earning between 8s and 25s a week. A third of the total 'were bad cases, probably requiring custodial care', while a fifth were 'doubtful', some of them were in blind alley jobs and future candidates for custodial care.[37]

With expenditure on defence and the new social services mounting, sheer cost ruled any extensive system of custodial care out of court as a practical political proposition. Apart from the expense involved such a policy would have revived old fears about the unwarranted detention of blameless and harmless individuals. Much of the legal process developed in the nineteenth century, to govern the detention of people of unsound mind, had had the aim of preventing the sort of abuses through which some unfortunates had been sent to a madhouse or asylum to suit the convenience of unscrupulous friends or relatives. This same concern for the freedom of the individual still made legislation on the care and control of feeble-minded children, as well as of adults, a politically and socially sensitive issue in the early twentieth century; it generated sustained and dramatic filibustering during the 1912 debates on the Mentally Deficient Bill.[38]

As with special education generally, feeble-minded children were among the last of the handicapped to receive any provision for their future training or welfare on leaving school. By the turn of the century London, Birmingham, and Bristol possessed after-care committees for blind and deaf children and, in some cases, for the physically handicapped as well. Moreover, the newly published regulations for evening schools made it worthwhile for blind and deaf schools to give training to children over sixteen. In addition a number of institutions provided for the young adult in workshops run alongside the school. Other organizations ran workshops unconnected with any school that the young adult could enter. Possibly because the deaf could usually find employment more easily than the blind, deaf schools did not normally have trade departments for the young adult. However, missionaries to the deaf in the large cities, together with an active After-Care Committee in London, helped children to find employment on leaving school. The lack of such committees for the feeble-minded caused the Radnor Commission considerable concern, for the only one they found which was run on a near city-wide basis was in Birmingham.[39] Without such a committee, information about children's subsequent careers could not be collected and children of a nomadic disposition could not be traced.

To remove the Radnor Report's grounds for criticism over this issue Dr Newman mounted a campaign, in his 1909 report, for the appointment of After-Care Committees. Not only did he describe the LCC's work in some detail, but he presented such information as was available from other cities. The main deficiency was obviously their patchwork incidence. Even where committees existed they did not provide information on a uniform basis. Hence, it was difficult to comprehend the reality behind categorizations of individuals as being in 'employment' or in an 'occupation', especially when the suspicion was that in many cases the money earned did not represent a living wage. For these reasons he saw the need for the compulsory establishment of committees covering both the cities and the countryside, providing a compulsory after-care service alongside colonies for those requiring custodial care. The following year he returned to the attack, pointing out that the current concern over children from ordinary public elementary schools entering blind alley jobs had led to the formation of local employment committees. Clearly, feeble-minded children were even more in need of such assistance. They needed not only assistance in finding employment, but after-care in the form of societies, clubs and similar voluntary associations 'with a view to continuing educational influences and preventing degeneration'. Another need was the power to establish residential institutions on the lines of the colony at Sandlebridge, Cheshire, providing custodial care for all ineducable feeble-minded children as well as those educable ones that had to be in detention.[40]

Newman also realized that if the special schools were to improve their record in placing children in employment, the training and education offered had to move away from the diluted traditional classroom syllabus that most schools were still providing. The heavy emphasis, in the timetable proposed by the Departmental Committee of 1898, on formal school work was a product of the concern of the 1880s, when the loss of grant through children failing to pass the tests of the Revised Code brought the problem of educating the feeble-minded child to the fore. As such children were largely seen as instances of arrested mental development, the most appropriate teaching methods had been thought to be those used by Froebel-trained teachers in the infants school. The idea that manual work might be a worthwhile educational and vocational activity for such children had not been fully recognized. The whole of the morning was devoted to ordinary school subjects in the hope that children might succeed if they were in smaller classes. Apart from their prowess in needlework, women teachers lacked the manual skills necessary for the afternoon lessons.

A new approach was needed. Teaching the feeble-minded child reading and writing was now thought unprofitable, for 'symbolic concepts do not come to him and he is unable to draw analogies', but there was a place for a well-organized scheme of manual training accompanied by suitable language and speech training:

> The introduction of manual instruction into the curriculum receives its practical sanction from the certainty that any attempt to train the feeble-minded child through the abstract methods of the elementary school must be doomed to failure, and that mentally defective children will never be able to earn their living entirely or partially by any other than manual means.[41]

The Board accordingly produced a three-stage curriculum which started with the kind of training that later became available in the interwar training centres run by the Board of Control. Children between the ages of five and eight or ten were to learn such basic social skills as dressing themselves, personal tidiness and cleanliness, and habits of tidiness in relation to the classroom and their clothing and other possessions. Semi-skilled and skilled training for the oldest children could cover a wide range of manual occupations. With the growth of special schools it was becoming possible for education authorities to follow London's example by providing junior schools and sexually segregated senior ones, a process seen as necessary if each group was to receive its specialist industrial training.[42]

'We find a want that is not met.' The 1899 Act had excluded dull and backward children from the benefit of the grant available for feeble-minded children but had offered them nothing in its place. Accordingly the Radnor Commission saw it as incumbent on local authorities to provide them with their own special classes, for they were ordinary children, not feeble-minded ones, whose poor scholastic performance was the result not of some innate mental defect but of factors such as insufficient sleep or food. The city of Mannheim, where intermediate classes for the observation, classification and education of such children had been run, provided Newman with a precedent that he wished local authorities to emulate.[43] Between 1909 and 1913 Newman gave increasing attention to the necessity for providing for these children and to the kind of arrangements that various authorities were making.

While idiot asylums had been able to admit patients of widely varying ability on a fee-paying basis in the past, the legalistic requirements of the 1899 Act, and public concern about the alleged threat of the feeble-minded to society at large, put a premium on using more precise forms of classification than had been available hitherto. The complexity of the problem, arising from a recognition that there were degrees of intelligence and that a patient's social status might affect an observer's judgement, had been realized as early as the 1860s: 'It is very difficult to distinguish between the lowest types of the normal mind and the highest among the feeble minded of the same age and social class, as well as between the young idiot and the very backward normal-minded child of the same age.' A few years later another observer put the same problem more colourfully after a visit to Earlswood: 'A jury would be puzzled to decide between a group of one's most stupid friends and acquaintances and the most intelligent of the idiots to decide which were the most capable of taking care of themselves and which were the most dangerous to the community.'[44]

Mental testing – the term was coined by J. M. Cattell, who had become interested in measuring differences between individual students at Columbia University – seemed to provide the answer. The first significant figure to enter the field had been Sir F. Galton, whose *Inquiries into Human Faculty* was published in 1883. The study of differences between individuals, a subject hitherto largely neglected by psychologists, was pursued by Galton at his Anthropological Laboratory at University College, London. As one who began to study the correlation between mental traits, a theme Karl Pearson, his biographer, and Charles Spearman pursued further, he was the true father of the mental test. The kind of tests devised up to the end of the century, mainly confined to the simpler, perceptive, and motor processes, reinforced the notion of a continuum of intelligence. In France the Ministry of Public Instruction commissioned Albert Binet to develop techniques for identifying children whose failure under normal classroom conditions might indicate their suitability for special education. He departed from his predecessors by using a wide variety of tests, involving vocabulary, spatial concepts, and other factors. By mixing together enough tests of different abilities he hoped to be able to assess a child's general potential. The first edition of his tests simply arranged them in an ascending order of difficulty. Three years later, in 1908, he assigned an age level to each task. Thus a child who was two years behind at the age of nine, or three years behind if over that age, was suspected of being mentally retarded. This gave an absolute measure of disparity. The German psychologist, W. Stern, gave a relative measure when he argued that a child's mental age should be divided by his chronological one, the resulting number to be known as his intelligence quotient or IQ. Stern's more unfortunate contribution was to 'pronounce without a shred of empirical evidence, that the IQ was constant'.[45]

It is important to emphasize what these tests did not purport to do. They were not intended to provide a way of ascertaining the relative intellectual powers of all children, or of classifying and grading them. They were, rather, a means by which a teacher might pick out the mentally backward child from, for example, the lazy one. As such the tests provided a rough first guide:

> The scale, properly speaking, does not permit the measure of intelligence, because intellectual qualities are not superposable, and therefore cannot be measured as linear surfaces are measured.

However, the wide spectrum of tests used could point to a 'defect of equilibrium', that is, where a child's retardation was more marked in some faculties than in others, as well as to individual differences of a pathological kind in his mental powers. It followed that a curriculum drawn up a stage behind that used for normal children was imperfectly suited to the defective. Using the profile of abilities revealed by the test, 'The first duty of the teacher is to take account of the faculties already developed, the aptitudes which are already apparent.'[46]

The new tests were first drawn to the attention of educationalists by Dr James Kerr in his report to the LCC for 1909. Newman's report of the following year gave them a cautious welcome: '. . . the results of these tests are at present barely sufficient to enable a definite opinion to be given as to their utility. Practical experience seems to show however useful they may be for children educated in France they are not always suitable for English standards.' H. H. Goddard, director of research at the Vineland Training Centre for Feeble-Minded Girls and Boys, New Jersey, translated them into English for use at his centre, where they practically became 'the sole test'. Newman then wrote, 'there can be no doubt as to their value and practicality when properly applied, and School Medical Officers are strongly advised to use them as part of their examination.' He accordingly added them as a coda to the 'Schedule of Medical Examination of Children for Mental Defect', first published in his 1909 Report. Yet if such tests were to be effective diagnostic instruments they had to be administered under carefully controlled conditions and not 'applied by anyone not fully understanding how to use them, and the conditions and appliances necessary for reliable results'. How many doctors, one may ask, heeded the warning that a successful response depended largely on the spirit of sympathy and encouragement they displayed.[47]

Thus, during the struggle between the Board of Education, then one of the most junior departments of state, and the Home Office, headed by one of the two most senior secretaries of state, the former had done much to strengthen its hand in resisting the Radnor Commission's proposals to hand over feeble-minded children, along with similarly afflicted adults, to one authority. Undoubtedly the fortuitously timed development of the Binet-Simon tests had done much to reinforce 'the contention that the care of children with mental defect should properly be located within the educational system', but so did many of the advances in the practice and administration of special education discussed above. By the time Home Office draftsmen were preparing the first of the two Mental Deficiency Bills presented to Parliament the Board of Education held a number of court cards in its hands. Most important, its development of a regular system of medical inspection allowed preliminary identification of children suffering from either mental or physical handicap. From the first school inspection children could be referred for a more careful assessment incorporating the best diagnostic tools yet known. If referred to a special school, the child could be offered a more enlightened curriculum than that of ten years earlier. On leaving school he might become the concern of an After-Care Committee, a cheaper and more humane alternative than any form of custodial care. Perhaps the final word lies with Newman. Whatever might be said in favour of the permanent detention of adults for life, he wrote, 'it seems to me a monstrous proposition to apply such treatment to young children whose powers are growing and concerning whose future we know little or nothing.'[48]

The upshot of the Mental Deficiency Act, 1913, and the Elementary Education (Defective and Epileptic Children) Act, 1914, was to make the provisions of the earlier 1899 Act compulsory in respect of mentally-defective children but to exclude the physically defecctive and epileptic children, who had to wait another four years. Under the 1913 Act local education authorities had the responsibility of ascertaining the existence of children suffering from mental defect. Children not thought capable of benefiting from education in a special school, those certified as requiring supervision or guardianship, and those on leaving school thought to need institutional treatment or guardianship, had to be notified to the new local mental deficiency authorities. As the 1914 Act was compulsory, LEAs, who had received no extra financial assistance in meeting the costs of medical inspection, understandably looked to the government for higher grants. The new scale sanctioned in 1914 gave LEAs £6 for each mentally deficient child in a day school and £12 for a residential school.

In briefing J. A. Pease, his political master, Newman justified the omission of the epileptic child from the 1914 Act on purely medical grounds. The condition was intermittent in its manifestations and severity, and therefore its responsiveness to treatment was uncertain.

Many of the worst cases were feeble-minded and would be covered by the new legislation. Only one-fifth to one-tenth required institutional treatment. Broadly speaking, Newman thought that there were about 5,000 epileptic children in all. Existing residential schools, capable of accommodating 530 children, had not achieved results 'of a very encouraging nature, and this of itself has not quickened the interests of local authorities in the education of these children'. A memorial from the Maghull Home, near Liverpool, recorded the perceived results of this omission: 'It is well known that epileptic children when excluded from the ordinary schools and compelled to remain at home . . . usually deteriorate in mind and become mentally defective.' The petitioners went on to argue that it was anomolous to leave them uneducated until they became ineducable, since 'their unstable minds if left uneducated and untrained, render them a source of danger and mischief to themselves and the community out of all proportion to their actual numbers'. Unswayed by these pleas J. A. Pease, president of the Board of Education, stuck to the official line when explaining the omission of epileptic children from the 1914 Act: 'Epilepsy is in itself an intermittent disease, very difficult to define, and the best method of treating it has not yet really been determined. . . . Its treatment is still in the experimental stage.'[49]

Largely as a result of pressure successfully orchestrated by Mrs Humphrey Ward, amendments made to the 1918 Education Bill provided for the compulsory education of physically defective, or crippled children, and epileptic ones. Mrs Ward, woman of letters and founder of the Passmore Edwards Settlements in London, had secured the support of Lyulph Stanley, later Lord Sheffield, and Graham Wallas in opening the first day school for crippled children certified by the Board of Education, thereby separating them from the mentally defective. Her survey of the London School Board area, which revealed the existence of 1,800 invalid children not at school, led to the opening of four centres for their education. Her other main work for crippled children was to inaugurate the Crippled Children's Training and Dinner Society.

A founder member of the Women's Anti-Suffrage Movement, she formed the Joint Advisory Committee in 1913, consisting of both pro- and anti-suffragists, to represent every field of social work in the belief that women should confine themselves to maintaining representation on municipal and other bodies concerned with domestic and social affairs. In 1918 she wrote to every MP, 95 LEAs, the Board of Education and *The Times* urging the inclusion of crippled children in the forthcoming legislation. Her son, Arnold Ward, put down a question in the House of Commons in March. Despite all this activity the interview she and Lady Edmund Talbot had at the Board of Education in April gave her little hope of eventual success. However, during the committee stage Major J. W. Hills, MP for Durham and a member of the Joint Advisory Committee, successfully introduced a clause making education compulsory for both physically handicapped and epileptic children. Hills's short speech putting the case for the physically handicapped child but ignoring the epileptic was sympathetically received by both sides of the House, possibly because of the severe wounds he had received in France. H. A. L. Fisher, president of the Board of Education, concerned about the financial problems facing county authorities, detracted from Hills's success by deferring the operation of the clause dealing with residential schools in the counties until seven years after the cessation of the hostilities then still in progress. However, that largely consolidating measure, the Education Act of 1921, seemed to redress the balance by requiring LEAs to provide board and lodging for defective and epileptic children if there were not less than 45 such children belonging to the area, for whom education could not provide in any other way.[50]

During the years before the outbreak of war in 1914 a considerable expansion in the number and type of schools provided under the Acts of the 1893 and 1899 had taken place. Medical inspection after 1907 had a dual role. Not only did it reveal large numbers of children requiring medical treatment but it also showed that certain physical conditions made their education in an ordinary public elementary school an unprofitable undertaking. Thus by 1911 there were day schools for children suffering from aphasia, ophthalmia, myopia, partial vision and deafness, and other complaints such as favus, ringworm, and phthisis. There were also residential convalescent and sanatorium schools. As Eichholz commented in a policy document that had some influence on the drafting of Newman's 1911 report,

> . . . we no longer confine action to those who fall within the four corners of these Acts [1893 and 1899]. Our duty is to the whole class of abnormal pupils of all ages and while many of these require special school training there are many for whom adaptations of arrangements which obtain in the ordinary public elementary schools will suffice.[51]

Although his suggestion appeared in print that special schools of observation should cater for children whose condition was of uncertain diagnosis his more expansive ideas concerning the 'preventive role of the medical officer' did not. However, Newman did concede that the school medical officer would be responsible, directly or indirectly, 'for any special treatment which the Authority or Managers may find it necessary to undertake', thereby making medical treatment one of his four main responsibilities.[52]

During the same years steps were taken to train teachers for the blind and deaf. With the establishment of the College of Teachers of the Blind under the auspices of the British and Foreign Blind Association and Gardner's Trust, founded in 1882 with a capital endowment of £300,000, the Board of Education became involved in the examination of teachers of the blind. Dr Eichholz, the Board's assessor, who attended the first examination in 1909 found 'the standard adopted . . . . was high almost to the point of severity'. At first the College met the full cost of running the examination – not until 1920 did it receive a Treasury grant of £10 a year. Seven years later, after gentle blackmail, the Treasury agreed to meet the full cost when it learnt that if it did not do so the Board of Education would have had to shoulder both the financial and the administrative burden of providing the examination.[53] The Board of Education also approved a scheme for training teachers of the deaf at the Fitzroy Square Training College for Teachers of the Deaf, in which the Ealing Training College participated. By 1912 a Joint Examinations Board had examined 193 candidates with a rigour that apparently equalled that of the College of Teachers of the Blind. Only 102 received their diplomas.[54]

The Annual Reports of the Chief Medical Officer to the Board of Education make clear what had been achieved by 1914. It is less easy to decide what had been left undone. On the one hand Newman had estimated that there were 32,000 educable feeble-minded children in 1911. The following year 13,110 were on the registers of day schools and 590 in residential ones. Of a possible 5,000 epileptic children, 415 and 473 were at day and residential schools respectively. Over the two decades during which the compulsory 1893 Act had been in force blind and deaf children seemed to have fared the best. The Radnor Report, for example, had little doubt about this, stating that it was 'probable that few blind or deaf children are now without suitable education.' It might be thought that it is comparatively easy to find out the number of children who should have been at school under the 1893 Act, for in the collection of census data one might expect that some of the problems relating to discovering the number of feeble-minded children, such as parental shame and the difficulties of diagnosis, did not apply. Yet although census officials were strongly critical of the accuracy of figures relating to the mentally handicapped, they also treated those relating to other handicaps with scepticism. 'We cannot, however, but express our decided opinion that statements made by persons as to the deficiencies, mental and bodily, of their children or other relatives, are not worth the cost and labour of collection and tabulation.' Ten years later the 1891 census characterized the figures as 'in all probability excessively inaccurate,' while officials in 1911 complained, 'as our experience gives us no reason to hope that the figures are appreciably more accurate on this than on previous occasions, we have not felt justified in entering upon an elaborate analysis of the figures. . . .' However, the 1911 census, using more restrictive criteria than those in the 1893 Act (see p. 00), returned 1,680 'totally blind' children between the ages of five and fifteen, 1,965 'totally deaf', and 2,988 deaf and dumb. A year later day and residential schools held 1,939 and 1,371 blind children respectively, including the partially blind, myopic, and ophthalmic. The corresponding figures for deaf children, including those partly deaf and the hard of hearing, were 3,747 and 2,545.

Best treated of all handicapped children were those cared for by the Roman Catholic Church which had made, Eichholz thought, the most systematic efforts of all religious communities to provide for its members. Accommodation for their blind and deaf children represented one-twentieth of all that was available for such children. While there were two small local authority residential schools, Roman Catholics had provided six accommodating 400 children. They had also built the only two residential schools for children suffering from ophthalmia and one-tenth of all accommodation for epileptic children. Their schools were run to high standards, with courteous staff and a domestic care that bore comparison with some of the best of the country. They had, stated Eichholz, been always the first to try new experiments such as the residential schools for the mentally defective at Hillingdon, for epileptics at Much Hadham, Herts, for ophthalmic children in Notting Hill, London, and Chigwell, Essex, and for blind and deaf children at Liverpool and Boston Spa.[56]

While the Roman Catholic Church's concern to preserve the faith amongst the young had brought it to the forefront in special education, the state more readily funded schools for delinquent children than for the handicapped. In 1911 state contributions to day and residential schools for blind children met 29 per cent and 12 per cent of the costs of maintenance respectively, while the corresponding figures for deaf schools were 27 per cent and 13 per cent. Yet the Treasury met 59 per cent and 40.4 per cent of the costs of running reformatory and industrial schools. The maintenance of law and social order had financial priority over compassion for the physically and mentally disadvantaged.[57]

THE INTER-WAR YEARS

In 1911 C. B. Davenport had propounded the first law of heredity: 'Two mentally defective parents will produce only mentally defective offspring.' His second law was that, apart from mongols, 'probably no imbecile is born except of parents who, if not mentally defective themselves, both carry mental defect in their germ plasm. . . . In view of the certainty that all the children of two feeble-minded parents will be defective, how great is the folly, yes, the crime of letting two such persons marry.'[1] Genetic research carried out by the end of the inter- war years had seriously undermined these 'laws'. By the 1920s the idea that each characteristic was represented in a single gene had been abandoned. The characteristics of a given individual were seen as the result of the interaction of hundreds of genes that produced combinations almost beyond calculation. Although a role was still allowed to heredity, it was no longer as previously thought the all-powerful factor, environment playing its part as well.

At the same time the earlier alarmist hereditarian studies came under a closer and more critical scrutiny. It began to be realized that as they were largely based on institutional inmates they did not represent a true cross-section of society. They were biased towards the poor and socially inadequate. Similarly, studies of juvenile delinquents had failed to allow for the possibility that the feeble-minded from economically and emotionally poor homes were more likely to be caught *in flagrante delicto* than brighter children from more stable backgrounds. By 1932 the Brock Report on Sterilization was able to dismiss the work of H. H. Goddard and his disciples in summary terms:

> Judged by modern standards the technique employed was unscientific and the instructions to the field workers so tendentious that it is not surprising that they succeeded in finding what they were told to seek. The criticism made by Dr Myerson[2] and others of this and similar enquiries has never been answered, and we do not think it necessary to spend time on any analysis of the dismal chronicles of the Kallikaks, the Jukes and the Nams.[3]

In addition such factors as trauma at childbirth and infectious diseases in childhood, such as meningitis, received greater recognition as did later the Rh factor and rubella in the early stages of pregnancy. These developments, however, still left a predisposing role for heredity, but the hereditarian 'laws' had been undermined.

As earlier studies had ignored barren women, they had inflated the number of births for feeble-minded women as a whole. In addition the importance of such cultural and social factors as low economic status and the lack of knowledge of efficient methods of birth control in determining family size began to receive their due. The Brock Committee found no evidence to support previously held beliefs about the philoprogenitive propensities of the feeble-minded: 'There is a widespread belief that one of the characteristics common to defectives is abnormal fertility. This is not borne out by the enquiry or by such studies as we have been able to collect. . . . The supposed abnormal fertility of defectives is, in our view, largely mythical. . . .'[4]

At the same time the relationship between heredity and the influence of environment was seen to be more complicated than previously supposed. Of what the committee described as the 'lowest social stratum' the Brock Report wrote: 'Cause and effect of the conditions found in the social problem group are debatable, but it is possible that selective mating may to a large extent account for this concentration of physical defects and mental defects and disorders. There is evidence that in the poorest districts neighbour marries neighbour, and like marries like',[5] a judgement that closely paralleled Dugdale's view on the causes of hereditary pauperism, on whose original work later glosses had overlaid the extent to which he found hereditary transmission less significant than environmental influences in determining the intellectual and moral traits of the Jukes. In short, the feeble-minded were now seen not so much as a social danger but as being at the centre of a nexus of social and economic problems, where 'mental deficiency, much physical inefficiency, chronic pauperism, recidivism, are all more or less closely related, and are parts of a single social problem'.[6]

At the same time as earlier alarmist fears concerning the feeble-minded were beginning to subside, financial constraints in the early 1920s made pre-war hopes of providing a comprehensive system of special provision for all handicapped children seem a pipe dream. The cost of enforcing the 1914 and 1918 Acts for physically and mentally handicapped children was 'so large as to appear prohibitive, at all events for many years to come'. Not for the first time, nor for the last, had educational policy outstripped resources. In March 1922 A. H. Wood, Assistant Secretary to the Board of Education, writing of the Special Services as a whole – the school medical service, special schools, the organization of physical training, the provision of evening centres and nursery education – recalled: 'The millenium was to arrive when every Authority provided each of the recognized forms of treatment for every child, when there was a school place for every defective child. . . . But this millenium . . . is no longer practical politics. . . . We have no longer to aim at developing each Service to the full with the comfortable knowledge that the money for it will appear almost automatically. We have rather to face a long series of lean years . . ., and the new problem is to decide how best to spend the money we have.'[7]

The problem was compounded by the uneven way in which the Special Services had developed between one authority and another. For instance, while Birmingham spent three times as much on special education as it did on the school medical service, Warrington's expenditure on special education was a quarter of what it spent on the school medical service. Moreover, the per capita cost of special education was higher than other branches of the special services. While £300 a year gave a reasonably satisfactory medical service or provided dental treatment for 1,200 children, or could offer spectacles to 1,000, it could send only four handicapped children to a residential school or ten to a day one. If all the services were properly provided for a county borough of 30,000 the cost would be £51,446 a year. Deciding that 'A strict observance of statutory requirements is financially impossible and must always remain so', Wood set out his priorities with a 'list in order of emphasis', ranking the priority of special schools as follows: blind, deaf, crippled, open air, and schools for tubercular children, with those for high grade and low grade mentally defective children trailing behind.[8] After a conversation with Wood, Newman minuted that 'The Board ought to endeavour to reduce expenditure' on special education, 'such reduction being confined as far as possible to the attempted education of the defective children whom no education will make breadwinners.' As Eichholz explained in a memorandum on mentally defective children, 'children of this type do not appeal to the popular imagination nor do they excite public sympathy as do the blind, the crippled and the deaf and dumb.'[9]

At the same time the Board did not know how many handicapped children required special education. At the beginning of 1922, 27 authorities were not making any provision for a handicapped child of any kind. With an annual expenditure of £1.5 million on special services and 5.2 million children on the registers the annual per capita expenditure per unit of average attendance in public elementary schools was 6s; 176 authorities spent less than half this figure and only 39 recorded above average expenditure. London, the leader, spent 17s 9d, a figure held to be 'probably just about what an authority ought to spend on the assumption that it really carries out its statutory duties'. If the proportions of children discovered in London with various forms of handicap were applied on a national basis, Wood estimated that such an exercise would produce 300,542 children, a figure that was more than double the 145,896 then known to the Board. Of this total 84,478 were in public elementary schools, 34,397 in special ones, 5,716 in institutions, while the remaining 21,305 were not at school at all. As the cost of putting all 300,542 children into day or residential schools would have been an estimated £16,863,360 a year, shared equally between the Board and LEAs, other means had to be found of dealing with the problem. Suggestions included hiving off tubercular children to the Ministry of Health, some low grade mentally defective children to the Board of Control, and putting higher grade mentally defective children into public elementary schools. As for bad cases of epilepsy, 'such persons are too short lived to make it an economical arrangement to spend much on training them for life'. In looking at the particular problem of mentally defective children, Eichholz suggested a compromise. If London's yardstick of one such child in a thousand were used, the total cost of new accommodation would be roughly £3 million, while the additional annual cost of maintenance would be £1.2 million. If, however, the Board aimed at half London's level, but still above that of the comparatively energetic authorities of Liverpool and Manchester, where the ascertainment rates were 0.36 and 0.37 a thousand respectively, 'we should have done very well'. This policy would have brought the additional cost of accommodation and maintenance to £1.5 million and £600,000, a target he suggested might be reached over the next ten years.[10]

To their credit, successive Presidents of the Board of Education made some effort to protect special education from the full rigours of the immediate post-war economy drive which was already under way before Lord Geddes published his reports. On 8 December 1920 the Lloyd George coalition Cabinet, believing that the doubling of public expenditure on public education between 1913–14 and 1920–1 was the result of the Education Act, 1918, ruled that 'schemes involving expenditure not yet in operation are to remain in abeyance'. Austen Chamberlain, Chancellor of the Exchequer, followed this by urging H. A. L. Fisher, President of the Board of Education, to 'seek, for, say, a couple of years, to incur the *least possible* expenditure'. Although Fisher had earlier pointed out that the Cabinet decision had omitted any reference to special education, he eventually had to concede the general principle that 'The onus will ordinarily lie on the LEA to show cause why they should incur new expenditure. The cases in which we should ask for or suggest new expenditure will be exceptional, and we are more likely to err on the side of leniency than on the side of severity' (in compelling authorities to carry out their statutory duties).[11] In 1924 C. P. Trevelyan, President of the Board of Education in Ramsay

MacDonald's first Labour government, proposing a net estimate of £41.9 million for 1924–5, had made a liberal building programme for special schools his third priority after replacing unsatisfactory elementary school accommodation and increasing the provision of secondary schools. In a letter to Philip Snowden, Chancellor of the Exchequer, he argued that his Conservative predecessor. E. F. L. Wood, later Lord Irwin, Lord and Earl of Halifax, had said that he had shrunk from making cuts that could have been seen to be reducing expenditure on special schools, because of possible objections from the House of Commons. 'It is obvious,' Trevelyan continued, 'that I cannot adopt expedients from which Wood shrank', an argument that helped to restore the cut of £900,000 Trevelyan found Wood had proposed for 1924–5. Despite this minor success a further note from Snowden, following a discussion between the two, shows what little chance Trevelyan had of building any special schools: 'I am rather dubious about your encouraging building. My suggestion was that you should deal only with really bad cases and that under your ordinary powers.' The following July Trevelyan began his offensive against the Treasury for the following year's estimates: 'There has been in this Department for three years past a regime of severe and in some respects of excessive parsimony. All modes of expenditure have been repeatedly examined with a view to their reduction, and, while I do not think that there is much left now for the axe, or the pruning knife, I shall always be on the watch for uninjurious economies.'[12] However, Ramsay MacDonald's government fell from office before the settlement of the Education estimate for 1925–6. Between 1924–5 and 1928–9 the net charge of the Board of Education vote, after allowing for teachers' superannuation contributions, remained almost stationary, falling from £41,900,000 to £41,726,000. On the other hand, the rates contribution rose from £30,713,000 to £34,300,000 over the same period. In 1929 when Trevelyan once more assumed office, in MacDonald's second Labour government, he omitted any mention of special education from the wide range of items on which he proposed additional expenditure. Although Snowden went some little way towards meeting Trevelyan's requests, his reply gave little hope for any future plans the Board might have had for building more special schools:

Finally I must say I am extremely perturbed at the forecasts of the future increases in your Estimates, increases which are far greater than can be accounted for by the raising of the school leaving age and I hope that you will bear with me if I say that I think that for the present we have made a sufficient advance in educational development, and that a task not less urgent than that of seeking to expand educational facilities is to make certain that we are getting value for our existing expenditure and that no practicable economies have been overlooked. To this second task I hope you will feel able to apply yourself.[13]

In the bleak economic and political climate of the inter-war years the Board could do little to expand special school accommodation. Circular 1245 issued in 1922 limited the grant for such schools to the level of that of 1921–2. A further Circular, 1297 of January 1923, by reducing standards made a further 887 places available. Yet the Board had to confess to the National Union of Teachers that the provision of special schools 'is admittedly inadequate, and their high cost makes it difficult, and indeed in present circumstances impossible, to secure their development'. At this time some 2,500 ascertained mentally defective and 14,000 physically defective children were not at school at all, while 16,000 and 14,000 of the respective categories were at special schools, and a further 10,500 and 74,000 were in ordinary schools. Although the Board sanctioned two new schools it withheld permission for seven others.[14] Following the publication of the May Report on National Expenditure in 1931 the Board imposed a virtual ban on all new school buildings. So severe was this restriction that it refused Leeds permission to start a new special school class at a cost of £190 a year, to relieve the city's five existing overcrowded schools and reduce the waiting list for admission. Later the same year, however, the Board saw its way to including some provision in the 1934–5 estimates for nursery and special school accommodation.[15]

Much of the progress in extending the availability of special education took place in conjunction with the growth of school medical and other social services. The most marked expansion of the inter-war years was in the provision of open-air schools housing children suffering from a wide variety of complaints including pulmonary and non-pulmonary tuberculosis. Here LEAs acted in cooperation with local health authorities, as part of a national campaign to provide free treatment of tuberculosis on the lines recommended by the Astor Committee in 1912. In addition, the development of maternity and child welfare services and of a system of home visits from trained health visitors helped to bring to light children with defective hearing or vision as well as a series of other disabilities. At the same time the Board of Education encouraged school medical officers to initiate research projects by publishing extracts from their findings or merely listing the subject matter. Amounting to 1,322 between 1908 and 1932,[16] such projects continued to run at this level until the outbreak of war in 1939.

The Board also managed to initiate a number of co-ordinated studies, some of which were conducted in partnership with the Ministry of Health. While the Wood Committee, in conjunction with the Board of Control, was set up to examine problems relating to the education of feeble-minded children, and the enquiry into encephalitis lethargica had direct implications for the management of special education, others were of wider concern. Enquiries into the prevention of tonsilitis and enlarged adenoids, the prevention of squint and defective vision, the incidence and significance of goitre, of disease among infants, of rheumatism, and the anthropometric enquiry, had implications for public health as a whole. Further studies in the 1930s focused on the problem of children with defective vision or hearing, whose smaller numbers made special provision for them financially viable. The Board published a report from its committee of enquiry into problems connected with defective vision in November 1931. A month later it appointed a committee to enquire into problems associated with partially sighted children, which reported in July 1934. Two years later a committee including members of the College of Teachers of the Blind, the National Institute for the Blind, and members of the Board of Education and Ministry of Health, published *The Education of the Blind – A Survey*. Then, after four years' deliberation, there appeared the *Report of the Committee of Inquiry into the Problems Relating to Children with Defective Hearing*.[17]

The problem of establishing the number of handicapped children, whatever their disability, which had bedevilled the costing exercises of the early 1920s, remained with the Board throughout the inter-war years. Newman's report for 1923 suggested criteria that would have produced 213,440 children, two-thirds the number Wood had estimated using the LCC's data, and five times the accommodation then available. To alleviate the situation Newman publicized the idea Departmental officials had already aired of leaving tubercular children to the health authorities, the use of orthopaedic services to reduce the number of crippled children, and cooperation between LEAs, especially when the number of handicapped children was too small for any one authority to supervise without incurring heavy per capita expense. For the large number of unprovided-for mentally defective children one possible solution was to send them to ordinary schools.[18] By the time Newman made this suggestion the Board had surveyed the extent to which LEAs used public elementary schools for mentally handicapped children. A subsequent memorandum to inspectors, accepting that 'The present financial stringency has made it clear that a uniform and comprehensive administration of the Defective and Epileptic Children Act of 1899 is quite impossible for many years to come', urged them to explore the idea of organizing classes for higher-grade defectives – the dull and backward children – and to encourage LEAs to consider schemes for this purpose. Such classes were to be called 'handicraft' or 'practical', have more attention from school medical officers, and to use open-air facilities, as mental deficiency often had a physical cause, while the children were to be separated as little as possible from their more fortunate fellows. Advice on these lines was given to LEAs in Newman's subsequent reports.[19] Circular 1349 of 12 January 1925 firmly put mentally-defective children, whose ascertained numbers had increased by 2,000 following the publication of Circular 1341 of 12 September 1924, at the end of the queue for special school accommodation. LEAs were to give priority to providing for blind and deaf children not already in school and to develop their orthopaedic services. As for mentally defective children, the Board's minima were assessment, notification of suitable cases to the Mental Deficiency Authorities, and supervision of those children not in special schools. After dealing with blind, deaf, and mentally-deficient children on these lines, LEAs were to attend to the problem of delicate and pre-tubercular children requiring Open Air schools. Between 1924–5 and 1928–9 the planned provision of Open Air school places nearly trebled, from 5,530 to 15,106, while accommodation for feeble-minded children remained virtually static.[20]

The deliberations of the Wood Committee, which eventually reported in 1929, gave the Board of Education further reason to urge caution on any authority that might have been contemplating additional expenditure on those children whose future was now under review. The Committee, whose remit was successively extended to include children of all grades of mental defect and then to consider adults as well, recommended the ending of the practice of certification of children, for it militated against the efficiency of the assessment process. Teachers, many of whom thought they could cope with children of low intelligence in the ordinary school system, were reluctant to refer children for examination. Parents were equally uneasy about seeing their children segregated from normal children and relegated to special schools, many of which were still housing low-grade defectives instead of the higher-grade ones for whom they were theoretically intended. Moreover, the wide range of variation in the incidence of mental defect reported, between 0.73 per thousand and 16.14 at the other extreme, showed how capriciously the system worked. Despite the Committee's evidence, however, medical certification survived for a further fifteen years.[21]

A survey made on behalf of the committee, held to be the most thorough and careful yet made in this country, by showing the extent of the problem revealed the inadequacy of existing provision. The total estimate of 105,000 mentally defective children between the ages of seven and sixteen was twice that of the Radnor Commission, three times the number ascertained by LEAs, and more than six times the available suitable school accommodation, which was spread unevenly over the country. For the 9,000 of the 33,000 ascertained children living in rural areas in 1927 there was one residential place for every seven or eight children. Forty of the 100 towns with a population over 50,000 had no special school places, the deficiency being worst in those towns under 60,000. Where classes existed for towns of under 50,000 inhabitants they were often underused. Moreover, with few potential pupils and high unit costs, the Board had refused to sanction small all age classes in small towns. The Committee also considered the educational needs of 300,000 dull and backward children, struggling in large classes in ordinary schools, a group whose needs the 1897 Departmental Committee had virtually ignored. In recommending that the whole 405,000 should form a special unit within the public elementary school system the Committee, faced with the virtually impossible task of implementing the 1899 and 1914 Acts within existing financial, social, and political constraints, legitimized and attempted to regularize and rationalize practices that many local authorities had already adopted and which the Board of Education condoned, if not actively encouraged, despite their questionable statutory basis.[22] Technically, to keep children who had been ascertained to be mentally defective was an infringement of the grant regulations: such children *ex hypothesi* could not benefit from education in an ordinary elementary school and rate expenditure on them was *ultra vires*. Yet the Board knew that if such children were turned out of ordinary schools there would have been an outcry that 'the Board would probably not care to face'.[23]

During the 1920s a greater understanding of the educationally retarded child helped to give respectability to the solution that the financial exigencies of the decade dictated. In 1923 Newman had written, 'The mentally defective child is not a worse degree of dullness or backwardness. It is a specific disease, whereas dullness and backwardness is (*sic*) mainly due to environmental conditions.' After reading C. Burt's *The Young Delinquent* (1925), from which he quoted in his report, he wrote, 'Nature knows no demarcation or breaks from what we are pleased to call the "normal" from the "abnormal", from the mentally sound to the mentally unsound, from the stable to the unstable, from the educable to the uneducable.' John Conolly would have approved. He went on to distinguish those children whose defect was social from those whose defect was educational, for whom 'every endeavour should be made to embrace the largest possible number within the fold of the public elementary school'. With fears abating of any social threat posed by the feeble-minded, he emphasized the importance of after-care and continued supervision *in the community*.[24]

Extracts from the Wood Report provide a convenient summary of the interplay between changing attitudes and policy recommendations:

> We have come to the conclusion that these two groups – the mentally defective child who is educable and the child who is dull or backward – can no longer be regarded as separate and distinct entities, but must really be envisaged as a single group presenting a single educational and administrative problem.
>
> What they need is not special care and control but a special form of

instruction, special teaching methods and a special syllabus of work.

Such children should be regarded as educationally defective rather than as mentally defective in the strict sense of the term.[25]

Despite the Committee's belief than their proposals on the restructuring of the education and training of mentally defective and retarded children would have involved 'little increased expenditure', they were published in a year of growing economic crisis and little came of them. On 1st August the County Councils' Association warned the Board that it was 'unable to accept any comprehensive obligation for the education of the retarded group of mentally defective children in special schools or classes'. Stirred into action by promptings from the Central Association for Mental Welfare and the Archbishops of Canterbury and York the Board set up an internal committee to consider the implications of the Report in December 1930. Its one positive step seems to have been to respond to the recommendation that schools for mentally defective children should become part of the public elementary school system. It transferred inspection of all special schools from the Medical Branch Inspectorate to the general inspectorate from 1 September 1934. Although the Board was not prepared to press LEAs to adopt arrangements involving additional expenditure on staff or premises, it took to task those that saw the Wood Report as a licence to neglect their assessment procedures or fail to fill vacancies in existing special schools by leaving eligible children in public elementary schools. After the *Annual Report of the Chief Medical Officer for 1933*, in which these strictures appeared, and a chapter published two years later on the diagnosis of mental deficiency, the Board made little further effort before the outbreak of war in 1939 to draw local authorities' attention to the plight of the feeble-minded child.[26]

Most deserving of implementation were the Wood Report's recommendations for training children deemed ineducable. In some cases their parents, despairing of obtaining institutional assistance from either the Board of Education or the Board of Control, put them into poor law institutions. Here they dwelt in an administrative limbo, enjoying the full protection of neither the Mental Deficiency nor the Education Acts. Guardians, seeing them primarily as paupers rather than as children, usually failed to make suitable provision for them. The number of feeble-minded children in poor law institutions, cottage homes, and boarded out by guardians was estimated by the Wood Committee to be about 5,400 in addition to a further 5,000 or more lower-grade children dealt with by the Poor Law Authorities. By contrast the number of children in residential schools run by local authorities and voluntary agencies was around 1,900.[27]

The Report found that 41 per cent of the lower-grade children in the areas surveyed were at home, receiving no form of training or supervision from a local authority. 24 per cent were in ordinary schools, while a further 11 per cent were at day or residential special schools. Only 13 per cent were in institutions maintained by local Mental Deficiency Committees, of whom nearly a third were in poor law institutions. Of the balance, five per cent were in non-certified poor law institutions, with the rest divided between private schools, mental hospitals, cottage homes, and other forms of care. If the child was under the supervision of the Local Mental Deficiency Committee training took place in either an institution or an occupation centre. If the former did not have a school department 'the children are allowed to sit all day or to run wild without any endeavour to instruct or interest them'. Occupation centres, first begun shortly before the outbreak of war in 1914, numbered 111 by 1929, with 1,200 on the registers. Yet there were an estimated 40,000 low-grade children in England and Wales between the ages of seven and sixteen. The training given in each type of institution concentrated on social skills, and simple hand and domestic work, as well as games and music to develop physical coordination. For abler children training and education could approach that of a special school.[28]

The system worked best in towns possessing both an occupation centre and a special school. If, for instance, there was no occupation centre in a town the special school found it had to accept 'ineducable' children, while an occupation centre in a town without a special school had 'educable' children on its register. Undoubtedly cooperation between the Boards of Education and Control in running institutions jointly would have solved many of the problems of doubtful classification, enabling children to transfer from one department to another without any administrative hassle. Unfortunately the Law Lords had ruled that, although the two Departments could contribute to a voluntary organization, they could not combine to build and support a local authority school or centre. The Board of Control's suggestion that they and the Board of Education should ask for amending legislation roused Wood's suspicions of the former's expansionist aims: 'They do not at all like the idea of having to cater only for idiots, imbeciles, and low-grade feeble-minded children.' Although the dividing line between the categories was hard to define 'there is no doubt that it is the policy of the Board of Control to move the line as high as they can'. Newman agreed. The Board of Education had not yet had sufficient experience of the workings of the 1913 and 1914 Acts, the latter seen by him as having been drafted to exclude as many children as possible – like, he might have added, The Mental Deficiency (Notification of Children) Regulations (Cd 7492, 1914). Thus mutual departmental suspicion prevented cooperation on a proposal that could have blurred the psycho-medical, legal and administrative divide between 'educable' and 'ineducable' and between 'training' and 'education', half a century before its removal in 1970.[29]

Children with hearing or visual handicaps and those who suffered from epilepsy faced problems similar to those confronting their less academically able siblings. Surveys made in the early 1920s suggest that the assessment of blind or deaf children could be as much a lottery as that of the feeble-minded. In 1922 there were 24 municipal boroughs claiming to have no blind children. While Dover and its near neighbour Deal claimed an incidence of 0.5 and 5.4 a thousand respectively, Portsmouth and nearby Southampton claimed 0.6 and 3.8 a thousand. A survey of 19 LEAs made the following year showed the percentages of blind children as varying between .002 and .097, while those for partially blind ones ranged between .009 and .349. For deaf children the range was .035 to .140, while partially deaf children showed percentages varying between a nil return, for Bradford, and 0.287. As with the assessment of mental deficiency school medical officers tailored their assessments to suit the length of their special-school cloth. One LEA returned as blind only those children in a blind school or on the waiting list for one, another returned only those children who were completely afflicted despite the definitions contained in the 1893 Act, while a third classified children as blind or sighted according to their proposed future occupation.[30] More serious was the possible mis-classification of children with visual or hearing difficulties as mentally defective. As late as 1936 the Board, describing methods of assessing mentally defective children that were then becoming available, found it expedient to issue this warning:

> Particular care should be given to the testing of the special senses. Where a child is said to be incapable of learning to read, or where his speech is at all defective in articulation . . . a defect of sight or hearing should in the first place be suspected. To apply the ordinary tests of intelligence to a child who is defective in sight or hearing is to do him serious injustice.[31]

The same Report went on to advocate the use of a gramophone audiometer in assessing hearing acuity, an instrument that Andrew Bell had described to the Egerton Committee half a century earlier.

Given the shortage of accommodation, the partially blind or deaf child was less likely to be put in a special school than were his totally afflicted siblings. For example, a ministerial briefing prepared in 1928 admitted that 257 ascertained deaf children did not attend any school while a further 200 were in ordinary schools. With the provision for partially deaf children 'admittedly incomplete', only 500 were in special schools. In addition the Board had reason to believe that a 'good many' had not been ascertained.[32] At the secondary school level prospects were even more bleak for any but a few fortunate parents who were able to secure places for their children at the Worcester College for the Blind, formerly the College for the Blind Sons of Gentlemen (1866), or the Northampton High School for the Deaf. As one mother complained, 'Many like us are forced to send our children to Council Schools to suffer the stigma which . . . attaches to children who cannot boast a public school education, to be taught by *women*. . . . May I appeal to you . . . to plead the cause of the *middle-class* parent of the unfortunate Deaf Child.'[33] However, one remedial step came with the passage of the Education (Deaf Children) Act, 1937, which from 1st April 1938 allowed deaf children to start school at the age of five, as did blind ones, a reform that Newman had wanted at least as long ago as 1913.[34]

A return made by the Permanent Committee on Epileptics of the Charity Organization Society, in 1925, shows the inadequacy of existing accommodation. 203 of the 316 LEAs circularized, the LCC being excluded, replied, covering 78 per cent of the average school attendance. Of 1,939 children suffering from severe epilepsy 379 attended certified special schools, 75 institutions other than special schools, 520 were in public elementary schools, and 965 (49.77 per cent) were in no school or institution. The number in public elementary schools, 520 or 26.82 per cent, exceeded the Board of Education's figure of 467 for the whole of England and Wales of those in ordinary schools, although it was conceded that a number of mild epileptic cases might have been included in the overall total. The numerically greatest offender making no provision was Manchester, with 102 children. Others with more than fifty were Lancashire and Salford. Sheffield, Liverpool, the West Riding of Yorkshire, Derbyshire, Warwickshire, and Kent had 40 to 50 for whom no provision existed. The incidence of cases detected varied from 0.0 a thousand in 16 areas to 2.0 in eight, the average being 0.55 which compared reasonably favourably with the Board's estimate of 0.48 and the LCCs 0.52. Although 68 of 132 LEAs admitted that their accommodation was insufficient, few had considered providing more, and there seemed little prospect of the deficiency being made good. Yet there were 873 epileptic children reported to be sane whose parents would have been prepared to let them go into residential accommodation if it were available. In other words existing accommodation, 525 places, needed to be at least doubled. However, an unofficial ruling on an ambiguity in the Educaion Act, 1921, made the likelihood of further accommodation being provided remote. The Act, after referring to defective and epileptic children, required local authorities to provide residential accommodation for 'forty-five such children' or more. Although this clause came into effect, outside London, on 1st April 1927 the Board delayed its ruling on whether the phrase meant 45 defective and epileptic children in all or 45 defective or 45 epileptic children. At a time of financial stringency the Board decided on the latter, the result being that 'the Section appears to exempt the great majority of authorities from the duty of establishing a Residential School for such [epileptic] children.' A year after sending its unofficial interpretation of the Act to the National Society for Epileptics, it met representatives of the residential schools for epileptic children to discuss means of making the best use of existing resources. With no superintendent of a school prepared to turn his school exclusively over to mentally-defective epileptics, the meeting agreed to a general tightening of admission procedures. As the subsequently published *Health of the School Child Report* indicated there was the possibility of freeing some 60 places if low grade mentally defective children were gradually weeded out. Such children were to be referred to the Mental Deficiency Authority to make room for abler epileptics and reduce the waiting time for admission, which could be as much as two years. This was the first time for twenty years that the annual reports had dealt with epileptic children at any length, an indication of the low priority accorded this group, whom many still thought inevitably deteriorated as they grew older. Thus the six residential schools, certified by the Board as early as 1910, were not augmented until the LCC opened a seventh with 29 places in 1935.[35]

By the late 1930s prospects, both clinically and educationally, for epileptic children were improving. In 1929 Dr Berger developed the process of electroencephalogy, a technique that measures the electrical activity of the brain. After further research this provided a means of assisting in the diagnosis of epilepsy and of distinguishing it from other neurological disorders. The range of anticonvulsant drugs increased, firstly with the development of luminal or phenobarbitone in 1912, a drug that came into use in the USA and Great Britain after clinical trials in the early 1920s. To this were added paraldehyde and phenytoin in 1924 and 1939 respectively.[36] Shortly before the outbreak of war the Board of Education had closely examined 585 cases in 26 LEAs in a survey that helped to refute long-held beliefs about the epileptic child. Nearly a third, 187, were considered slight cases suitable for public elementary schools, just on half, 261, were suitable for residential schools, only 26 were categorized as mentally defective, while a further nine had been notified to or were already in mental institutions. For the first time the Board had a detailed analysis of a large sample of epileptic children and some idea of the nature and extent of the problem and the amount of various types of provision needed.[37]

The Board of Education and other authorities also fostered preventative measures to reduce the demand for special education. Not only did this help to reduce the imbalance between supply and demand but it offered the lure of cost effectiveness. The development of orthopaedic services, Open Air schools, a school medical service, and a rudimentary schools meals service helped to alleviate conditions that, if left untreated, might have brought children within the ambit of the special schools. Medical advances such as the introduction of the Wassermann reaction for syphilis and the discovery of salvarsan made possible more effective treatment of venereal disease. Wartime urgency brought an unparalleled swiftness in implementing the recommendation of the Royal Commission on Venereal Diseases in 1916 that treatment should be free. With the sanctioning of wards where necessary for parturient women with venereal disease, the following year, it became possible to reduce the number of children born with various sight and mental handicaps. Similarly, the compulsory notification of ophthalmia neonatorum, after which its treatment also became generally available, assisted in reducing the number of children born with sight defects.[38] The provision of beds in municipal hospitals for whooping cough, measles, and scarlet fever, a complaint that became less virulent in the twentieth century, all helped to reduce the sequelae of these diseases. The net effect of such measures, requiring more discussion than can be attempted here, must remain a matter of speculation for medical science, but the extension of public health facilities undoubtedly helped to keep children alive who might previously have died of their physical or mental impairment.

The introduction of child guidance clinics provided the means for treating children considered emotionally or psychologically disturbed, in an attempt to improve their classroom performance or behaviour. Although the study of child development has a respectable ancestry running from Plato, through Comenius, Rousseau and Pestalozzi, to Froebel, it only began to receive specialist attention towards the end of the nineteenth century. Early pioneers such as Herbert Spencer and G. Stanley Hall were not essentially concerned with the wide range of individual differences, and it was Francis Galton who deserves the credit for being the first practitioner of a form of individual child guidance. After conducting tests on a child at his anthropometric laboratory, he would recommend treatment for him at home or school, and give advice on the career he should choose. John Sully, who founded the British Child Study Association, the forerunner of similar branches in the provinces, distinguished in his *Studies in Childhood* (1895) three main types of deviation: intellectual dulness, emotional instability, and deviation from commonly accepted moral conduct. To him the so-called abnormal child, in the vast majority of cases, was a maladjusted one, that is he had not adjusted himself to his environment. He was not a pathological defect. After the 1899 Act the experience of teachers in special schools, who found that in some cases they were able to return their charges to ordinary schools after tuition in smaller groups, and the realization that so-called moral defectives could become well behaved on removal from their previous environment, raised the question of the wisdom of leaving the selection of children for special education to doctors. Such doubts led to the appointment of Cyril Burt as child psychologist to the LCC in 1913, at first on a part-time basis, the first such appointment in the country. In 1920 Dr Crichton Miller established the Institute of Medical Psychology, later known as the Tavistock Clinic, the children's branch of which received recognition from the University of London for training postgraduate students in child guidance. Through the initiative of Mrs St Loe Strachey, a JP with considerable experience of juvenile courts, and her husband, the editor of the *Spectator*, an approach was made to the Commonwealth Fund of New York for assistance. Although there was now some postgraduate training in child guidance there was no systematic psychiatric or psychological training in the universities or elsewhere in the courses run for probation officers, home visitors, care committee workers, and similar social workers.[39] Thus when the Charity Organization Society, which was supporting the project, wrote to the Board of Education, it adopted a defensive stance: 'It is possible that the idea of child guidance might suggest psycho-analysis or other psychiatric devices which do not command universal confidence, and which are in any case too new to expect a complete recognition from a great public authority like the Board of Education.' The letter went on to reassure the Board about the solid and conservative character of the Fund's work in New York by instancing their publications, *The Problem Child in School* (1926) and *Three Problem Children*. To oversee the project the Central Association for Mental Welfare formed a sub-committee, the Child Guidance Council, which with the parent body had Miss Evelyn Fox as its honorary secretary.[40]

One feature of the beginnings of the study of child psychology had been a reassessment of the young delinquent, who became seen not so much as a youngster embarking on a lifelong career of crime, but as a person passing through a period of emotional and behavioural disturbance. The study of juvenile crime, and even of criminology as a whole, had received little attention in the half-century following the appearance of Mary Carpenter's works in the 1850s. On the Continent, following the founding of the Société d'Anthropologie de Paris in 1859, a number of racial anthropologists had become interested in the subject, amongst whom was Cesare Lombroso whose *L'Uomo di genio* and *L'Uomo delinquente* appeared in 1888 and 1889 respectively. Havelock Ellis, translator of Lombroso's earlier work, published *The Criminal* in 1890, for which Lombroso had provided the main inspiration and to whom he owed the idea 'that the criminal and the genius were complementary forms of degeneration'. Here, despite his interest in physiognomy, he argued for a more scientific study of crime.[41] By this time the British Parliament had passed the Probation of First Offenders Act, 1887, some nine years after the State of Massachusetts had introduced its first probation law. The Probation of Offenders Act, 1907, rectified one of the main deficiencies of the earlier Act which had failed to make provision for the appointment of official probation officers. In England the first juvenile court opened in 1905, six years after the State of Illinois had introduced separate juvenile courts; the first such court at Chicago soon began to take into consideration reports from the Juvenile Research Department of the University of Chicago when dealing with children. In England Parliament passed the Prevention of Crimes Act, which set up the Borstal system, and the Children Act, in 1908. The latter Act ordered the creation of juvenile courts throughout the country, gave officiating magistrates a wide range of discretionary powers and abolished imprisonment under the age of sixteen unless the offender was 'of so unruly a character that he cannot be detained in a place of detention provided under this . . . act'. In accordance with recommendations in the *Report of the Departmental Committee on Reformatory and Industrial Schools* (1911) the Home Office started the Children's Branch in 1914 to oversee reformatories, industrial schools, juvenile courts, the probation service, street trading, and other matters affecting children.[42] By the mid-1920s, with the publication of Cyril Burt's *The Young Delinquent*, there had come about a better understanding of both the child thought to be intellectually retarded and the one prone to anti-social conduct. In both cases there was an infinite degree of variation between the 'normal' and the 'abnormal'. In his report for 1925 Newman quoted from Burt's recently published work:

> This graded continuity, the normal meeting with the abnormal by almost imperceptible shades, is entirely in accord with what we now know of most other forms of mental deviation. The insane, the neurotic, the mentally deficient, are none of them to be thought as types apart'. . . . It is the same with the moral faults of children; they run in an uninterrupted series, from the most heartless and persistent of crimes . . . to the mere occasional naughtiness to which the most virtuous will at times give way.[43]

Through the generosity of the Commonwealth Fund of New York Dr Ralph Crawley, the Board's senior medical officer, visited the USA where child guidance clinics were already working in conjunction with children's courts handling cases of delinquency, or with an educational, health, or hospital service dealing with cases of functional neurosis and family problems. In addition philanthropic societies were referring children before initiating boarding-out procedures. England, apart from the Tavistock Clinic, could offer only the clinic at the Jewish Free

School, the work of Drs Shrubsall, Auden, and Hughes in London, Birmingham, and Stoke-on-Trent, and a recently established clinic in Bath.[44]

Initially child guidance clinics had to look to outside support for financial aid, as did the East London Clinic and the London Child Guidance Clinic. A number owed their origins to the enthusiasm of individual psychologists, psychiatrists, and school medical officers who became interested in this work. In such instances local appeals and charitable funds met the daily running expenses. However, the Board in 1932 approved expenditure on a clinic at Oxford at the same time stipulating that the example was not to be taken as a precedent for approving such expenditure as part of the school medical service. It reversed this decision three years later in less financially austere circumstances when it approved a grant for Birmingham's clinic. By the late 1930s there were 37 clinics represented on the Child Guidance Council, together with an unknown number not represented, perforce geographically scattered. Children from Blackpool, for example, had to travel to Liverpool or Manchester, a considerable undertaking for a mentally disturbed patient. Initially teachers seem to have referred backward children but gradually, by 1939, children with behavioural problems and functional neuroses became more typical of those sent.[45]

As with other aspects of the development of special education the early history of child guidance clinics had followed a traditional path. First there had been the efforts of voluntary pioneers, eager to make use of a new expertise and try out new ideas, then with growing credibility had come a wider demand for a service that voluntary agencies could not meet, and finally the state had supplemented these earlier efforts. On the other hand reliance on local initiative, whether voluntary or official, and the intervention of the Great War, followed by years of financial stringency that were only beginning to ease just before the outbreak of another war, meant that the provision of special education services was still incomplete. An unknown number of children, because of their geographical location or the inadequacy of the assessment process, to mention just two factors, suffered physical or mental handicaps that remained untreated either by the school medical service or by the special schools, while others remained officially 'ineducable'.

FROM BUTLER TO WARNOCK

Discussions on the post-war structure of the education system for England and Wales began with the publication of a Green Paper, classified as 'Strictly Confidential', followed for a wider audience by the White Paper, *Educational Reconstruction* (Cmnd 6458). In both papers handicapped children appeared in chapters dealing with the health and welfare of children, a practice dating from their inclusion as one of the topics covered in the annual reports in the Board's chief medical officer. The 1941 Paper, while acknowledging that much of the accommodation for blind and deaf children was old and inconveniently distributed, found it quantitatively adequate, a tribute more to the declining incidence of these handicaps than to the lavishness of earlier provision. The White Paper of 1943 dismissed special education in a short paragraph, evidence perhaps not so much that 'the foundations of reform had already been laid' but of the low priority legislators, administrators, and the general public attached to the needs of the handicapped child.[1]

While it is true to say that the consolidating Act of 1921 had been the first to include the education of handicapped children in a general education Act, such children had remained a separate category relegated to a special section. The 1944 Act however brought them in theory, if not in administrative practice, into the mainstream of education. In carrying out its new statutory duty of providing adequately for pupils of different ages, abilities, and aptitudes, LEAs were to have particular regard to securing provision for pupils 'suffering from any disability of mind or body by providing, either in special schools or otherwise, special educational treatment'. Where the disability was serious, education where practicable was to be given in special schools; where this was impracticable or the disability less serious education could be given elsewhere.[2] In other words LEAs could continue to use ordinary schools providing a pupil's disability was not serious and the school made any necessary special arrangements required for coping with it. Although the change in terminology from 'defect' to 'handicap' and 'disability' suggested a greater understanding and sympathy, the existing structure of special education remained basically unchanged, in contrast to the post-war reconstruction of other fields of education, matters that had aroused far more public concern.

The new Act abolished certification, a process associated with the procedures under which patients had been admitted to lunatic asylums; such children now became known as educationally sub-normal. Instead there was to be an assessment of all children over the age of two whose disability, whether of mind or body, appeared to be of such a nature as to make them incapable of receiving education in an ordinary school. Under regulations issued in 1945 and further elaborated in *Special Educational Treatment* (1946) the minister defined eleven categories of disability, all of which had received at least tacit recognition before. For instance, although the 1893 Act had recognized only blind and deaf children, a number of authorities had made provision for the new groups of partially blind and partially deaf children whose education, in both cases, had been the subject matter of pre-war reports. Diabetic children, whose chances of survival had improved following the isolation in 1921 of insulin, a complex protein, were a new category only to be included amongst 'delicate children' in 1955. While children with speech defects formed a new grouping, there had been some pre-war division for the asphasic. Again the maladjusted child, administratively a new phenomenon, had had his existence tacitly recognized once the Board of Education started to give grants to Child Guidance Clinics.[3]

The triumphs and occasional failures of medical science, together with a rise in the standard of living, smaller and wider-spread families, improved housing, and other forms of environmental reform over the previous sixty years, had brought considerable changes in the type of physical handicap from which pupils now suffered. Before 1914 the chief disabling diseases suffered by children in cripple schools, as they then were known, had been tuberculosis of the bones and joints. This condition had accounted for the presence of three-quarters of the pupils in special schools in Manchester and Birmingham. By 1964 the number of children in all the special schools in England and Wales so affected had fallen to 31, whereas in 1912 there had been 863 in London's day schools alone.[4]

The incidence of rheumatic fever, once a scourge of childhood, also declined. In the twelve areas in England and Wales, where juvenile rheumatism was a notifiable disease, the incidence fell from 5.5 per 10,000 children under the age of fifteen in 1948 to 0.5 per 10,000 by 1963. By 1970 there were 704 children with either rheumatic or congenital heart disease in special schools in England and Wales, whereas in 1937

Manchester alone had had 575 children under supervision with heart disease. By the end of 1945 Manchester had 12 in its special schools with a further 15 on the waiting list. By the end of 1964 the number of children in all the special schools in England and Wales suffering from a rheumatic heart condition was 76. The fall in their numbers now made children with congenital heart disease the majority, thus reversing the situation prevailing twenty years earlier. The provision of cardio-rheumatic clinics after the Second World War enabled diagnosis to distinguish between those with innocent heart murmurs from those requiring treatment. Developments in surgery enabled a growing proportion of children with congenital heart disease to attend ordinary schools whereas earlier they would have required special ones.[5]

With a decline in cases of tuberculosis of the joints and of rheumatic fever the commonest disability suffered by children in special schools became cerebral palsy. Commonly known as spastics, sufferers' motor and sensory deficiencies led to an underestimation of their scholastic abilities. 'As far as is known at present, there are not many cerebral palsied children who are capable of tackling grammar school work', declared the Ministry of Education in 1954. However, the opening of schools specifically for cerebral palsied children gave them opportunities previously denied when they had been educated in schools for the physically handicapped generally. More recent findings suggest that about a quarter of all cerebral palsied children are of average or above average intelligence.[6]

Second to cerebral palsied children, who accounted for a third of all physically handicapped children in special schools in 1970, were those with spina bifida forming nearly one-sixth of the pupils. A series of surgical techniques developed in the 1950s and 1960s not only increased the life expectancy of such children but also made it possible for them to attend school. The ileal bladder operation, combined with new techniques for mastering incontinence, made them more acceptable in the classroom. The fitting of a Spitz-Holter valve made possible the draining off of excess cerebrospinal fluid in treating the associated condition of hydrocephalus, while early surgery could improve the chances of survival for babies born with meningomyelocele, the protusion of a portion of the spinal cord and its enclosing membranes through a bony defect. A survey of babies treated in the neonatal surgical unit at Sheffield between 1959 and 1964 showed that out of every hundred babies treated, 70 lived of whom 55 then had normal mental development. The Department of Education and Science, anticipating an increase in the number for whom education would have to be provided, asked all LEAs in 1967 to review the likely demand for places for spina bifida children when formulating their building programmes. To encourage LEAs to take appropriate action, the following year the DES promised priority to those programmes that included such provision. The first special school for these children had been provided by the Shaftesbury Society in 1959, and a nursery school was added to it in 1967. By the end of the decade two more schools had opened or were at the planning stage.[7]

When LEAs were asked in 1954 to supply information about physically handicapped children awaiting admission to special schools, the group second in size to cerebral palsied children was those with post-poliomyelitis. The outbreaks in 1947 and 1950 were larger even than in 1955, when the 6,331 reported cases that year were treble those of 1954. The disease tended to attack the young, with over two-thirds of those affected being under the age of fifteen in both 1954 and 1955. Its incidence began to fall following the inauguration of an inoculation programme for young children in the summer of 1956. By 1961, with the Sabin oral vaccine available in England, the number of notified cases had fallen to 874. It dropped to 51 two years later, and 16 by 1967. As post-poliomyelitis cases gradually worked their way through the school system, numbers fell from 674 in 1964 to 316 six years later.[8] While the number of these cases fell, there was a sudden increase in the number of those born with limb deformities. Between 1958 and 1961 some 250 children whose mothers, while pregnant, had taken thalidomide, a sedative drug, were affected in this way. More than half were able to attend ordinary primary schools with support from their teachers and the local medical services. Studies of their subsequent progress showed a normal spread of ability and achievement.[9]

By the mid-1950s blindness in children was largely the result of congenital, hereditary, and developmental defects. Thanks to improved perinatal services the prevention of ophthalmia neonatorum, phlyctenular ophthalmia, and interstitial keratitis had been the main factor in reducing the number of blind children over the previous twenty-five years. For instance, the number of cases of ophthalmia neonatorum fell from 5,050 in 1937 to 606 thirty years later. While in 1925 36.9 per 100,000 children aged between five and fifteen had been registered as blind, by 1950 the proportion had fallen to 21.1 only to rise to 24.3 by 1954. During the same period overall numbers fell from 2,720 to 1,364 but rose to 1,680 by 1955. Much of the increase of the early 1950s resulted from the excessive use of oxygen on premature babies, a practice that produced retrolental fibroplasia, a disease first identified in 1942. By 1955 its cause was discovered and the number of babies so afflicted fell. While 38.4 per cent of children born blind between 1951 and 1955 had suffered from this condition, the proportion fell to 10 per cent over the next five years: 'Seldom has a disease, so apparently enigmatic in its causation, so intractable to treatment and so tragic in its effects, been so rapidly brought under control.'[10]

Under pre-war legislation special education was only available to partially-sighted children if they were classified as blind. *The Report of the Board of Education on Partially Sighted Children* (1934) had recommended that such children be taught in ordinary schools, providing attention was given to their need for good lighting and other requirements. Only two schools had implemented this suggestion by 1939. Consequently partially-sighted children had to attend such blind schools as were prepared to accommodate them, a practice the Committee had condemned. It also called for a relaxation in the existing school curriculum, advocating only short periods of reading and writing, and the avoidance of strenuous physical exercise. Although three blind schools became available for partially-sighted scholars soon after the end of war in 1945, there remained a general reluctance to liberalize the curriculum. Accordingly the Ministry ran a conference in 1947 to persuade teachers and others that they could safely follow the 1934 Committee's advice. In an attempt to wean medical officers and others away from older attitudes, *The Health of the School Child* (1949) contained a summary of the conference proceedings and a synopsis of the existing state of medical and ophthalmological opinion, in support of the Ministry's contentions. When the Vernon Committee on the Education of the Visually Handicapped met in the late 1960s it found that in one respect little had changed since 1934: 'Comparatively little experience has been gained in this country of educating visually-handicapped children in ordinary schools.' Possibly as a result of this its members reversed their predecessors' recommendations. Blind and partially-sighted children should be taught in the same schools. However in 1977, five years after the publication of the report, there were only two schools, with a total of 221 pupils, that provided for both blind and partially sighted children; the remaining 1,017 blind and 1,559 partially sighted were still in separate schools.[11]

The number of deaf children in special schools had remained remarkably static between 1908 and 1946, rising by only 43 to reach 3,461 by the end of the war. Over the next ten years a variety of factors combined to raise the total to 5,206. Not only did LEAs have a definite duty towards the partially deaf as well as to the deaf but the 1944 Act required them to begin assessing all children who were in possible need of special education, at the age of two. This was of particular benefit to partially hearing children as it enabled training to begin at the most important stage of a child's life, that is, under the age of three. Certain special circumstances also increased the numbers requiring special education. Following an outbreak of rubella in 1940, it was found that mothers who were infected during the first three months of their pregnancy could give birth to children with a hearing defect, or cataract, or both. Other possible disabilities included heart problems and impaired intelligence. The use of streptomycin in treating tubercular meningitis added to the toll by saving some lives at the expense of making some recipients of the drug deaf. Last, the lowering of the school age from seven to five had added to the numbers in deaf schools.

In the long term the most important factor was an improvement in the process of assessment. The training of health visitors in testing a baby's hearing, the use of the Sweep Frequency Test, the building of audiology centres in hospitals and health centres, made failure to detect a child's hearing impairment less likely. By 1967, for the first time, the number of ascertained partially deaf children, 3,307, outnumbered the deaf, 3,118. Although the Ministry of Education had conducted a survey in 1960 to find out how many audiometers were used in the school health service and had issued a joint circular with the Ministry of Health the following year, a decade later not all LEAs had satisfactory assessment procedures. Of the 146 asked for returns in 1971, one significantly failed to comply with the DES's request, while 18 still did not arrange routine audiometry tests for all school entrants at the age of five. Moreover, ten of these authorities did not screen the hearing of all infants. In global terms, 60 per cent of all school children had their hearing tested as a matter of routine during their first year at school, 26 per cent during their second year, 4.5 per cent at a later stage, while 7.8 per cent either had no tests or had them only on referral. (Unfortunately the return did not require LEAs to state how often they used the calibration service provided by the Royal National Institute for the Deaf, which began in 1962.) Last, two other developments in the education of the deaf in the post-war years require noting. The supply of hearing aids through the National Health Service – 714 in 1957 and 6,006 in 1967 – allowed an increasing number of children with a hearing defect to attend ordinary schools. In common with audiometers these required inspection and servicing, as a pilot scheme run by the RNID in 1967 discovered. Just how effective the testing and the prescribed remedy (the hearing aid) were, must remain a matter of some speculation. For some children, also, the quality of education improved following the opening of a grammar school for the deaf in 1946 and of a school for boys with a technical and art bias ten years later.[12]

It will be remembered that the Board of Education had recognized expenditure on child guidance as falling within the remit of the Education Act, 1921, before war broke out in 1939. By that year there were 17 clinics wholly maintained and five partially maintained by LEAs, as well as a further 46 schools for 'nervous, difficult, and retarded children' approved by the Child Guidance Council and the Central Association for Mental Welfare. The evacuation of children to reception areas in September 1939 made a number of children, previously manageable at school and at home, unbilletable as they had become emotionally disturbed following their arrival in an alien environment. Special hostels for such children became part of the government evacuation scheme. Where possible staff attached to existing child guidance clinics practised in them. By this means and through the wartime dispersal of staff the number of clinics had increased to 79 by 1945. Under the Education Act, 1944, the Minister, who now had a specific responsibility for maladjusted children, approved some of these hostels as schools.[13]

In the immediate aftermath of war doubts grew about the provision being made by the Ministry of Education for its newly-acquired responsibility, the maladjusted child. The publication of D. H. Stott's *Delinquency and Human Nature* (1950) reinforced the conviction that if maladjustment in childhood could be properly treated, juvenile delinquency would diminish. The lure of cost effectiveness finally produced action. George Tomlinson, then Minister of Education, announced the appointment of the Underwood Committee in October 1950. When the committee reported in 1955 it found such a severe shortage of public-sector accommodation that LEAs had to make extensive use of independent schools. In December 1954, while there were 1,077 maladjusted children in voluntarily run schools, there were 1,157 in maintained boarding schools with a further 681 children waiting up to six months or longer for places. There were also three day special schools, one in Oxford dating from 1930, a second founded two years later in Leicester, and a third in London which had only opened in 1954. In addition the LCC provided 17 part-time day special classes, the only authority in the country to do so. Overall, the number of children receiving some form of day treatment but excluding attendance at a child guidance clinic, in proportion to those in boarding schools, was one in seven.[14]

As the maladjusted child formed a new category for which the Ministry now had responsibility, a major task facing the Committee was that of estimating potential demand for the new service, a matter on which there had been little research. For the guidance of LEAs in planning their services the Ministry had estimated in 1946 that about one per cent of pupils aged five to fifteen would require special educational treatment, an estimate the Committee understood to refer to any one year. On the assumption that the figure referred to new cases the committee estimated that over the ten-year span of compulsory education five per cent of the school population would need treatment at some time during their school careers. Pilot surveys made by three LEAs possessing well-developed child guidance services, Berkshire, Birmingham, and Somerset, produced estimates of 5.4, 7.7, and 11.8 per cent respectively. Not only did these figures include children whose disability had previously remained unrecognized in areas where the chances of detection should have been high, but the differences between them illustrate the wide range of criteria adopted by the three authorities. By taking eight per cent as the average of these surveys, the Committee argued that the proportion of children requiring treatment at any time in an LEA with fully developed facilities was approaching two per cent. Unfortunately, there was plenty of evidence in the Report to show that the areas surveyed were the exception rather than the rule in making adequate provision.[15]

After approaching 32 of the 96 LEAs that had a child guidance service the Committee based its staffing recommendations on the authorities' perceived needs. The total number of child guidance staff needed for England and Wales was the equivalent of 140 full-time psychiatrists, 280 educational psychologists, and 420 psychiatric social workers. Yet in 1955 the number of full-time equivalents in post was 56, 141, and 109 respectively. The target establishment would have provided one team for every 45,000 school children, in spite of Essex LEA's experience that one team could only cope with 35,000. Although proportionally and absolutely the greatest increase was to be in the number of psychiatric social workers, the Underwood target was still 80 less than that recommended by the *Report of the Committee on Social Workers in the Mental Health Services* (the Mackintosh Committee) four years earlier.[16]

Despite the expansion of training facilities and improvements in pay the Underwood Committee's pious hope, that 'it would indeed be gratifying if the comparatively modest objective we have set were attained during the next decade', was never realized. During the 1960s child guidance clinics had to compete with the increasing demands for staff made by the health and welfare services. 1959 was the year of publication of the Younghusband Committee's Report, *Social Workers in the Mental Health Services* (Cmnd 8260) which forecast that these services would require 240 full-time officers within ten years. The Mental Health Act of the same year, with its emphasis on a 'change from custody to care and from care to treatment', further intensified demand for social workers and others trained in psychological and psychiatric skills. However, while in 1955 there had been 50 LEAs with no child guidance facilities at all, by the early 1960s the DES could guardedly report that all areas had some form of child guidance service.[17]

Further pressure for improving staffing levels came from both official and unofficial bodies. In 1960 the Royal Medico-Psychological Association backed Essex LEAs estimate that one team was needed for every 35,000 children. The report of the Summerfield Committee, *Psychologists in the Education Services* (1968), wanted one educational psychologist to every 10,000 children. In turn the Warnock Committee more than doubled this by advocating one to every 5,000 children and young persons under the age of nineteen. Seventeen years after the publication of the Underwood Report the 638 educational psychologists in post comfortably exceeded the Underwood target of 386 but fell short of the Summerfield figure of 850. The 163 child psychologists, not all of them in the consultant grade and thirty short of the Underwood requirement, had reached two-thirds of the RM-PA's goal of 243. Last, the 438 psychiatric social workers were 141 short of the Underwood total of 579 and 291 short of the Summerfield Committee's. The global figures mask regional disparities. In and around London the clinics had more child psychiatric staff than the RM-PA had thought necessary, while the South-East and South-West had generally met the Underwood criteria. Elsewhere, apart from Wales, the number of psychiatrists in service was still less than half Underwood's recommendations.

The demand for the services of the child guidance clinics seemed almost open-ended once the new services started. Although the number of clinics doubled between 1955 and 1972, as did the proportion of children treated which rose from four to eight per 1,000, each clinic despite its better staffing dealt with only three more cases a year. In other words more generous staffing produced more in-depth treatment, not greater productivity. Further studies suggested that some earlier estimates of the incidence of various forms of mental and emotional disturbance needed to be revised upwards. An Isle of Wight survey revealed that 6.8 per cent of the ten-to-eleven year-old age group needed some form of treatment, while a national survey put 14 per cent of the seven-year-old group in the maladjusted category, levels well above the estimate made in 1955 that one to two per cent of the child population would require treatment at any one time. Although the Underwood Committee had underestimated the strength of potential demand for child guidance services, it had seen the necessity for expanding existing special school provision through more day special schools and classes. Not only did non-residential facilities have the attraction of being cheaper than boarding schools, but they could be seen as therapeutically acceptable by making treatment of the family as a unit possible. Day treatment also forestalled any parental opposition that placement in a boarding school might have aroused. By the end of 1971 there were 2,133 maladjusted children in special classes. The previous January, with 83 day maintained classes, 3,914 day children slightly exceeded the 3,774 boarders.[18]

Mentally defective children, known after 1945 as educationally subnormal (ESN) and estimated as ten per cent of all school children, formed the largest handicapped group. They encompassed feebleminded, dull, and backward children, a group the Wood Report had renamed 'retarded'. The cut-off point between 'educable' and 'ineducable' remained at the Wood Report's level of an IQ of 50 to 55. LEAs were firmly reminded of the consequences of misplaced kindness:

> In the past, numbers of children who have been recognized by their teachers and even by School Medical Officers to be ineducable or detrimental to others, have, on sentimental grounds, been allowed to attend school. In future this practice should cease. One detrimental or low-grade child in a class can cause havoc in a class. . . . It is too great a price to pay. . . . He should be reported to the local mental deficiency authority.

The balance, with IQs between 50 to 55 and 80 now became the sub-normal groups.[19]

Leaving aside the controversies over selection procedures for secondary education at the age of eleven, the division between 'educable' and 'ineducable' made in section 57 of the 1944 Act caused more parental anguish than any other part of the Act. A departmental minute shows that in the year ending 31 March 1955 section 57 attracted 319 appeals, a figure that made it easily outstrip the next most contentious clause, s.90 dealing with the compulsory purchase of land, against which there were 78 appeals. Section 116, which excluded persons of unsound mind and those detained by a court order under various lunacy and mental treatment acts, attracted criticism from the Socialist Medical Association on grounds that George Newman would have approved. As 'a child may vary in its capacity for education at different times', a once and for all decision about its fate was manifestly unjust.[20]

A table published by the Department of Education and Science in 1972 suggests that doctors became progressively less ready to certify children as ineducable. The proportion of appeals halved between 1951 and 1969, falling from 5.8 per thousand to 2.9. Over the same years appeals from parents of children deemed ineducable fell from 11.6 per cent to 6.09 from 1966 onwards. The proportion of children the Department's own medical staff examined, which for most years up to 1965 was one-third, but as high as 40 per cent in 1960 and 1964, had fallen to 14.3 per cent by 1969. Such trends suggest that medical officers were only certifying as ineducable those children with the severest learning difficulties, whose parents realized that appeals stood little chance of success.[21]

The period covered by this return was one in which a more sympathetic and informed attitude towards mental illness and handicap was developing in certain circles. 'We believe that most people today would at least pay lip-service to the principle . . . that the mentally ill are sick people and that mental hospitals should be thought of primarily as hospitals for the treatment of illness', professed the Report of the Royal Commission on the Law Relating to Mental Illness and Handicap. Their admission that 'Few people know what the distinction between mental deficiency and mental illness is', possibly tempered their optimism. Despite half a century of development in mental testing they found an overlap between the type of child in special schools in some areas and those in occupation centres in others. One suggested remedy was to build more special schools to take children of a lower level of ability. For children referred to a training centre, the Commission recommended the extension of the Education Act, 1944, to make attendance there or at a hospital during the years they were required to attend school.[22] The subsequent Mental Health Act, 1959, gave local health authorities the duty of providing training for children of compulsory school age 'suffering from a disability of mind'.[23]

However, neither the 1944 nor the 1959 Acts defined education or training, an unfortunate omission as the earlier Act required local education authorities to ensure children received efficient full-time education suitable to their ages, abilities, and aptitudes. The 1957 Report gave some guidance: 'The basis of occupation centre training is habit training, teaching the children to keep themselves clean and to feed and dress themselves, sense training to improve alertness, movement and speech, and carefully graduated handwork of all kinds.' There could also be instruction in reading, writing, and arithmetic for those thought capable of developing a rudimentary understanding of writing and figures.[24]

Meanwhile the credibility of the eleven-plus examination as a means of selecting children accurately for a grammar, technical or secondary modern school education had come under attack. In 1957 one survey concluded that 10 per cent, or about 60,000 children a year, were sent to the wrong type of school. Two years later the *Crowther Report, 15–18*, suggested that the major impulse for the establishment of extended courses in secondary modern schools was the realization that classification, however accurate it might seem when made, became inaccurate with the passage of time: 'The longer the period for which a system of selection is asked to predict, the greater the subsequent need for redistribution.' By the age of 15 about 14 per cent of pupils should have been redistributed between selective and non-selective schools; by the time of enlistment for National Service this 14 per cent had become 29 per cent in the case of RAF recruits.

> The problem is not confined to selection for secondary schools. It occurs whenever it is necessary to select candidates – for employment quite as much as for education. With human beings, no selection can be regarded as final.[25]

The declining lack of confidence in the effectiveness of the eleven-plus examination as a predictor of future academic performance, a topic that can only be briefly sketched here, was one of a number of factors that led to the publication of Circular 10/65 in July 1965 announcing the government's declared intention of ending selection at eleven-plus and eliminating separatism in secondary education.

Once this change in policy was announced it became less easy to justify a system by which children were tested for their suitability for training or education. Just over a year later the Central Council for Education (England) published its report *Children and Their Primary Schools* (the Plowden Report). Members heard evidence casting doubt on the efficacy of selection at the lower end of the ability range: 'Some witnesses have made the point that there can be no firm and accurate division between children who are suitable for "education" and those who are not.' The Report quoted findings of a study made by the British Psychological Society on 155 testable children in a hospital for the subnormal. 24 per cent had IQs over 50, 14 per cent over 70, and four per cent over 100. The Committee also remarked on the delay that occurred in identifying educationally subnormal children. While one in four physically handicapped children in a special school was under the age of eight in 1964, the corresponding figure for the educationally subnormal child was one in eighteen. To minimize parental anguish the Report suggested that the term 'educationally subnormal' be replaced by 'slow learners', a term which implied a common ground between children in special schools and those in normal ones. This followed a study of 17,000 babies born in March 1958, tested for their ability to read seven years later, which had shown that half the sample had 'not achieved a sufficient mastery of this subject . . . to use it as an effective tool for future learning, while a further 24 per cent were either non-readers or poor readers.'[26]

1966 was also the year in which the Guild of Teachers of Backward Children approached the Ministry of Health and the Department of Education and Science for an enquiry into special education needs. In November 1967 Sir Edward Boyle pressed for a committee to study all aspects of special education needs including those children excluded from the school system: 'I think we ought to consider their needs very closely.'[27]

A year later the government announced its intention of transferring the junior training centres to the DES, a promise it kept when it introduced the Education (Miscellaneous Provisions) Bill in 1970. Although this failed to reach the statute book that year because of the dissolution of parliament, the new administration reintroduced the relevant clauses in the Education (Handicapped Children) Bill which received the Royal Assent in July 1970.

The Under Secretary for State for the DES, William van Straub-enzee, stated that the progress made in special educational techniques justified the proposed changes:

Experience has . . . led many of those who are concerned to the conclusion that every child, no matter how severely handicapped, should have the opportunity to develop to the fullest extent of which he is capable, and that it cannot be right to exclude any child from the scope of the educational services.[28]

Members also showed their concern for the plight of the autistic child, whose condition had first been defined in 1942. Earlier the condition had led to diagnoses such as childhood schizophrenia or childhood psychosis, and it still remained easy to confuse sufferers with the mentally retarded. The National Society for Autistic Children, established in 1962, in one survey had found 60 of 460 children aged five to 14 in mental hospitals because they had been wrongly classified. With the number of autistic children variously estimated at 5,000 to 7,000 there could have been a thousand children in this situation. Specialist schools for autistic children were a recent development, the first having opened in 1965. By 1970 there were 250 school places, most of which were in the south of England. Those of the remaining children who were in large understaffed institutions were particularly vulnerable, for their condition easily led to neglect. Of other mentally handicapped children in hospital in 1970, about half attended hospital schools, while the other half were ward-bound. Overall the transfer of functions from the Ministry of Health to the DES affected 32,837 children in various institutions on 31 December 1969. Of these 7,711 were in-patients in subnormality hospitals while the remainder attended junior training centres or special care units. The 1,340 attending independent establishments made a grand total of 34,177 ascertained under the Education Act, 1944, as being unsuitable for school. This represented 3.3 per thousand of the two to 15 year-old child population. Yet the DES knew that some of these children had an IQ over 50 and that others were under the age of two. Since recent surveys had put the incidence of severe mental handicap at 3.7 a thousand, it was clear that a considerable number were still escaping the LEAs' screening processes.[29]

The new Act brought the number of handicapped children attending or awaiting admission to special schools to around 145,000, two-thirds of whom were in ESN schools which were either ESN(M) for the 'moderately' or ESN(S) for the 'severely educationally subnormal', terms defined for use in the Mental Health Act, 1959. By 1977 the number of children in special schools in England and Wales had reached 176,688 or 1.8 per cent of the school population. Quantitatively this was a remarkable achievement, for the number of special school places had fallen from 51,152 to 38,499 during the course of the Second World War, only reaching 60,417 in 1957.[30]

There still remained the problem of securing some degree of nationwide uniformity of assessment. In 1970 the number of handicapped children receiving special education could vary between 52.5 per 10,000 of school population in one LEA and 220.6 in another. The greatest discrepancies in a sample of nine authorities were amongst the educationally subnormal, whose proportions receiving special education ranged from 13.5 per 10,000 to 116.5. In January 1977 the proportions ascertained as in need of special education ranged from below 120 per 10,000 in certain predominantly rural areas to over 300 in a few LEAs in better equipped large urban areas. Variations between the ascertainment of specific handicaps were even wider. For example one London borough had apparently ten times as many maladjusted children as another. Such differences could not be accounted for by social and environmental factors alone. As ever, they also reflected variations in local policy, the commitment individual LEAs had to various branches of special education, the strength and availability of the relevant assessment services, and a tendency to tailor the thoroughness of assessment to the availability of special school accommodation, child guidance clinics, and other services.[31]

As regards the Education Act, 1981, the Plowden Report was in many ways a seminal document. It endorsed the current policy of the DES, enshrined in the 1944 Act and reiterated in Circular 276 of 1954: 'No handicapped child should be sent to a special school who can be satisfactorily educated in an ordinary school.' Nearly all witnesses to the Plowden Committee agreed that 'the unnecessary segregation of the handicapped is neither good for them nor for those with whom they must associate. They should be in an ordinary school wherever possible.' As well as questioning the validity of the concepts 'educable' and 'ineducable' the Report called into question the practical utility of the categories of handicap into which the DES's regulations divided handicapped children, a list that omitted the child with acute and prolonged difficulties in learning to read. The assessment of a child, which should begin at as early an age as possible, the Report saw as a continuous, not once-and-for-all, process that required the cooperation of teacher, doctors, and parents. The latter required advice and support and to be associated as closely as possible with their child's education. They also needed a counselling service, which should be available as soon as the handicap was identified, in order to coordinate all the services involved in their child's welfare and future – health visitors, doctors, teachers, hospital almoners, and others. Teachers in training were to be equipped to help deal with slow-learning and other handicapped children in ordinary schools. Last, there was a need for a detailed enquiry to be made into the needs of handicapped children and the provision made for them. Seven years later in a written answer Margaret Thatcher, Secretary of State for the DES, announced her intention of appointing a committee that was to be headed by Mrs (later Lady) H. M. Warnock.[32]

Meanwhile the National Bureau for Co-operation in Child Care had published *Living with Handicap* (1970). Significantly, its first chapter gave a detailed account of the harrowing experiences of parents whose children had been born handicapped; the financial hardship to those on low incomes, a sense of social isolation, and the sheer lack of information and advice. Yet in one respect there had been improvement. The post-war years had brought into existence a number of local and national voluntary associations of parents with children suffering from such conditions as cerebral palsy, spina bifida, epilepsy, and Down's syndrome. These groups gave their members mutual support and advice, thereby helping parents to cope with some of the emotional and physical stress that the arrival of a handicapped child brings to a family, as well as supplementing services that doctors and the para-medical services sometimes failed to supply. Nationally they acted as pressure groups on parliament and the public at large by preaching a more informed and tolerant attitude towards the handicapped. The regard shown for parents of such children from the 1960s onwards was part of a wider trend marked also by the formation of the National Association of Governors and Managers to secure a greater voice for parents on the managing bodies of schools. It was these years of economic prosperity that also saw the introduction of attendance allowances in the Social Security Act, 1970, and the passage of the Chronically Sick and Disabled Persons Act the same year, followed by the White Paper *Better Services for the Mentally Handicapped* (Cmnd 4638, 1971) and the publicity pamphlet *Help for Handicapped People* (1972). The Plowden Report, The National Children's Bureau's Report, the Court Report *Fit for the Future* (1976), the Warnock Report *Special Educational Needs* (1978), and the Education Act, 1981, all paid some attention to the needs and opinions of parents, as had the earlier Education Act, 1970.[33]

The report *Living with Handicap* also highlighted some of the main defects of the assessment procedures, the lack of professionally trained and suitable personnel, and the fragmentary nature of the planning and provision of relevant services for handicapped persons, both as children and later in life on entering employment. In particular the report saw assessment as a multi-disciplinary task requiring teams competent to make a physical, intellectual, emotional, and social assessment of a child suspected to be suffering from a handicapping condition.[34] The fragmented nature of these services, in particular of the National Health Service itself, became a major theme of the Court Report. Although its main concern, appearing as it did a few months after the first twelve-month period in peacetime for 140 years in which recorded deaths had exceeded births in Britain, was with child health as a whole, it included some consideration of the particular problem of the handicapped child.

In this area the NHS was found wanting: 'The standard of diagnosis, assessment, treatment and care for children suffering from physical, mental, or multiple handicaps does not reach that largely achieved by the National Health Service for the treatment of acute illness.' With the services for handicapped children seen as being characterized by overlap and poor coverage, the Report repeated earlier calls for doctors, teachers, psychologists, psychiatrists, social workers, and others to come together to tackle the problem of learning disorders.[35]

In a flight of purple prose the Report asserted that since 1944 'a sea-change has come over the special educational scene, leaving no aspect the same'. Formal ascertainment procedures had been widely discarded as unnecessary and undesirable, and the previously closely defined categories of disability were now seen as less useful with the realization that handicaps often overlapped and were inter-related. The earlier sharp division between a special school and an ordinary one had broken down with the development of such features as special classes, remedial centres, child guidance centres, and home tuition. With a greater desire to have the handicapped child in an ordinary school where possible and practicable, a post-1981 trend was already developing. With more children with serious physical handicaps remaining in the ordinary schools, the composition of pupils in special schools was changing. They were more likely to be severely handicapped in more ways than one. This was especially marked in the case of severely mentally handicapped children, now constituting a fifth of the population of special schools.[36]

Shortly before the publication of this report the Education Act, 1976, the main purpose of which was to bring into line those LEAs that had not yet introduced comprehensive education, also brought the principle of educating handicapped and non-handicapped in the same school a stage closer. Whereas the 1944 Act had permitted integration, or 'mainstreaming', in cases where the disability was not serious or where it was impracticable to provide education in a special school, the 1976 Act made integration the norm, except where it would interfere with the provision of efficient education in an ordinary school or where it would involve unreasonable public expenditure.[37] However, this particular clause was repealed by the 1981 Act before it had been brought into effect.

Thus, when the Warnock Committee sat, the legal framework for introducing integration was already on the statute book, albeit un-adopted, by which time 12 per cent of all children ascertained as handicapped were already in special units or classes in ordinary schools. Of the 21,245 children so educated, 64 per cent were described as ESN(M), 17 per cent had partial hearing and 11 per cent were maladjusted. In addition some 40 per cent of maintained schools in England and Wales were running special classes, other than those designated as 'special'; they catered for 458,087 children – 4.7 per cent of the school population – who had learning difficulties, emotional or behavioural problems or a combination of these. 82 per cent of them spent less than half their time in the special classes. In addition there were a number of handicapped children attending ordinary classes whose education was supplemented by special assistance.[38]

In all, the Warnock Report calculated that up to one in five children were likely to require special education provision at some time during their school career, while about one in six would require such provision at any one time. These proportions were remarkable close to those contained in the Ministry of Education's pamphlet, *Special Education Treatment* (1946), which suggested that around 15 per cent would require special education.[39] Such education would normally take place in the special school as the following passage, which conveniently summarizes the basic thinking of the Report, indicates.

> The wider concept of special education proposed in this report, embracing as it does all those children in ordinary schools who, though not at present accounted handicapped, need additional support in a variety of forms, is directly in line with the principle that handicapped and non-handicapped children should be educated in a common setting as far as possible. The great majority of these children will continue to attend ordinary schools in the future. Moreover, we have made very clear our determined opposition to the notion of treating handicapped and non-handicapped children as forming two distinctive groups, for whom separate educational provision has to be made. It follows that we wholeheartedly support the principle of the development of common provision for all children.[40]

Children whom the committee did not propose to integrate included those with severe physical, sensory or intellectual difficulties, children with severe emotional or behavioural difficulties, and those with less severe disabilities but who despite special help had been unable to perform well in an ordinary school. Possibly aware that special schools, catering solely for the children suffering from the severest learning difficulties, would become educational ghettos, the committee suggested a number of means by which they might become less isolated, through a mutual exchange of facilities and expertise with ordinary schools.[41]

Subsequent legislation, the Education Act, 1981, theoretically gave parents more opportunities than before for participating in decisions affecting their children's education, as had the Education Act of the previous year. The new Act implemented the recommendation of the Warnock Report advocating the assessment, where necessary, of children under the age of two. In pursuance of his promise to the House of Commons the Secretary of State issued regulations prescribing the offering of medical, psychological, and educational advice where necessary for an assessment. Although a parent could now ask for an assessment, make representations, give evidence, be present at all examinations, and appeal if necessary to the Secretary of State, these rights, some of which he already held, are only of value to those who are already well informed on matters requiring much specialized knowledge. The new Act, however, made no provision for the setting up of an advisory committee to the Secretary of State on children with special education needs, or of a special education research group, or for the training of teachers, measures that the report had recommended.[42]

Although the Board of Education early in the century had taken steps to ensure that teachers with specialist qualifications were appointed to schools for the blind and deaf, mentally handicapped children had suffered comparative neglect. In 1908 the Board had issued regulations requiring teachers of the blind and deaf to obtain an approved qualification, for recognition as permanent assistant or headteachers, but no such demands were made of teachers of the feeble-minded despite the introduction of short courses by the Central Association for the Care of the Mentally Defective a few years later. Thus in January 1977 about 57 per cent of teachers in special schools for the blind, 67 per cent in schools for the deaf, and 74 per cent in those for the partially hearing had an appropriate recognized qualification. As teachers of other disabilities still did not have to possess a specialist qualification, only about 22 per cent of teachers in all special schools in England and Wales were so qualified. Only in 1984, when the DES revised the initial teacher training courses, did it require all trainee teachers to pay some attention to the problems confronting children with learning difficulties.[43]

However, the greatest shortcoming was in the manner of implementation of the new Act. In a time of financial stringency the government refused to make available any additional financial resources, thereby giving LEAs little incentive to implement the spirit of it. Those who wanted to do so could turn to Section 2 of the Act, under which children with learning difficulties were indeed normally to be taught in ordinary schools but subject, *inter alia*, to the 'efficient use of resources', a less liberal proviso than that of the 1976 Act which had spoken only of 'unreasonable public expenditure'. The Leader of the Opposition denounced the bill as 'a Michelin guide to nowhere'. How justified he was remains to be seen; the recent abolition of the Secretary of State's obligation to make an annual report to Parliament under the Education Act, 1986, does not facilitate such monitoring. Fortunately there are other opportunities for holding him and his successors accountable to Parliament.[44]

CONCLUSION

Pioneers of education 'outside the mainstream' were motivated by a desire for a more orderly society and a genuine concern for the socially, physically, and mentally disadvantaged. In a number of cases the pioneers of schools for the blind and deaf had personal experience of such handicaps within their own families. Accordingly, one way of making some provision for their kind was by forming a blind or deaf asylum for a group of children suffering a similar handicap. As many forms of congenital disability do not respect social class there has been a nucleus of locally or nationally influential, knowledgeable, and articulate people to take a lead in forming *ad hoc* pressure groups. Again, the disabled are usually able to find a parliamentary advocate; the debates in the two Houses on the Education Bill, 1970, for instance, contain contributions from Members which show what seems to be personal experience of autistic children.

At the same time this humanitarian conviction has been intertwined with considerations of social control, as the waxing and waning of fears about the feeble-minded vividly shows. One factor in the legislation of 1893 and 1899 was the belief that special provision for the handicapped could be cost-effective, keeping beggars off the streets and the indigent out of the workhouse. Earlier, magistrates wishing to find a cheaper, more effective, and humane means of dealing with young offenders had begun searching for alternatives to the various forms of punishment then available. In doing so those country gentry who initiated reformatory schools were finding a new means by which they could discharge their traditional duty of upholding the Queen's peace. The debate on the treatment of the young offender – whether it should be punitive in order to express society's disapproval, express the desire for revenge on the wrongdoer, be seen as a deterrent to other possible wrongdoers, or be a form of rehabilitation – remains with us still today, as the recent House of Commons debates on the restoration of the death penalty remind us. Indeed the penological discussion has its political overtones as the recent introduction of the 'short, sharp shock' for juvenile offenders shows. Although it has ceased to be a shock because it is not short and the offender becomes habituated to the regime, its introduction has satisfied the hard-line lobby. The pattern of juvenile crime remains much as it did a hundred years ago when John Watson went to a reformatory for stealing rabbits. Today he would be stealing video recorders. The *Criminal Statistics: England and Wales, 1985* (CM 10, 1986) show that of offenders found guilty of indictable offences or cautioned in 1985 about 30 per cent were juveniles aged 10 to 17. The proportionate indictment of juveniles was highest for the relatively less serious crimes of burglary, theft and handling stolen goods, and indictable offences of criminal damage. In the same year the peak age of known offending was 15 for males and 14 for females, the same as in nearly every year for the previous decade. Those in the 16 to 24 age group were also most at risk from serious wounding, 'other' wounding, or assault.[1] The young, the most likely to sin, were also the most likely to be sinned against. With known delinquency peaking in the teens the juvenile offender seems no more likely to become a lifelong criminal, the spectre haunting criminologists a hundred years ago, than he was then.

In making provision for education outside the mainstream the Poor Law authorities, the Home Office, and the central government education department have faced a common problem, that of giving due regard to the English tradition of local government and suspicion of the encroaching power of the central executive while attempting to obtain a degree of uniformity in the service they are administering. Hence at the local level there has been and, in the case of special education, still remains, the problem of securing the implementation of central government directives and guidelines. Ranged against the Poor Law and Home Office inspectorate in the nineteenth century there were not only various statutory and departmental limitations on their power, and a comparative absence of effective financial sanctions that could be used to improve standards, but also a strong sense of personal autonomy felt by local leaders in their communities.

Hence the attitudes of the various poor law boards, of management boards of reformatory and industrial schools, of their individual members, and of the officials they employed, could profoundly affect a child's experience in one of the custodial institutions. Accordingly some workhouse children were boarded out, while others went to the local school, long before these became common practices. Some had generous benefactors who alleviated the monotony of the daily routine, others had none. Outside these institutions the situation was similar. Whether or not a child picked a precarious living in an urban struggle for survival or ended up in some voluntary or state-provided custodial institution was almost a matter of lottery. Initially the constable on the beat exercised his discretion. If the child was taken to the local police station the duty officer in charge could exercise further discretion, even to the extent of giving unauthorized corporal punishment on the spot, a practice still prevalent in the 1930s. Again, much depended on the attitude and normal practice of an individual bench. To explore day-to-day policy at this level requires the use of police station incident books and petty session records.

However, the mere existence of such privately run homes as Dr Barnardo's, which handled nearly 60,000 children during his lifetime, points to the inadequacy of the state's provision for those who, to use today's terminology, needed to be taken into care. The London District Schools, for instance, apparently refused to take children over the age of 12, yet Lord Shaftebury had estimated in the late 1840s that there were 30,000 destitute children in London alone. Later in the century the extent of London's destitute juvenile population became an issue of ideological contention between the Charity Organization Society, arguing that the indiscriminate type of charity practised by Dr Barnardo (who boasted that he never refused shelter to a needy child), merely increased London's mendicant population and undermined the poor law ethos, and the voluntary organizations who maintained that they were responding to a social need.[2]

Whether children came to a voluntary or a state-run haven their subsequent careers were broadly similar: unskilled jobs for the boys and domestic service for the girls were usually their next ports of call. A small proportion of boys and girls emigrated, while some boys went to sea or enlisted in the Army. We know little of the subsequent careers of these children. Letters written by ex-reformatory boys who had made good in the Army or the colonies, reproduced in the reports of the Home Office inspectorate, seem no more typical of their peers than the novelist Leslie Thomas seems a typical ex-Barnardo's boy. Apart from odd hints of the bullying of younger inmates by older ones the internal culture of these institutions still awaits exploration. However, learning the art of self-survival in a reformatory or industrial school seems to have been useful preparation for the Western Front. Ex-inmates won six VCs, three DSOs and 204 DCMs, while 145 were commissioned – a tribute to the army's sense of democracy in a time of need.[3]

It will be remembered that the institutions discussed above held an unknown number of physically and mentally handicapped children for whom the state made no special educational provision before the last decade of the nineteenth century. England lagged behind a number of Western European countries and certain states in the USA, both in making public provision for the handicapped and in developing the necessary pedagogic expertise. The integration now advocated on educational, social, and humanitarian grounds is a legacy of past administrative pragmatism. Obviously before the legislation of the 1890s, the handicapped child, if he went to a school at all, attended an ordinary one. The Departmental Committee of 1898 accepted the teaching of both feeble-minded and physically-defective children in ordinary schools:

> We recommend that inspectors shall make inquiry, when inspecting ordinary schools, as to the methods used for teaching [mentally] defective children with a view of suggesting such special provision as may appear to be suitable.
> . . . we think that physical defect alone is not sufficient cause for the admission of a child to a special class, but that children of normal intellect, if they can attend school at all, should attend ordinary schools.[4]

As we have seen, physically and mentally handicapped children attended ordinary schools during the financially lean years of the 1920s and 1930s. The 1944 Act made some provision for integration, a policy carried further by the largely stillborn 1976 Act, which was still on the statute book when the Warnock Committee was sitting and to whose implications the Report gave considerable attention.

One legacy of the Revised Code had been to see feeble-mindedness as an educational problem, manifesting itself in a child's inability to keep pace with his peers in the basic subjects. Hence the early special schools had worked mainly on the premise that such children were education-ally backward, requiring smaller classes taken by staff trained as infant teachers. Another consequence was to divide the educable from the ineducable, the high-grade feeble-minded from the low-grade. Al-though this became the basis of the demarcation line between the Boards of Education and Control, in practice there was always an overlap. Children, especially those coming from a deprived back-ground, learnt social skills in infants' classes and the lower forms of elementary schools. Some children, the responsibility of the Board of Control, began learning a basic numeracy and literacy. Finally, what had been essentially an artificial division ended with the implementation of the Education Act 1970, from the following April onwards.

Two factors assisted these developments. First there was a widening of the nature and purpose of education in ordinary schools, a subject deserving further analysis in its own right. At the same time there was a growing realization that many handicapped children possessed a previously unsuspected potential for education. This was particularly true of those put into institutional care, where they frequently lacked mental stimulation. A series of studies made in the 1960s and later suggested that Down's Syndrome children cared for at home were generally more advanced, possessed greater emotional maturity, had wider interests and activities and more diverse social skills, than those nurtured in institutions. The 1970 Act reinforced the process. Earlier, Down's children, if they had attended a Junior Training Centre, had usually been supervised by personnel lacking a teaching qualification. Now such children are more likely to be with trained teachers, some of whom have appropriate specialist qualifications, who implement a curriculum designed with the profile of learning difficulties of the individual child in mind.[5]

A second consequence of the 1970 Act has been to bring children with severe learning difficulties within the field of further education. Now that they are 'educable', LEAs have as much of a duty towards them, as towards any other young persons between the ages of 16 and 19, to provide for their further education under the 1944 Act. Yet in 1977 the age of 16 marked the end of formal education for young persons with disabilities, as it had done ever since the Acts of 1893 and 1899. It required action by a group of parents in Oxfordshire, convinced that their children did not suddenly lose the ability to learn at the age of 16, to remind LEAs of a duty 'not widely recognized.'[6]

LEAs also have powers under the National Health Service Act, 1977, to provide educational facilities in Adult Training Centres. In implementing the Acts the central problem is one of allocating limited resources and deciding priorities at a time of financial stringency when public expenditure is discouraged. For there is an ambivalence towards spending money, whether public or private, on special education. Much has been made, to some extent as an act of political necessity, of the cost-effectiveness of investment in special education and of its role in social engineering. Public money flows more readily towards the disadvantaged during times of prosperity, as it did in the 1960s and early 1970s. Although in less prosperous times it may be politically in-expedient to cut such expenditure, it remains equally difficult to direct extra resources towards it when other sectors of education are experiencing cuts. Hence the Education Act, 1981, the cultural legacy of a more prosperous period, has lacked the resources necessary for its effective implementation.

The final word on this cruel dilemma may rest with the Board of Education official who was faced sixty years ago, also during a recession, with the problem of providing special places for 65,000 children. He wrote:

> Only a nation which has provided adequately for all its other children and still has superfluous money to spend, could justifiably embark on an adventure of this kind.[7]

NOTES

Chapter 1, pp. 11–34

1 *Report of the Royal Commission on the State of Popular Education in England (Newcastle Report)*, Parliamentary Papers (PP) 1861, XXI, A, p. 382.

2 Public Record Office (PRO) MH 19/17, Education Department (Ed. Dept.), to Poor Law Board (PLB), 12 Jan. 1867.

3 *Bowyer's Report*, PP 1852–3, LXXIX, pp. 91–2 (587–8). Poor Law Amendment Act (PLAA) 1844, ss. 40, 41. PLAA 1866, s. 16 removed the distance limit.

4 *Report from the Select Committee (SC) on the Poor Laws*, PP 1817, VI, pp. 14–15. W. Monnington and F. J. Lampard, *Our London Poor-Law Schools* (1898) pp. 160–1.

5 *Report from Her Majesty's Commissioners for Inquiry into the Administration and Practical Operation of the Poor Laws*, PP 1834, XXVII, 'Instructions to Assistant Commissioners', Appendix A, Part I, p. 248–55 (262–9).

6 S. and B. Webb, *English Local Government: English Poor Law History Part II* (1) (1929), pp. 70–2. PP 1834, XXVII, p. 205 (209).

7 D. Paz, *The Politics of Working-Class Education in Britain, 1830–50* (1980), pp. 55–6. *Fifth Report from the Poor Law Commissioners*, PP 1839, XX, pp. 13–15 (17–19). *Report to the Secretary of State for the Home Department: Report from the P.L.C. on the Training of Pauper Children* (1843), pp. 19–20. On Kay's ambivalent attitude towards the causes of poverty, see also D. Paz, 'Sir James Kay-Shuttleworth: the man behind the myth', *History of Education XIV*, III (1985), pp. 185–98.

8 *J. C. Symons' Report*, PP 1849, XLII, p. 224 (518).

9 *40th Report from the S.C. on the Poor Law Amendment Act 1834* PP 1838, XVIII, III, Q 13200. G. C. T. Bartley, *Schools for the People* (1871), p. 273.

10 *1st Report from the S.C. on the Poor Law Amendment Act, 1834* PP 1838, XVIII, I, p. 39. *4th Report*, PP 1838, XVIII, I, Q 4405, 4410.

11 *4th Annual Report of the P.L.C.*, PP 1838, XXVII, p. 60. D. Paz, *op cit*, p. 59. Poor Law Amendment Act, 1844, ss. 40, 41. An Act to Amend the Law for the Formation of Districts, 1848, sI. PLAA 1849, sI. Divided Parishes and PLAA, 1882, s. 12.

12 PP 1847, XLIX, 'Report by S. Tremenheere on Mr Drouet's Establishment for Pauper Children at Tooting', pp. 171–5. *House of Lords Sessional Papers*, 1841, XXXIII (I), 'Report on the Norwood School of Industry', p. 104. *The Times*, 14, 16 April 1849.

13 *Newcastle Report*, PP 1861, XXI, A., pp. 368, 384. W. Chance, *Children under the Poor Law: their education, training and aftercare* (1899), p. 287. R. A. Leach, *Pauper Children: their education and training* (1890), p. 287.

14 *5th Annual Report of the P.L.C.*, PP 1839, XX, 'Instructional Letter to the Chaplain of Mr Aubin's Establishment . . .' pp. 46–8 (50–2). J. P. Kay, *A Report on the Training of Pauper Children* (Clowes, 1839, Morten, 1970), p. 13.

15 *Newcastle Report*, PP 1861, XXI, E, 'E. C. Tufnell's evidence', Qs 3142–3.

16 D. Paz, *op cit.*, p. 57. *4th Report from the S.C. on the Poor Law Amendment Act, 1834*, PP 1838, XVIII, I, Qs 4446–7, 4490–5.

17 A. Brundage, *The Making of the New Poor Law* (1978), pp. 145, 165–5.

18 PRO MH 19/14, 'J. C. Symons to Committee of Education', 27 Mar., 4 Oct. 1848. *Bowyer's Report*, PP 1854, LI, p. 51 (617).

19 PP 1849, XLII, 'Paper from Kay-Shuttleworth to Sir George Grey dated 5 Aug. 1846', pp. v–xiv (247–56).

20 This unequal contest will end with the centralization of the training of bandsmen for HM Forces. *Moseley's Report*, PP 1854–5, XLI, pp. 1–16 (391–406). *Ibid.*, 'Return relating to the education of pupil-teachers', p. 2 (184).

21 PP 1849, XLII, 'Letter containing instructions to HMIs of Schools of Parochial Unions in England and Wales', pp. xviii–xxiii (260–5).

22 PRO, MH 19/14, 'PLB to Ed. Dept.', 31 May, 12 Dec. 1848, 8 Mar. 1854. MH 19/16 'Ed. Dept. to PLB'. 14 Jul. 1857, 'C. Gibson's minute of 21 Jul. 1857'.

23 PP 1847–8, LIII, 'Amount of Salaries and Emoluments paid to School-masters and Schoolmistresses of each Poor Law Union in England and Wales in the Year 1847', pp. 353–374. *Newcastle Report*, PP 1861, XXI, E, 'E. C. Tufnell's Evidence', Q. 3172. PRO MH 19/21, 'List in file relating to petition of the Board of Guardians of St Mary, Islington, London, 9 May 1889'.

24 *Bowyer's Report*, PP 1850, XLIII, p. 42 (106). PP 1856, XLVII, 'Kay-Shuttleworth's letter of 5 Aug. 1846', pp. 10-11 (252–3). PP 1856, XLVII, 'Comm. of Cncl's letter of 13 Dec. 1855', pp. 8–10 (638–40).

25 In June 1852, 25 schools had 100 or more pupils, 30 had 75–99, 101 had 50–74, 568 had less than 50. PP 1854, LI, p. 52 (618).

26 PRO MH 19/15. 'R. R. Lingen's letter of 15 June 1852 to the PLB', 'PLB's reply of 17 June 1852'.

27 *Newcastle Report*, PP 1861, XXI, A, pp. 638–40. *Report of the Royal Commission on Schools not comprised within H.M.'s two recent Commissions on Popular Education and Endowed Schools (Taunton Report)*, PP 1867–8, XXVIII, A, pp. 241, 243, *Ibid.*, vol. G, p. 166, *Ibid.*, vol. H, pp. 24, 307, 353. *Newcastle Report*, PP 1861, XXI, F, Q. 3365.

28 *Bowyer's Reports*, PP 1850, XLIII, p. 46 (110), PP 1854–5, XLIII, pp. 74–5 (840–1). *Symons' Report*, PP 1852–3, LXXIX, p. 171 (669).

29 *2nd Report from the S.C. on Poor Relief*, PP 1862, X, Qs. 4361–3, 4371. Using restrictive criteria it seems that approximately 15,500 of 52,125 children in workhouses on 1 Jan. 1862 could be considered permanent residents. *The Report of the R.C. on the Poor Laws and Relief of Distress*, PP 1909, XXXVII, p. 41 (57) shows 36,573 of 62,426 indoor children being relieved without having parents in the workhouse. For a recent survey of private schools used by the working classes, see P. Gardner, *The Lost Elementary Schools of Victorian England* (1984).

30 H. Jenner-Fust, *Poor Law Orders* (1907), p. 52.

31 *Newcastle Report*, PP 1861, XXI, A, pp. 662–3, 666–7.

32 PRO MH 19/16, 'J. F. Stephen to the PLB', 11 Oct. 'Lord Courtenay's minute', 13 Oct., 'W. G. Lumley's minute', 15 Oct. 'Lord Courtenay to J. F. Stephen', 20 Oct., 'John Jenkins to the PLB' 15 Nov., 'PLB to Jenkins', 18 Nov. 1858.

33 *Newcastle Report*, PP 1861, XXI, B, 'Fraser's Report', pp. 89–90. *Ibid.*, vol. C, 'Hedley's Report', pp. 151–2, 'Hodgson's Report', pp. 522–3.

34 *Ibid.*, vol. A, pp. 355–6, 373, 384. *Ibid.*, vol. C, 'Cumin's Report', pp. 38–9.

35 *Newcaste Report*, PP 1861, XXI, A, p. 357.

36 PRO MH 19/16, 'Return dated 20 April 1860'. *Symons' Report*, PP 1859, XXI, I, p. 521.

37 *Newcastle Report*, PP 1861, XXI, A, pp. 355–7, 373, 384.

Chapter 2, pp. 35–61

1 'Report on Kneller Hall by the Rev H. Moseley', PP 1854–5, XLI, pp. 10–12 (400–402).

2 L. Twining, *Recollections of Workhouse Visiting and Management during Twenty-Five Years* (1880), pp. 6, 9, 21–3. *Journal of the Workhouse Visiting Society* (Jan., 1859), pp. 12–18 reprints 'The Union Workhouse', *Church of England Magazine* (1852). *Ibid.*, (Jan. 1862) reprints H. Archer, *A Scheme for Befriending Orphan Pauper Girls* (1861). L. Twining, 'Workhouses', *Trans. of the National Assoc. for the Promotion of Social Science*, 1857 (*Trans N.A.P.S.S. 1857*) (1858), pp. 571–4. *Trans N.A.P.S.S. 1858*, (1859), p. xxxi fn, *1st Report from the S.C. on Poor Relief*, PP 1861, Qs. 1351–3.

3 PRO MH 32/117, 'Libraries and Newspapers in Workhouses', undated, *c.* 1890.

4 G. Haw, *From Workhouse to Westminster: the life story of William Crooks, M.P.* (1907), p. 106. H. Fenner-Just, *op. cit.*, pp. 74–5.

5 A. Brundage, *op. cit.*, pp. 122–3, 143. *Journal of the Workhouse Visiting Society* (July 1860), pp. 238–44.

6 *2nd Report from the S.C. on Poor Relief*, PP 1862, X, Qs. 4876–7, 4885– F. Davenport and F. Fowke, *op. cit.*, pp. 179–80.

7 F. Davenport and F. Fowke, *Children of the State* (1889 edn.), pp. 183–4. (9), PP 1870, LVII, 'Report . . . on the Boarding Out of Pauper Children in Certain Unions in England', pp. 121–89 (191–259).

8 *23rd Report of the PLB*, PP 1871, XXVII, 'Circular Letter from the PLB to Boards of Guardians of Certain Unions', 25 Nov. 1870, pp. 11–21 (61–73) (63–73).

9 *3rd Report of the L.G.B.*, PP 1874, XXV, 'Education of Girls in Pauper

Schools', pp. 311–94. PP 1875, LXIII, 'Observations on the Report of Mrs Senior . . . by E. C. Tufnell, pp. 299–342. For Mrs Senior's riposte see, *Ibid.* 'Letter by Mrs Senior being a reply to the Observation of Mr Tufnell', pp. 343–65.

10 *R.C. on Poor Laws and the Relief of Distress*, PP 1910, LII, 'Report on the Condition of Children', pp. 2–3 (10–11). *Report upon the Educational Work in Poor Law Schools, and in Twenty-Two Schools, certified under the Poor Law (Certified Schools) Act, 1862, which are inspected by the Board of Education by J. Tillard and M. B. Synge (Report by Tillard and Synge)* (HMSO, 1908), p. 24.

11 PP 1897, LXXVI, II, 'Report upon the Ophthalmic State of Poor Law Children in the Metropolis', pp. 3–5, 9–15, 34, 36, 103, 105, 113–16. The Report also contains a detailed description of the schools Stephenson visited, pp. 102–204. *Report of the Departmental Committee on the Education and Maintenance of Pauper Children in the Metropolis (Poor Law Schools' Commission)*, PP 1896, XLIII, p. 149. PRO MH 32/110, 'Memorandum of 19 Jan. 1875, signed by J. H. Bridges, W. Holgate, and F. J. Mouat'.

12 W. Monnington and F. J. Lampard, *op. cit.*, pp. 1–7, 14–15, 108. *Poor Law Schools Commission*, PP 1896, XLIII, pp. 9, 10, 13, 16, 168, 171. *Report from the S.C. of the House of Lords on Poor Relief*, PP 1888, XV, Q. 3944.

13 *32nd Report of the L.G.B.*, PP 1903, XXIV, p. cxiii.

14 *Report of the Royal Commission on the Poor Laws and the Relief of Distress*, PP 1910, LII, p. 5 (13).

15 *15th Report of the L.G.B.*, PP 1886, XXXI, pp. 51–61 (201–11). *18th Report of the L.G.B.*, PP 1889, XXXV, pp. xcv (289). *21st Report of the L.G.B.*, PP 1892, XXXVIII, p. 195. *24th Report of the L.G.B.*, PP 1894–5, L, p. 89. A case that attracted much notoriety involved a Miss Hockley sentenced to twelve years' penal servitude for ill treatment, causing death in some cases, of babies farmed out to her. One child involved was the responsibility of the Plympton Board of Guardians' Boarding-Out Committee. See *22nd Report of the L.G.B.*, 1893–4, XLIII, pp. 117–19.

16 *R.C. on Poor Laws and the Relief of Distress*, PP 1910, LII, 'Report on the Condition of Children', pp. 90–2. *Ibid.*, PP 1909, XXXVII, p. 805 (825).

17 By 1909 there were three women inspectors. For the various Orders, see *39th Report of the L.G.B.*, PP 1910, XXXVIII, p. xxiii *40th Report of the L.G.B.*, PP 1911, XXXI, p. xxiii, *41st Report of the L.G.B.*, PP 1912–13, XXXV, p. xxiii.

18 *R.C. on the Poor Laws and the Relief of Distress*, PP 1909, pp. 810–12 (830–2).

19 *Ibid.*, p. 182 (202), 'Report on the Condition of Children', PP 1910, LII, p. 8 (16).

20 *Report of the Care of Children Committee (Curtis Report)*, PP 1945–6, X, p. 160 (718).

21 *Report of the Royal Commission Appointed to Inquire into the Working of the Elementary Education Acts (Cross Commission)*, PP 1887, XXX, 'W. Holgate's Evidence', Qs. 49813–6, 49975. H. Jenner-Fust, *op. cit.*, p. 551.

22 Elementary Education Act, 1876, ss. 5 and 48. PRO MH 32/109, 'H. G.

Bowyer to LGB 16 April 1877', 'E. C. Tufnell to LGB 19 April 1875'. For the PLB's regulations in detail, see R. A. Leach, *op. cit.*, pp. 16–24. The Rev J. C. Clutterbuck, who wanted a more rigorous scrutiny of workhouse teachers, was sentenced to four years' penal servitude in 1891 for obtaining £1,500 by false pretences.

23 *Cross Commission*, PP 1887, XXX, 'W. Holgate's Evidence', Qs. 50025–6.

24 *Ibid.*, Q. 50049.

25 PRO MH 19/20. 'Minute of 12 April and 31 July 1875'. PRO MH 19/21, 'Minute of Jan. 1890'. *Report of the R.C. on the Poor Laws and the Relief of Distress*, PP 1909, XL, Q. 28346.

26 PP 1849, XLII, 'Minute of 18 Dec. 1847', pp. xvi–xvii (258–60), PRO MH 19/16 'Education Dept. to PLB', 4 July 1862. PRO MH 19/17, 'List dated 25 July 1863'. *Report from the S.C. of the House of Lords on Poor Relief*, Qs. 4987–8. *Report by Tillard and Synge*, p. 11. T. Adkins, *The History of St John's College, Battersea* (1906), pp. 261–5.

27 *Report by Tillard and Synge*, pp. 6–15 *passim*.

28 *Times Education Supplement*, 1 Jan., 25 Nov. 1920. *Education in 1930*, PP 1930–1, XII, p. 16 (758). *Education in 1931*, PP 1931–2, IX, p. 19 (71). *Education in 1938*, PP 1938–9, p. 11 (685).

29 *Poor Law Schools' Commission*, PP 1896, XLIII, pp. 54, 56. *27th Report of the P.L.B.*, PP 1898, XXXIX, pp. 5–8. *Report by Tillard and Synge*, p. 13.

30 *Cross Report*, PP 1887, XXX, 'W. Holgate's Evidence', Q. 49812.

31 *Poor Law Schools' Commission*, PP 1896, XLIII, Q. 12627.

32 *Ibid.*, pp. 50–1.

33 *18th Report of the P.L.B.*, PP 1866, XXXV, 'Dietaries for the inmates of Workhouses', pp. 19, 51 (343, 375). *5th Annual Report of the L.G.B.*, PP 1876, XXXI, 'Report on Metropolitan Pauper Schools', pp. 122–3 (194–5). V. Johnston, 'Local Prison Diets 1835–78', in D. J. Oddy and D. S. Miller, *Diet and Health in Modern Britain* (1985), pp. 207–30. *Journal of the Workhouse Visiting Society* (Jan. 1859), pp. 25–7. *Ibid.*, (Feb. 1860), pp. 155–6.

34 F. K. Prochaska, 'Female Philanthropy and Domestic Service in Victorian England', *Bull. Inst. Hist. Research* LIV, 129 (1981), pp. 79–85.

35 *4th Report from the S.C. on Poor Relief*, PP 1861, IX, Qs. 13021–2, 13070, 13072.

36 *Ibid.*, Qs. 12659, 12693, 12695, R. A. Leach, *op. cit.*, pp. 208–10.

37 W. I. Jennings, *The Poor Law Code, and the Law of Unemployment Assistance* (1936), p. 7.

38 *Curtis Report*, PP 1945–6, X, pp. 38, 40, 44 (596, 598, 602).

39 *Ibid.*, pp. 55–7, 69 (613–15, 627).

40 Home Office, *5th Report of the Children's Branch* (1938), pp. 90–107. P. Paterson, 'A Ghost of Christmas Past', *Spectator*, 18 Dec. 1982.

41 *Curtis Report*, PP 1945–6, X, pp. 71, 80–1, 84 (629, 638–9, 642).

Chapter 3, pp. 62–91

1 *Report of the Royal Commission on Reformatory and Industrial Schools (Aberdare Report)*, PP 1884, XLV, 'Appendix B', pp. 734–6 (836–8).

2 G. Rusche and O. Kirchheimer, *Punishment and Social Structure* (New

York, 1939), p. 59, J. Hawes, *Children in Urban Society: juvenile delinquency in nineteenth-century America* (New York, 1971), p. 59. G. Wagner, *Children of the Empire* (1982), p. 256.

3 B. Rodgers, *Cloak of Charity: studies in eighteenth-century philanthropy* (1949), pp. 18, 48. S. Trimmer, *The Oeconomy of Charity* (1801), pp. 314, 317. *Newcastle Report*, PP 1861, XXI, C, p. 34. *Aris' Gazette*, 6 Aug. 1794. Quoted by P. B. Cliff, 'The Rise and Development of Sunday Schools in England, 1780–1880' (Unpublished PhD thesis, University of Birmingham, 1982), p. 57.

4 M. Lewis, *The Navy of Britain: a historical portrait* (1948), p. 309. L. Radzinowicz, *A History of English Law and its Administration from 1750*: vol. IV *Grappling for Control* (1968), pp. 43, 50, 53. S. Low, *The Charities of London (1850)*, pp. 109, 314. R. Porter, *English Society in the Eighteenth Century* (1983), p. 315. The Foundling Hospital had sent its first children to sea at the earlier date of 1752. R. K. McClure, *Coram's Children: the London Foundling Hospital in the eighteenth century* (New Haven and London, 1981), p. 126.

5 E. Bradlaw, 'The Children's Friend Society at the Cape of Good Hope', *Victorian Studies* XXVII, No. 2 (Winter, 1984), pp. 155–77.

6 L. Radzinowicz, *op. cit.*, Vol. I: *The Movement for Reform* (1948), pp. 12, 14, 176 footnote 50.

7 M. Ignatieff, *A Just Measure of Pain: the penitentiary in the industrial revolution* (New York, 1978), pp. 24, 28, 81.

8 *Report from the Select Committee on Criminal and Destitute Juveniles*, PP 1852, VII, 'Captain J. Williams' Evidence' Q. 181.

9 *First Report of the Select Committee on Juvenile Offenders and Transportation*, PP 1847, VII, 'Evidence of Lt A. F. Tracy, RN, Governor of the House of Correction, Tothill Fields', Qs. 1769–83.

10 L. Radzinowicz, *op. cit.*, Vol. I, pp. 585–6, 597, 597 footnote 20.

11 D. Philips, *Crime and Authority in Victorian England: the Black Country, 1835–70 (1977)*, p. 96 *et seq.*

12 D. Philips, *op. cit.*, p. 134.

13 I. Pinchbeck and M. Hewitt, *Children in English Society*, Vol. II *From the Eighteenth Century to the Children Act, 1948* (1973), pp. 447, 548, 549 footnote 1.

14 *loc. cit.*, PP 1817, VII, p. 327.

15 V. A. C. Gatrell and T. B. Hadden, 'Criminal statistics and their interpretation', in E. A. Wrigley (ed.), *Nineteenth-Century Society: essays in the use of quantitative methods for the study of social data* (Cambridge, 1972), pp. 387–8. For concern over juvenile unruliness in pre-industrial England, see G. Pearson, *Hooligan: a history of respectable fears* (1983), pp. 183–202.

16 D. J. C. Jones, 'The New Police, Crime and People in England and Wales 1829–1888' in *Transactions of the Royal Historical Society. Fifth Series*, Vol. LXXXIII (1983), pp. 151–68.

17 *Report from the Select Committee Appointed to Inquire into the Present State of the Education of the People in England and Wales*, PP 1835, VII, Part II, 'Evidence of Francis Place', p. 68 (834).

18 *Report of the Commissioners Appointed to Inquire into the Condition and*

Treatment of Prisoners Confined in the Birmingham Borough Prison, PP 1854, XXXI, pp. iii–xxxviii *passim*. Evidence of the ill-treatment of at least a dozen other juvenile prisoners came to light.

19 M. Hill, 'Juvenile Delinquency' in Micaiah Hill and C. F. Cornwallis, *Two Prize Essays* (1853), pp. 201–4. M. D. Hill, *Suggestions for the Repression of Crime contained in the Charges Delivered to Grand Juries of Birmingham: supported by additional facts and arguments* (1857), p. 128.

20 S. Low, *op. cit.*, pp. 388–96. K. Heasman, *Evangelicals in Action: an appraisal of their social work in Victorian England* (1962), pp. 77–80. *Household Words*, 7 June 1866. *Reformatory and Refuge Journal* (1861), p. 30.

21 C. F. Cornwallis, *The Philanthropy of Ragged Schools* (1851), p. 48.

22 G. F. A. Finlayson, *Lord Shaftesbury (1981), pp. 346, 369 note 98.*

23 J. Guthrie, *Seed-Time and Harvest of Ragged Schools or a Third Plea with New Editions of the First and Second Pleas* (Edinburgh, 1860), pp. 193–4.

24 H. W. Schupf, 'Education for the Neglected: Ragged Schools in Nineteenth-Century England', *History of Education Quarterly* XII (1972), pp. 162–83.

25 M. Hill *op. cit.*, p. 207.

26 The Reformatory Schools' Act, 1893, s. 2 allowed JPs to send children on remand to places other than prisons.

27 The Children Act 1908, s. 101 (1) abolished imprisonment for a child under 14; s. 102 (2) abolished penal servitude for a young person under 16 but allowed imprisonment of one certified as too unruly or depraved for other forms of custodial treatment.

28 E. A. Clark, 'The Superiority of the "Scottish System": Scottish Ragged Schools and their Influence', *Scottish Educational Studies* IX (1977), pp. 29–39. *Newcastle Report*, PP 1861, XXI, A, pp. 399–402. *Aberdare Report*, PP 1884, XLV, 'Appendix A', summarises the relevant provisions of the then extant acts.

29 *1st Report . . . of the Inspector appointed . . . to visit . . . Reformatories and Industrial Schools of Great Britain (1st Reformatories' Report)*, PP 1857–8, p. 5 (816). *2nd Reformatories' Report*, PP 1859 (Session II), XIII, II, p. 15. *6th Reformatories' Report*, PP 1863, XXIV, p. 9 (505).

30 *Newcastle Report*, PP 1861, XXI, C, p. 369. *23rd Reformatories' Report*, PP 1880, XXXVII, p. 6. *Report of the Departmental Committee on Reformatory and Industrial Schools* PP 1913, XXXIX, p. 31. *Report of the Inter-Departmental Committee on the Provision of Funds for Reformatory and Industrial Schools*, PP 1906, LIV, p. 3 (9). By 1913 the Departmental Committee reported 42 certificated teachers in reformatory schools, *loc. cit.*, PP 1913, XXXI, p. 20 (22). The Royal Philanthropic Society's reformatory moved to Redhill following the Rev S. Turner's visit to Mettrai described in S. Turner and T. Paynter, *Report on the System and Arrangements of La Colonie Agricole at Mettray* (1846). In turn the reformatory at Mettrai owed much to J. Wichern's *Rauhe Haus* founded in the mid-1830s. J. Hawes, *op. cit.*, pp. 78–80.

31 The *Reformatory and Refuge Journal* by the 1880s carried advertisements of goods for sale made in various institutions. *Reports of the D.C. on*

Reformatory and Industrial Schools, PP 1913, XXXIX, pp. 33–6, 47. (35–7, 49).

32 *Ibid*. p. 34.

33 PRO Ed. 11/149, 'Report on Reformatory and Industrial Schools', J. O. Peet, 16 Nov. 1918.

34 *1st Reformatory's Report*, PP 1857–8, XXIX, p. 6 (816). For the role of the landed classes in establishing reformatories see J. A. Slack, 'The Provision of Reformatory Schools, the Landed Class, and the Myth of the Superiority of Rural Life in Mid-Victorian England', *History of Education* VIII (1), pp. 33–44, B. Elliott, 'The Provision . . . mid-Victorian England: a footnote', *History of Education* IX (1), (1980), pp. 63–4. *J. C. Symons' Report on Reformatories*, PP 1857, (Sess II), XXXIII, p. 228 (1074).

35 *23rd Report of the P.L.C.*, PP 1871, XXVII, p. 158. *5th Report of the P.L.B.*, PP 1876, XXXI, p. xxv–xxvi. *19th Reformatories' Report*, PP 1881, LIII, p. 16 (404). *22nd Reformatories' Report*, PP 1884, XLIV, p. 12 (452). *27th Reformatories' Report*, PP 1889, XLII, p. 26 (542). *31st Reformatories' Report*, PP 1893–4, LVIII, p. 12 (488).

36 PRO HO 45/9840/B10830. 'J. G. Legge's report of 5 June 1895'. For a fuller account of events aboard *Wellesley* see J. Hurt, 'Reformatory and Industrial Schools before 1933', *History of Education* XIII, No. 1 (1984), pp. 45–58.

37 PRO HO 45/9840/B10830, 'G. Lushington's minutes of 15 Dec. 1892 and 10 Jan. 1896'.

38 R. A. Leach, *Pauper Children* (1890), p. 212. Home Office, *Sixth Report of the Children's Department*, HMSO, (1951), p. 84.

39 G. Patterson, 'The Shipping Industry: life and death at sea', in R. W. Sturgess (ed.), *The Great Age of Industry in the North East* (Durham County Local History Society, 1981), pp. 135–61.

40 C. Hocking, *Dictionary of Disasters at Sea during the Age of Steam, 1824–1962* (1969), *20th Report of the P.L.B.*, PP 1867–8, XXXIII, p. 133. *The Times*, 28 July 1898. Board of Trade, *Report of the Boy Seaman Committee* (1907), gives further evidence on this theme.

41 *Fishing Apprentice System*, PP 1894, LXIX, pp. 9–14 (769–74).

42 E. M. Spiers, *The Army and Society, 1815–1914* (1980), pp. 35, 37, 40, 41. A. R. Skelley, *The Victorian Army at Home: the recruitment and terms and conditions of the British regular, 1859–99* (1977), pp. 262–3.

43 G. Wagner, *Children of the Empire* (1982), p. 259. J. Parr, *Labouring Children: British immigrant apprentices to Canada, 1869–1924* (1981), pp. 11, 34. *Aberdare Report*, PP 1884, XLV, 'J. Trevarthen's Evidence', Q. 3922. *38th Reformatories' Report*, PP 1900, XXXIII, pp. 16–18 (203–5). *Report of the Departmental Committee on Agricultural Settlements in British Colonies*, PP 1906, LXXVI, p. 17 (599).

44 For an account of malpractices at the London School Board's truant school at Homerton, see J. Hurt, ref. 36 *supra*.

45 PRO HO 45/9629/A22484, 'V. Harcourt to Lord Aberdare, 27 Dec. 1884'. HO Circulars of 22 Nov. 1884, and 31 Jan. 1885. 'Harcourt to Lushington', 16 Jan. 1885. PRO HO 45/9838/B10399A. 'Circular letters to inspectors of reformatory and industrial schools', 2 June 1892.

46 *Aberdare Report*, PP 1884, XLV, 'Evidence of Dr J. Watts', Qs. 5672, 5683.

Report of the Dept. Committee on Agricultural Settlements in British Colonies, PP 1906, LXXVI, 'J. G. Legge's Evidence', Qs. 6801, 6809.

47 Swinton Public Library, Manchester. Ms. J. 879.

48 G. Wagner, *op. cit.*, p. 259. *Poor Law Schools' Commission*, PP 1896, XLIII, 'Major Gretton's Evidence', Qs. 16, 561–16, 655 *passim*. *Report of the Departmental Committee on Agricultural Settlements*, PP 1906, LXXVI, 'J. G. Legge's Evidence', Qs. 6775, 6779.

49 For the rigours of domestic service in a prairie homestead see E. C. Sykes, *A home-Help in Canada* (1912). For a study of the subsequent lives of British emigrants to Canada see, *The British Immigrant: his social and economic adjustment to Canada* (Toronto, 1935), PRO HO 45/421663/41, 'A. H. Norris's minute of 26 April, 1928'. The Children Act, 1908 authorized a Treasury grant for the emigration of reformatory and industrial children. PRO HO 45/46505/43 'Memorandum re emigration of children from reformatory and industrial schools', shows 2,782 children were sent from such schools in the years 1901–13 inclusive.

50 PRO HO 45/46506/46. 'Letter from C. E. B. Russell to W. Beecher Smith, 5 Sept. 1913', and 'Smith's reply, 8 Sept. 1913'. PRO HO 45/9992/A46506, 'Minute of TDR, 11 Mar. 1910'.

51 PRO HO 45/16538 contains Ministry of Health circular, May 1922. *The Times*, 2 June 1934. PRO HO 45/421663/41 'Minute of FSS 1 Aug. 1936'.

52 *Aberdare Report*, PP 1884, XLV, p. XIV, 'Appendix A5', p. lxxix. *Report of the Inter-Departmental Committee on the Provision of Funds for Reformatory and Industrial Schools*, PP 1906, LIV, pp. 2, 8 (8, 14).

53 H. T. Holmes, *Reformatory and Industrial Schools* (Fabian Tract 111, 1902). Liverpool Education Authority retained its truant school until 1934. In addition there were five voluntarily maintained industrial schools in existence until the 1940s. J. B. May, *Education and the Urban Child* (Liverpool, 1962), p. 22.

54 *Report of the Departmental Committee on Reformatory and Industrial Schools*. PP 1913, XXXIX, p. 15. 'Evidence of Inspector T. D. Robertson', Qs. 283–7. B. Elliott, 'Mount St Bernard's Reformatory, Leicestershire, 1851–81', *Recusant History* XV, I (1979), pp. 15–22.

55 J. Carlebach, *Caring for Children in Trouble* (1970), p. 88. Home Office, *Report of the Committee on Salaries and Conditions of Service of Officers in Reformatory and Industrial Schools* (1919), *passim*.

56 The earlier Probation of First Offenders Act, 1889, did not provide any system of supervision.

57 Home Office, *Report on the Work of the Children's Branch* (1923), pp. 18–21. Home Office, *Education in Reformatory and Industrial Schools: Circular Letter of H.M. Chief Inspector of Reformatory and Industrial Schools to the managers and staff of schools* (1919). Home Office, *Second Report of the Children's Branch* (1924), p. 37.

58 C. Burt, *The Young Delinquent*, (1925), p. viii. This work ran to four editions. The seminal two-volume G. S. Hall, *Adolescence: its psychology and relations to physiology, anthropology, sociology, sex, crime, religion, and education* (1904), was reprinted fourteen times. For a fuller account of the child-guidance movement see G. Keir, 'A History of Child Guidance',

British Journal of Educational Psychology XXII (1952) pp. 5–29.
59 *Loc. cit.* p. 23.
60 *Ibid.*, p. 24.
61 Home Office, *Fifth Report of the Children's Branch* (1938), pp. 59–84.
62 *Curtis Report*, PP 1945–6, X, pp. 91–101 (649–659) *passim*.

Chapter 4, pp. 91–106

1 *Report of the R.C. on the Blind, Deaf and Dumb etc. of the U.K. (Egerton Report)* PP 1889, XIX, pp. xiii, xviii, xiv, liv, (15, 20, 47, 56) PLAA 1834 s. 56, PP 1887, LXX, 'Blind and Deaf-Mute Persons, (England, Wales and Ireland)', pp. 3, 43.

2 *Loc. cit.*, Nov. 1774.

3 M. Anagnos, *Education of the Blind* (Boston, 1882), pp. 15–18. H. G. Wagg, *A Chronological Survey of Work for the Blind* (1932) *passim* is used here and elsewhere.

4 E. Chapman, *Visually Handicapped Children and Young People* (1978), p. 71. T. R. Armitage, *The Education and Employment of the Blind: what it has been, is, and ought to be* (2nd edition, 1886), pp. 64–7.

5 S. Low, *The Charities of London* (1850), p. 182. C. Carton, *The Establishments for the Blind in England: a report to the Minister of the Interior and for Foreign Affairs* (Bruges, 1838, London, 1895), pp. 9, 38.

6 S. Low, *op. cit.* p. 184, 186. *An Address in Favour of the School for the Blind in Liverpool Institute in the Year 1791* (Liverpool, 1811) p. 24. *Training of the Blind: Report of a Special Committee of the Charity Organization Society* (1876), p. 32.

7 C. Carton, *op. cit.*, pp. 19, 38.

8 *Egerton Report*, PP 1889, XIX, pp. xix–xx. (21–2).

9 C. Cantor, *op. cit.*, pp. 20, 25–6, 33.

10 E. C. Johnson *Tangible Typography or How the Blind Read* (1853), pp. 11, 17, 28, 41, 44. J. G. Knie, *A Guide to the Proper Management and Education of Blind Children* (Translated by W. Taylor, 1861) p. 2 note. E. C. Johnson, *The Blind of London* (1860), p. 16. T. R. Armitage, *op. cit.*, pp. 42–3. J. Gall, *An Account of the Recent Discoveries which have been made for facilitating the education of the blind* (Edinburgh, 1837, London, 1894), pp. 36–7. *Statement of the Education, Employments, and Internal Arrangements . . . at the Asylum for the Blind*, Glasgow (Glasgow, 1842; London, 1894), pp. 36–7, 39–43, 58. T. R. Armitage, *op. cit.*, pp. 4, 42–3. *Egerton Report*, PP 1889, XIX, pp. 391–407 (527–43) gives examples of Braille, Braille musical, Moon, Lucas, Frere, two types of Alston and American Scripts. 'C' in Moon is the same as the symbol for 'D' in Lucas, and the symbol for 'U' in Moon is easily confused with that for 'N' in Lucas.

11 T. R. Armitage, *op. cit.*, pp. 46, 115. *Egerton Report*, PP 1889, XIX p. xxxiii.

12 R. W. Flint, 'History of Education for the hearing impaired', in L. J. Bradford and W. G. Hardy, *Hearing and Hearing Impairment* (New York and London, 1979) pp. 19–37. 'On Some Methods Employed for the instruction of the Deaf and Dumb', *Quarterly Journal of Education* (III) VI (1832), pp. 203–18. *Egerton Report*, PP 1889, XIX, 'Appendices 12 and 25', pp. 214–6, 278 (546–8, 610).

13 D. G. Pritchard, *Education and the Handicapped, 1760–1960* (1963), pp. 21, 29, 42, 88–9.

14 *op. cit.*, pp. 82–90, 201.

15 *Egerton Report*, PP 1889, XIX, pp. lxxii (74).

16 H. G. Wagg, *op. cit.*, pp. 183, 185. *Egerton Report*, PP 1889, XIX p. xv (17).

17 F. Martin, *Elizabeth Gilbert and Her Work for the Blind* (London and New York, 1871), pp. 240–2. Unlike the ladies accompanying Miss Preusser a year later, Miss Gilbert's lady companions remained at the Westminster Palace Hotel while the gentlemen went to the Education Department's office in Downing Street.

18 COS *Training of the Blind* (1876), pp. 5, 7–9, 12–13, 21.

19 Greater London Council Record Office, SBL 756. Folio 214.

20 *Egerton Report*, PP 1889, XIX, 'Appendix 13', pp. 218–21 (350–3), 'Appendix 26', pp. 280–8 (412–20).

21 PP 1886 XXV, 'Reports by H. E. Oakley and L. T. Munro on the Education of Deaf and Dumb Children', pp. 566, 568.

22 *Egerton Report*, PP 1889, XIX, pp. xxxvii, lxxx (marginal note) PRO Ed. 31/128, 'Memorial from Grimsby School Board, 30 March 1899'. London School Board teachers had initially paid for the guides for blind children out of their own pockets until the LSB recompensed them. GLCRO, SBL 755 Folio 178.

Chapter 5, pp. 107–126

1 G. Sutherland, *Ability, Merit and Achievement: mental testing and English education, 1880–1940* (1984), pp. 8–9, discusses this episode in greater detail. *Egerton Report*, PP 1889, XIX, p. civ (106).

2 *Report of the Mental Deficiency Committee (Wood Report)* HMSO (1924), p. 14. M. F. Bridie, *An Introduction to Special School Work* (1917), p. ix quotes from *Natura Brevium*.

3 J. Locke, *An Essay Concerning Human Understanding*, Everyman edn., 2 Vols. (1965) I, pp. 127–8.

4 Quoted by A. T. Scull in *Museums of Madness* (1979) p. 64 from J. Cox, *Practical Observations on Insanity*, 3rd edn. (1813), p. ix. For the action of Conolly and Pinel see I. Macalpine and R. Hunter, *George III and the Mad Business* (1969), pp. 273, 286.

5 I. Macalpine and R. Hunter, *op. cit.*, p. 56.

6 H. Lane, *The Wild Boy of Aveyron* (1977), pp. 19–26, 56, 167, 269–73, 281–2. Victor of Aveyron lived with Madame Guerin, Itard's housekeeper, until his death in 1828.

7 R. Hunter and I. Macalpine (eds.), *An Inquiry Concerning the Indications of Insanity with Suggestions for the Better Care of the Insane, John Conolly, 1830* (1964) pp. 171–2, 174.

8 I. Macalpine and R. Hunter, *George III and the Mad Business* (1969), pp. 310, 316–7.

9 Poor Law Amendment Act 1834, s. 45. Factory Act 1833, s. 11.

10 'Visit to the Bicêtre', 'Education of Idiots at Bicêtre', *Chambers' Edinburgh Journal*, VII (1847), pp. 20–4, 70–3, 105–7, 'Education of Idiots', *ibid.*, VII (1847), pp. 169–71, 262–5. 'The Bicêtre Asylum', *Westminster Review* XLIX

(1849), pp. 70–84. Samuel Gaskell, the author of the articles in *Chambers' Edinburgh Journal*, had been the medical officer of the Lancaster Asylum before becoming a Lunacy Commissioner.

11 A. and C. Reed (eds.), *Memoirs of the Life and Philanthropic Labours of Andrew Reed D.D.* (1863), pp. 392, 396, 399, 414, 418. L. Kanner, *A History of the Care and Study of the Mentally Retarded* (Springfield, Illinois, USA, 1964), pp. 55–6.

12 E. Turner, 'On Teaching the Idiot', *Journal of the Society of Arts* II (1853–4), pp. 651–3.

13 *loc. cit.*, pp. 12, 70–1, 90, 124.

14 *Report of the Commissioners for Lunacy for 1865*, quoted by the *Egerton Report*, PP 1889, XIX, pp. xcvi–xcvii.

15 K. Jones, *Mental Health and Social Policy, 1845–1959* (1960), p. 12, D. K. Henderson, *The Evolution of Psychiatry in Scotland* (1964), p. 220. R. Hunter and I. Macalpine, *Psychiatry for the Poor: 1857 Colney Hatch Asylum – Friern Hospital, 1973* (1974), p. 17. R. Hunter and I. Macalpine, *George III and the Mad Business* (1969), pp. 308–9. L. S. Hearnshaw, *A Short History of British Psychology, 1840–1940* (1964), pp. 45–6. R. Hunter and I. Macalpine, *The Indications of Insanity; John Conolly 1830* (1964), p. 22 fn. P. M. Duncan, 'Notes on Idiocy', *Journal of Mental Science* VII (July 1861), pp. 22–52. For the 1868 Act see ref. 30.

16 L. Kanner, *op. cit.*, pp. 87–8.

17 Quoted from E. Séguin, 'Psycho-Physiological Training of an Idiotic Hand', in M. Rosen *et al.*, *The History of Mental Retardation: collected papers* Vol. I (Baltimore, 1976), p. 163.

18 L. Kanner, *op. cit.*, p. 17; *ibid.* pp. 28–30 suggests a fall from earlier standards.

19 S. P. Davies and F. E. Williams, *Social Control of the Mentally Defective* (1930), p. 37. D. Greenwell, *On the Education of the Imbecile* (1869), p. 20. *Egerton Report*, PP 1889, XIX, 'G. M. Tait's evidence', Q. 468.

20 R. Hunter and I. Macalpine, *Psychiatry for the Poor: 1857*, pp. 20, 25, 28. A. Scull, *Museums of Madness* (1979), pp. 116, 198.

21 W. L. Parry-Jones, *The Trade in Lunacy: a study of private madhouses in England and Wales in the Eighteenth and Nineteenth Centuries* (1972), pp. 126–7, 162–3. G. M. Ayers, *England's First State Hospitals and the Metropolitan Asylums Board, 1867–1930* (1971), pp. 17, 45, p. 82 fn, p. 308. K. Jones, *Mental Health and Social Policy, 1845–1959* (1960), p. 45. I. Macalpine and R. Hunter, *George III and the Mad Buisness* (1969), p. 279.

22 L. Kanner, *op. cit.*, p. 94. H. A. Husband, *The Students' Handbook of the Practice of Medicine* (1878), G. M. Gould, *An Illustrated Dictionary of Medical Biology and Allied Sciences* (1911).

23 S. J. Gould, *The Mismeasure of Man* (New York and London 1981), p. 73.

24 J. L. Down, 'Observations on an Ethnic Classification of Idiots', *Clinical Lectures and Reports, London Hospital* III (1866), pp. 259–62. J. Conolly, *Treatment of the Insane without Mechanical Restraints* (1856, reprinted with an introduction by R. Hunter and I. Macalpine, 1973) p. xliii fn. 136. S. J. Gould, 'Dr Down's Syndrome', in *The Panda's Thumb: more reflection in Natural History by the author of Ever Since Darwin* (Harmondsworth, 1980) pp. 133–9. L. Kanner, *op. cit.*, pp. 103–4.

25 Quoted from H. Maudsley in S. Collini, 'The Idea of "Character" in Victorian Political Thought', *Transactions of the Royal Historical Society (Fifth Series)*, XXXV (1985), pp. 29–50.

26 V. Skultans, *English Madness: ideas on insanity, 1580–1890* (1979), p. 63. O. Temkin, *The Falling Sickness* (Baltimore, 1945), p. 3.

27 H. Maudsley, *Responsibility in Mental Illness* (1874), pp. 62–3. Charity Organization Society (COS), *The Feeble-Minded Child and Adult* (1893), p. 6 quoting Shuttleworth. A. F. Tredgold, *Mental Deficiency (Amentia)*. (2nd edn., 1914) pp. 123,421. The 12th edition of this book edited by M. Croft appeared in 1979. A. Lewis, 'Henry Maudsley – his work and influence', *Journal of Mental Science* XCVII (Apr. 1951), pp. 259–77.

28 H. Maudsley, *op. cit.*, pp. 22, 47, 269, 276. There are broad parallels between the texts of Maudsley's *Body and Mind* (1873) and his *Responsibility in Mental Disease* (1874). J. Barlow, *On Man's Power Over Himself to Prevent or Control Insanity* (London, 1843), p. 12.

29 PP 1882, XXIII, *Minutes for 1881–2*, 'The Revised Code for 1882' Articles 109e (v), 109 (iii); PP 1884, XXIV, *Minutes for 1883–4* 'The Revised Code for 1884', Articles 109d (vi), W. T. Darby's Report', p. 292, 'H. E. Oakley's Report', p. 349, 'T. W. Sharpe's Report', p. 380, 'H. Waddington's Report', p. 435, 'R. Wilde's Report', p. 449, 'F. Wilkinson's Report', p. 465.

30 *Egerton Report*, PP 1889, XIX, pp. xciii, cv (95, 107) The seven asylums were: Eastern Counties Asylum, Colchester, Essex; Royal Albert Asylum, Lancaster; Earlswood, Surrey; Western Counties, Starcross, near Exeter, Devon; Downside Lodge, Chilcompton, Bath; Midlands Counties, Knowle, Birmingham; Normansfield, Hampton Wick. In addition the Metropolitan Asylums Board had a training school at Darenth, Kent. The Poor Law Amendment Act, 1868, went further. S. 13 provided that idiots, imbeciles, or insane paupers might be placed in any hospital, institution, or licensed house registered, under the Act, for the *care, education, and training of idiots or imbeciles* (author's italics).

31 *Ibid.*, pp. xcvii, xcix – c, 'G. E. Shuttleworth's evidence', Q. 19328.

32 *Egerton Report*, PP 1887, XIX, cvi (108).

33 *Ibid.*, xcv, cv (97, 107).

Chapter 6, pp. 127–152

1 PP 1898, XXVI, *Report of the Departmental Committee on Defective and Epileptic Children (Defective and Epileptic Children Report)*, pp. 1, 3. PRO Ed. 14/43, 'Memorandum of London School Board Delegation to Education Department', 18 June 1896, 'Memorandum of A. Eichholz', 7 January 1899.

2 PRO Ed. 50/9 'Eastbourne S. B. to Ed. Dept.', 18 July 1893. PRO Ed. 50/29 'Circular Letter from Ed. Dept.', 9 April 1895. PRO Ed.14/43 'Memorandum of London School Board Delegation to Education Department, 18 June 1896.

3 *Report of the Departmental Committee on the Poor Law Schools*, PP 1896, XXIII, pp. 78, 81, (84, 87) *Egerton Report*, PP 1889, XIX, pp. xliii, xci, xcvi, cvi (45, 93, 97, 108).

4 PP 1898, XXVI, *Defective and Epileptic Children Report*, p. 4 (10).

5 *Ibid.*, 'Sir Douglas Galton's evidence', Q. 5957.

6 *Ibid.*, 'Dr Coleman's evidence', Q. 6111.

7 *Ibid.*, P4 (10), 'Dr F. D. Harris's evidence', Qs. 1059, 'Dr G. E. Shuttleworth's evidence', Q. 53.

8 *Ibid.*, pp. 12–13. (18–19).

9 *Ibid.*, pp. 28–9 (34–5).

10 R. I. Macalpine, *Three Hundred Years of Psychiatry, 1535–1860* (1963), pp. 148, 152, 778, 1044–7.

11 PP 1898, XXVI, *Defective and Epileptic Children Report*, 'Dr F. H. Walmsley's evidence', Qs. 4068–72. W. W. Ireland, *The Mental Affections of Children, Idiocy, Imbecility, and Insanity* (1898), pp. 12, 152.

12 H. Maudsley, *Responsibility in Mental Disease* (1894), p. 41.

13 PP 1898, XXVI, *Defective and Epileptic Children Report* 'G. Penn Gaskell's evidence', Q. 4364, pp. 30–2 (36–8).

14 *Ibid.*, pp. 18–21 (24–7).

15 *Ibid.*, p. 16 (22).

16 Elementary Education (Defective and Epileptic Children) Act, 1899, ss. 1(1), 2, 3, 4, 8. Elementary Education Act Amendment, 1903, PRO Ed. 50/148. 'List date stamped 12 Jan. 1914'.

17 PRO Ed. 31/16. 'Treasury's letters, 8 Feb. 1899, 16 May 1899', 'Education Department's letters of 25 Jan., 2 May 1899'. *Report of the Royal Commission on the Care and Control of the Feeble-Minded (Radnor Report)*, PP 1908, XXXIX, 'H. F. Pooley's evidence', Q. 242.

18 *Loc. cit.*, pp. 97–8.

19 G. R. Searle, 'Eugenics and Class' in C. Webster, *Biology, Medicine and Society, 1840–1940* (1981), pp. 217–42. S. A. K. Straham, *op. cit.* pp. 81, 91, 249–50, 256–7.

20 *Loc. cit.* PP 1908, XXXIX, pp. 1, 7 (185, 191).

21 *Ibid.*, pp. 181–3 (365–7).

22 *Ibid.*, p. 185 (369).

23 *Ibid.*, p. 198 (382).

24 *Ibid.*, p. 185 (369).

25 *Ibid.*, p. 185 (369).

26 *Ibid.*, p. 188. For Kerlin on moral imbecility, see M. Rosen (et al.), *The History of Mental Retardation*, Vol. I (University Park Press, Baltimore, 19776), pp. 305–10.

27 *Radnor Report*, PP 1908, XXXIX, p. 88 (272).

28 *Ibid.*, PP 1908, XXXV, 'H. F. Pooley's evidence', Q. 358.

29 *Ibid.*, pp. 96, 102 (280, 286). The witness was a COS worker.

30 *Ibid.*, pp. 354–7 (538–41) give the Report's recommendations on education and training.

31 S. P. Davies and F. E. Williams, *Social Control of the Mentally Deficient* (1930), pp. 59–67. See also S. P. Davies with the collaboration of K. G. Ecob, *The Mentally Retarded in Society* (Columbia University Press, New York, 1959 edn.), pp. 33–6. (1918). S. J. Gould, *The Mismeasure of Man* (1984).

32 S. J. Gould, *op. cit.*, pp. 231–2. S. P. Davies with K. G. Ecob, *op. cit.*, pp. 51–4.

33 *Loc. cit.* p. 24.

34 *Ibid.*, p. 25.
35 A. F. Tredgold *op. cit.*, (1908 edn.) p. 2, (1914 edn.), p. 8. C. P. Lapage, *Feeblemindedness in Children of School Age* (Manchester, 1911), p. 203.
36 *Report of the Chief Medical Officer of the Board of Education for 1911 (Report of the C.M.O. for 1911)*, PP 1912, p. 200 (644) *Report of the C.M.O. for 1908*, PP 1910, XXIII, p. 115 (119), *Report of the C.M.O. for 1909*, PP 1910, XXIII, p. 137 (315).
37 *Report of the C.M.O. for 1909*, PP 1910, XXIII, p. 164 (312).
38 G. Sutherland, *Ability, Merit and Measurement: mental testing and English education, 1880–1940* (Oxford, 1984), p. 42. J. Woodhouse, 'Eugenics and the Feeble-Minded: the parliamentary debates of 1912–14', *History of Education* XI (1982), pp. 127–37.
39 *Report of the Board of Education for 1905–6*, PP 1906, XXVIII, pp. 32–3. *Report of the C.M.O. for 1909* PP 1910, XXIII, p. 140 (318). *Radnor Report*, 1908, XXXIX, p. 100 (284).
40 *Loc. cit.*, PP 1910, XXIII, pp. 162–71 (340–9), *Report of the C.M.O. for 1910*, PP 1911, XVII, p. 214 (666). For Children's Care Committees, see J. S. Hurt, *Elementary Schooling and the Working Classes, 1860–1918* (1979), pp. 143–51 *passim*.
41 *Report of the C.M.O. for 1909*, PP 1910, XXIII, p. 159 (337).
42 *Ibid.*, pp. 157–61 (335–9) for a more detailed discussion.
43 *Radnor Report*, PP 1908, XXXIX, p. 78 (262). *Report of the C.M.O. for 1909*, PP 1910, XXIII, p. 162 (340).
44 P. M. Duncan, 'A description of some of the most important Physiological Anomalies of Idiots', *Journal Mental Science* VII (June 1862), pp. 515–29. J. C. Parkinson, *A Day at Earlswood* (Reprinted from the *Daily News*, 1869).
45 For a fuller account see G. Sutherland, *op. cit.*, pp. 111–27, A. D. B. and A. M. Clarke, 'Mental Testing: origins, evolution and present status', *History of Education* XVI (1985), pp. 263–72. J. C. Flugel, *A Hundred Years of Psychology, 1833–1933* (1933), pp. 208–10. S. J. Gould, *op. cit.*, pp. 146–58.
46 A. Binet and Th. Simon (with an introduction by A. Darroch), *Mentally Defective Children* (1914), pp. v–viii, 14.
47 *Report of the C.M.O. for 1910*, PP 1911, XVII, p. 208 (660) footnote, *Report of the C.M.O. for 1911*, PP 1912–13, XXI, p. 196 (640). G. Sutherland and S. Sharpe, ' "The Fust Official Psychologist in the Wurrld": aspects of the professionalisation of psychology in the early twentieth century', *History of Science* XVIII (1980), pp. 181–208.
48 For a fuller account see G. Sutherland, *Ability, Merit, and Measurement* (Oxford, 1984), Chapter II. The quotations are from pp. 47 and 56.
49 PRO Ed. 50/150A, 'Sir George Newman's minute of 23 May 1913', PRO Ed. 31/196 'Memorial from the Committee of Moghull School', 27 June 1913. *Hansard*, 4th series. House of Commons debates, 4 March 1914, Vol. LIX, c. 476.
50 PRO Ed. 50/152 contains details of her negotiations with the Board of Education in 1918. G. M. Trevelyan (Mrs Janet Penrose), *The Life of Mrs Humphrey Ward* (1923), pp. 131–2, 137–8, 140, 240, 294–5. *Hansard*, 4th series. House of Commons debates, 3 July 1918, Vol. CVII, c. 1797–8, *ibid.*, 16 July 1918, CVIII, c. 963. Education Act, 1921, s. 56, ss. 2(ii).

51 PRO Ed. 50/149 'A. Eichholz's memorandum of 10 November 1911'.

52 *Report of the C.M.O. for 1911* PP 1912–13, XXI, pp. 170–4 (614–8). The Open Air Movement is described more fully by R. A. Lowe, 'The Early Twentieth Century Open Air Movement: origins and implications', in N. Parry and D. McNair (eds.) *The Fitness of the Nation: physical and health education in the nineteenth and twentieth centuries* (History of Education Society, Leicester, 1983), pp. 86–99.

53 PRO Ed. 50/16. 'A. Eichholz's memorandum of 7 September 1909'. PRO Ed. 50/85. 'Treasury to Board of Education. 24 April 1920', and 29 January 1927. J. M. Ritchie, *Concerning the Blind* (1930), p. 94.

54 *Report of the C.M.O. for 1912*, PP 1914, XXV, pp. 227–8 (631–2).

55 PRO Ed. 24/167, 'G. Newman's minute of 24 November 1911', quoted by G. Sutherland, *op. cit.* p. 47. The statistical data for numbers on school registers comes from *Report of the C.M.O. for 1913*, PP 1914–16, XVIII, pp 190–1 (482–3). *Radnor Report* PP 1908, XXXIX, p. 85 (269), *Census of 1911*, PP 1913, LXXIX, pp. iv–v (794–5), 'Table 1', p. 1 (807). The 1881 census officials in their subsequent report also recorded that an investigation of admissions to one lunatic asylum in 1882 showed that one half of the admissions as indisputable idiots between the ages of five and fifteen had not been recorded on the census schedule the previous year.

56 PRO Ed. 24/1383, 'A. Eichholz's minute of 15 July 1918'.

56 PRO Ed. 50/107, 'Memorial of a deputation representing Committees of Schools and Institutions and LEAs dealing with the education of the blind and deaf', 23 January 1914. Grants for blind and deaf schools were raised at the same time as those for mentally defective children, to £7 and £13 for day and residential schools respectively.

Chapter 7, pp. 153–170

1 C. B. Davenport, *Heredity in Relation to Genetics* (1911) quoted in L. Kanner, *op. cit.*, p. 130.

2 See for example A. Myerson, *Inheritance of Mental Diseases* (Baltimore, 1925).

3 PP 1933–4, XV, *Report of the Departmental Committee on Sterilisation*, p. 13 (623).

4 *Loc. cit.*, p. 18 (628).

5 *Ibid.*, p. 21 (631).

6 On Dugdale see M. Rosen et al. (eds.), *The History of Mental Retardation Vol. 1 (Baltimore, 1976), pp. 269–82. Report of the Mental Deficiency Committee (Wood Report)* (1929) Part II, 'The Adult Defective', p. 39.

7 PRO Ed. 50/150B, 'A. H. Wood to President of the Board of Education: 10 January, 1922'. PRO, Ed. 50/104. 'A. H. Wood's memorandum of 27 March', 'G. Newman's minute of 28 Mar. 1922'.

8 *Ibid.*

9 PRO Ed. 50/140 'A. H. Wood's memorandum of 27 March 1922.' A. Eichholz, 'Mentally Defective Children: Additional Provision for Education', 1 June 1923.

10 PRO Ed. 50/104, 'G. Newman's memorandum of 28 Mar. 1922.', PRO Ed.

50/150B. 'A. H. Wood's memorandum of 8 June 1923', A. Eichholz 'Mentally Defective Children', 1 June 1923.

11 PRO T161/98/S7422. 'Memorandum of F. Phillips', 11 Dec. 1920, 'A. Chamberlain to H. A. L. Fisher', 31 Dec. 1920, 'H. A. L. Fisher's memorandum' 29 December 1920, 'H. A. L. Fisher to Austen Chamberlain', 31 Dec. 1920.

12 PRO T161/227/S23263 'C. P. Trevelyan to P. Snowden', 1 Jan. 1924, 9 Feb. 1924. 'P. Snowden to C. P. Trevelyan', 16 July 1924.

13 PRO T161/281/S32668 'H. W. Orange to Treasury', 22 Nov. 1927. PRO T161/300/S35267 'G. P. Trevelyan to P. Snowden', 29 Oct. 1929, 'P. Snowden to C. P. Trevelyan', 28 Jan. 1930.

14 G. Sutherland, *op. cit.*, pp. 59–60. PRO Ed. 50/154 'Blackpool Borough Council to Board of Education', 28 June 1923.

15 PRO Ed. 50/48, 'A. W. Maudslay's minutes', 9 Aug., 15 Aug. and 14 Oct. 1933.

16 G. Sutherland, *op. cit.*, p. 84.

17 *The Health of the School Child; Annual Report of the C.M.O. . . . for . . . 1932,* (1933) *Health*, (1924), pp. 134–40. For a summary of reports published in the 1930s, see *Health . . .* (1932), pp. 71–77, *Health . . .* (1934), pp. 102–6, *Health . . .* (1937), pp. 88–94, *Health . . .* (1938), pp. 101–8.

18 *Loc. cit.*, pp. 63–9, *Health . . .* (1925), *Health . . .* (1926), p. 85.

19 PRO Ed. 11/115 gives the returns from various LEAs on the use of ordinary schools for mentally defective children. 'A. Eichholz to A. H. Wood', 1 May 1922, 'Memorandum to Inspectors E224', 11 May 1922. *Report for . . . 1923* (1924), pp. 66–7.

20 *Health . . .* (1925), pp. 81–2 and 85–6 summarizes Circulars 1341 and 1349. *Health . . .* (1929), p. 27.

21 *Loc. cit.*, Part I, pp. 1–3, p. 85.

22 *Ibid.* pp. 57–9, 84, 132. *Defective and Epileptic Children Report*, PP 1898, XXVI, Qs. 506–13, 962–6, 4251 are the only indexed references to 'dull children'.

23 PRO Ed. 50/119. 'A. H. Wood's minute', 17 Sept. 1923.

24 *Health . . .* (1926), pp. 81–2, 85.

25 *Loc. cit.*, pp. 92–3.

26 PRO Ed. 24/1365, 'County Councils Association', 1 Aug. 1929, PRO Ed. 50/124, 'Letters of the Central Association for Mental Welfare', 11 Nov. 1930, 'Archbishop of York' 29 Nov. 1930, 'Archbishop of Canterbury' 18 Nov. 1930. *Health . . .* (1934), p. 143. *Health . . .* (1936), pp. 119–27.

27 PRO Ed. 50/122 'Interview memorandum', 18 Feb. 1925. *Wood Report* Part I, p. 122, Pt. IV, p. 92.

28 *Wood Report* Pt. I, pp. 63–8, pp. 86–7, *passim*, Pt. IV, Table 16b, p. 189. See also PRO Ed. 50/121, 'Mrs E. F. Pinsent's minute', 21 Feb. 1925.

29 PRO Ed. 50/112, 'A. H., Wood's memorandum', 4 Aug. 1920. 'G. Newman's minute', 10 June, 1921.

30 PRO Ed. 50/150B; Ed. 50/98, 'Eichholz's memorandum' 23 Nov. 1923.

31 *Health . . .* (1930), p. 122.

32 PRO Ed. 50/108, 'Memorandum for Lord Charnwood's Motion in the House of Lords on 18 June 1928'. Viscount Gage omitted these damaging

admissions in his reply. See *Hansard* 5th series, House of Lords Debates, Vol. LXXI, c. 500–1.

33 *Ibid.* 'Mrs Buckley to the Duchess of Atholl', 12 Jan. 1926. Original emphasis.

34 PRO Ed. 24//622, 'Minute of W. R. Barker', 20 Feb. 1913. See also marginal comment on the draft Defective Children Bill.

35 PRO Ed. 50/103, 'Return by the Permanent Committee on Epileptics', December 1925. 'Board of Education to National Society for Epileptics', 4 June 1931. 'Report of conference with representatives of special schools for epileptic children', 28 Oct. 1932. *Health* . . . (1933) pp. 74–7. *Health* . . . (1949), p. 81.

36 I. A. Darling, 'Phenobarbital (luminal) treatment of insane epileptics', *Archives of Neurology and Psychiatry* (IX, 1923), pp. 477–86. J. Collier, 'Epilepsy', in *A Short History of Some Common Diseases* (Oxford 1934) p. 129. D. Scott, *About Epilepsy* (3rd edition, 1978), p. 98.

37 PRO Ed. 50/103, 'J. Lumsden's minute', 18 July 1939.

38 G. M. Ayers, *England's First State Hospitals, 1867–1930* (1971), pp. 183–5.

39 G. Keir 'A History of Child Guidance', *British Journal Ed. Psych.* (XXII, 1952), pp. 5–29. M. Bridgeland, *Pioneer Work with Maladjusted Children* (1971), pp. 48–50.

40 PRO Ed. 'COS to Board of Education', 26 Mar. 1927. For a brief account of the Commonwealth Fund, see *The Commonwealth Fund: historical sketch, 1918–1962* (New York, 1963).

41 P. Grosskurth, *Havelock Ellis; a biography* (190), pp. 115–16, 168.

42 J. W. D. Pearce, *Juvenile Delinquency* (1952), pp. 6–9; J. Carlebach, *Caring for Children in Trouble* (1970), p. 87; L. W. Fox, *The English Prison and Borstal Systems* (1952), p. 334.

43 *Health* . . . (1926), p. 82.

44 *Health* . . . (1928), pp. 31–2.

45 *Health* . . . (1935), pp. 114–16. *Health* . . . (1938), pp. 62–4.

Chapter 8, pp. 171–188

1 *Special Educational Needs: Report of the Committee of Enquiry into the Education of Handicapped Children and Young Adults (Warnock Report)* (Cmnd 7212, 1978), pp. 18–19.

2 Education Act, 1944, s. 33(2).

3 Ministry of Education, *Special Educational Treatment, Pamphlet 5* (1946), p. 11. The eleven categories were blind, partially sighted, deaf, partially deaf, delicate, diabetic, epileptic, educationally subnormal, maladjusted, physically handicapped, and children with speech defects.

4 *Health* (1958), pp. 136–7, *Health* (1966), pp. 52–3.

5 *Health* (1958), pp. 30–1. *Health* (1966), p. 53. *Health* (1972), p. 42.

6 *Health* (1954), p. 95. *Health* p. 42. R. Gulliford, *Special Educational Needs* (1976 edn.), p. 177.

7 *Health* (1969), p. 75. *Health* pp. 43–4.

8 *Health* (1956), pp. 81–3. *Health* (1964), p. 37. *Health* (1966), p. 54. *Health* (1972), p. 42.

9 *Health* (1969), p. 71. R. Gulliford, *op. cit.*, p. 179.

10 *Health* (1956), pp. 105–7. *Health* (1958), p. 21. R. Gulliford, *op. cit.*, p. 158.

11 *Health* (1934), p. 103. *Health* pp. 108–13. DES, *The Education of the Visually Handicapped Child* (1972), pp. 43, 48. DES *Statistics of Education* Vol. I, 'Schools' (1977), p. 48.

12 *Health* (1958), p. 20. *Health* (1960), pp. 95–99. *Health* (1969), p. 51. *Health* (1974), pp. 32–4.

13 Ministry of Education, *Report of the Committee on Maladjusted Children* (1955), (*Underwood Report*), p. 12.

14 *Times Educational Supplement*, 6 Oct. 1950. D. H. Stott, *loc. cit.*, pp. 375–6. *Underwod Report*, pp. 13, 53–9.

15 *Underwood Report*, pp. 96–7, 172.

16 *Ibid.*, pp. 98–9.

17 *Ibid.*, p. 98. M. Penelope Hall, *The Social Services of Modern England* (Sixth Edition, 1965), p. 330. *Health 1961* (1962), p. 87.

18 *Health* (1974), pp. 7–11, 71. *Warnock Report* (1978), pp. 26, 267. *Underwood Report* pp. 53, 60. DES *Statistics of Education* Vol. I, 'Schools' (1977), 'Table 26', p. 48.

19 *Special Educational Treatment*, p. 20.

20 PRO Ed. 50/562, 'Minute of 31 March 1955'. Socialist Medical Association to Ministry of Education', 3 Dec. 1947.

21 *Health* (1972), pp. 39–40.

22 *Report of the Royal Commission on the Laws Relating to Mental Illness and Mental Deficiency (Percy Report)* (Cmnd 169, 1957), pp. 22, 23, 219, 220.

23 Mental Health Act, 1959, s. 12. The Second Schedule refers to children as 'suitable or unsuitable for education in a school' to replace the earlier terms 'educable' and 'ineducable'.

24 *Loc. cit.* p. 218.

25 M. Hyndman, *Schools and Schooling in England and Wales; a documentary history* (1978, pp. 106–7).

26 *Loc. cit.*, Vol. I, pp. 298 and footnote, 301. Vol. II, 'First Report of the National Child Development Study (1958 Cohort)', p. 533.

27 Hansard 5th Series, Vol. DCCLIII, c. 492. House of Commons debate, 3 Nov. 1967.

28 Hansard, 5th Series, Vol. DCCCXXI, CC1301–2, 1310, 1685–6. House of Commons Debates, 13 July, 15 July 1970. Hansard, 5th series, House of Commons debates, Vol. DCCCIII, c. 1291, 13 July 1970.

29 Hansard, 5th Series, Vol. CCCIX, cc. 357, 361. House of Lords Debate, 14 April 1970. *Health of the School Child, 1969–79* (1972), pp. 35–6. R. Furneaux and B. Roberts, *Autistic Children, teaching, community and research approaches* (1977), p. 5.

30 *Health* (1972) p. 34. *Special Educational Needs: Report of the Committee of Enquiry into the Education of Handicapped Children and Young Persons (Warnock Report)* (Cmnd 7212, 1978), p. 37.

31 National Bureau for Cooperation in Child Care, *Living With Handicap* (1970), pp. 356–7. *Warnock Report*, pp. 37–8.

32 *Children and Their Primary Schools: A Report of the Central Advisory Council for England (Plowden Report)* (1967), pp. 296–304 *passim*. *Hansard*, 5th series, *DCCCLXIV*, 'Written answer 22 Nov. 1973'.

33 J. Mays et al. (eds.), *Penelope Hall's Social Services of England and Wales* (9th edn., 1975) pp. 109, 255–6.

34 *Loc. cit.*, pp. 11–12.

35 *Fit for the Future: The Report of the Committee on Child Health Services (Court Report)* (Cmnd. 6684, 1976), pp. 2, 11, 222.

36 *Ibid.*, pp. 154–5.

37 Education Act 1976, s. 10.

38 *Loc. cit.*, pp. 38, 104.

39 *Loc. cit.*, p. 41.

40 *Loc. cit.*, p. 100.

41 *Loc. cit.*, pp. 123–5.

42 Education Act, 1981, s. 2. DES Circular 8/81. 7 Dec. 1981.

42 PP 1910, XXIII, 'Annual Report . . . of the CMO', p. 119 (123). Warnock Report, p. 233. Teachers of trade, craft, or domestic subjects in special schools for the blind and deaf were not required to have a specialist qualification. DES Circular 3/84, 13 April 1984.

43 *Hansard*, House of Commons debates, 2 Feb. 1981. c. 27–8, 35. Education (No. 2) Act, 1986, s. 60.

Conclusion, pp. 189–193

1 *Loc. cit.*, pp. 19, 71.

2 G. Wagner, *Barnardo* (1976), pp. 92–4, 298.

3 Home Ofice, *Report on the Work of the Children's Branch* (1923), p. 16.

4 *Defective and Epileptic Children Report*, PP 1898, XIX, p. 28.

5 C. Cunningham, *Down's Syndrome: an introduction for parents* pp. 133–5.

6 *Times Educational Supplement*, 16 Jan. 1981. *Warnock Report*, pp. 17–18.

7 PRO, Ed. 50/155, 'A. H. Wood's memorandum, 20 Jul. 1923'.

INDEX